I0453451

Emotionally Connected

A Guide to Recovering from Anxious, Avoidant
Attachment Styles and Enhancing Emotional Intelligence
for Stronger Connections

Anxious Attachment Recovery

Avoidant Attachment Recovery

Emotional Intelligence

Amy Harper

To my family, my steadfast anchors, your love fuels my every endeavor.

Thank you for being my guiding stars.

Contents

Avoidant Attachment Recovery

5 Steps to Overcome Fear of Intimacy, Strengthen Connections and Transition from Avoidant to Secure Attachment

Emotional Intelligence

A Practical Guide for Personal Growth and Building Stronger Connections

Anxious Attachment Recovery

A Practical Guide to Emotional Freedom and Lasting Relationships

Amy Harper

Introduction

"As we familiarize ourselves more with secure attachment, our relationships become easier and more rewarding—we're less reactive, more receptive, more available for connection, healthier, and much more likely to bring out the securely attached tendencies in others."

Diane Poole Heller.

Understanding and awareness of anxious attachment can aid individuals in building healthier and more secure relationships. This book will provide comprehensive insights into anxious attachment, helping individuals overcome it and establish lasting and fulfilling relationships.

While characterized by sensitivity and attentiveness to their partner's needs, an anxious attachment style often necessitates constant reassurance and affection to feel secure within a romantic relationship. Failure to receive validation in the desired manner can cause feelings of worry and stress for those with an anxious attachment style.

Individuals with an anxious attachment style often internalize a perceived lack of affection and intimacy as a sign that they are unworthy of love, leading to intense fears of rejection. To avoid abandonment, they may exhibit clinginess, hypervigilance, and jealousy within their relationships.

The anxiety of being alone drives attachers to exert significant efforts to maintain their relationships, viewing their partner as the solution to their emotional needs. I'll touch upon these efforts throughout the book.

Anxious Attachment in Relationships

Although individuals with an anxious attachment style yearn for romantic connections, they often find relationships to be a source of stress and anxiety.

Anxious attachers possess a high level of sensitivity and attentiveness to their partner's needs, willingly accommodating them. However, their insecurities and doubts about their self-worth lead them to project these uncertainties onto their partner's behavior. If their partner fails to respond to their needs in the specific way they desire, it reinforces their belief that they are unworthy of love.

For individuals with an anxious attachment style, relationships are a double-edged sword. On one hand, they deeply fear rejection and abandonment, leading to hypervigilance and a constant need for reassurance from their partner. They constantly seek validation and confirmation of their partner's love. On the other hand, being in the presence of their loved one provides solace and comfort. The presence of their partner serves as a balm to their anxieties.

Who Is This Book For?

This book is for anyone feeling stuck in a cycle of worry and uncertainty in their relationships, especially if you often feel insecure or anxious about your partner's feelings for you. If you've ever felt like you're constantly waiting for reassurance or overthinking things in your relationships, this guide can help. It's also great if you've faced challenges trusting others or want to understand why you feel like you do in relationships. Think of it as a roadmap to understanding yourself better and building healthier connections with others.

Why Do You Need This Book?

Your feelings of insecurity or anxiety in relationships can stem from patterns developed over time, possibly from past experiences or early relationships. This book offers practical insights and tools to help you recognize and understand these patterns better. By gaining this understanding, you can start making positive changes in how you approach relationships, helping you feel more secure, confident, and fulfilled in your connections with others. It's a step-by-step guide to addressing those underlying concerns and building healthier relationship habits.

What's Next?

Let us delve into the book's first chapter, where we will explore all aspects of anxious attachment and equip ourselves with the tools to overcome its challenges and foster healthier relationships.

Chapter 1

What is Anxious Attachment

"The key to finding a mate who can fulfill those needs is to first fully acknowledge your need for intimacy, availability, and security in a relationship - and to believe that they are legitimate. They aren't good or bad, they are simply your needs. Don't let people make you feel guilty for acting "needy" or dependent." Don't be ashamed of feeling incomplete when you're not in a relationship, or for wanting to be close to your partner and to depend on him."

Amir Levine & Rachel S.F. Heller.

A nxious attachment refers to a specific type of insecure relationship children develop with their mothers or primary caregivers. This attachment style can have significant and lasting effects on their relationships as adults. Attachment is the innate ability to form emotional bonds with others, and it begins at birth and continues to shape how individuals relate to others throughout their lives. I will speak about relationships and how insecurity develops later in the book.

The attachment style that is established in early childhood, particularly with the primary caregiver, serves as a blueprint for future relationships. If the emotional needs of the child are consistently not met or responded to, it can lead to the development of an insecure attachment style, specifically anxious attachment.

Individuals with anxious attachment may struggle with trust, intimacy, and forming secure emotional connections in their adult relationships. They may constantly fear abandonment or rejection and feel the need for reassurance and constant attention to alleviate their anxieties. This can create challenges in establishing and maintaining healthy, fulfilling relationships.

It is important to note that while anxious attachment can have its challenges, it is not a life sentence. With self-awareness and a willingness to heal and grow, individuals with an anxious attachment can work towards developing more secure attachment patterns. This may involve seeking therapy or counseling, learning effective communication and emotional regulation skills, and building relationships with securely attached individuals who can serve as positive role models.

Attachment Styles

Attachment styles can significantly impact how individuals behave and react to relationships, particularly in romantic contexts. There are four main attachment styles: Secure, Anxious, Avoidant, and Disorganized (Cherry, 2022). Understanding these patterns can help individuals identify their needs and overcome relationship challenges.

Secure attachment is characterized by individuals with high self-worth and can set boundaries. They feel satisfied in their close relationships and have a sense of safety and stability. Usually, as children, their caregivers were consistent and healthily responded to their needs.

Anxious attachment is characterized by neediness, anxiety, and low self-esteem. Individuals with this attachment style want to be close to others but fear rejection. As children, their caregivers were likely inconsistent in their responses, leading to feelings of anxiety and uncertainty.

Avoidant attachment is characterized by individuals who avoid emotional closeness with others. They might rely on themselves, crave freedom, and struggle with emotions. In childhood, their caregivers were likely unavailable, rejecting their needs and emotions, leading to a learned avoidance of closeness.

Disorganized attachment is characterized by an intense fear of being unloved, often stemming from childhood trauma, abuse, or neglect. Individuals with this attachment style might feel they don't deserve love. They likely had caregivers with chaotic or scary behavior, leading to emotional problems in adulthood.

By understanding their attachment style, individuals can identify their needs and behaviors in relationships and work towards healthier patterns. Seeking therapy or counseling can also help develop more secure attachment styles and build fulfilling relationships.

Impact of Anxious Attachment

An anxious attachment can significantly impact a person's ability to handle stress and adapt to change. This can manifest in difficulties in various relationships, including romantic relationships, friendships, and other connections.

Anxious or disorganized attachments often arise as a result of certain factors, such as trauma, neglect, early separation from parents, lengthy hospitalizations, inconsistent or inexperienced parenting, emotional un-availability from caregivers, or a caregiver's depression (Brennan, 2021).

If a person faced challenges or struggles during their early childhood, as an adult, they might find it difficult to trust others. Some signs of an anxious attachment include a fear of emotions, intimacy, and emotion-al closeness, a desire to distance oneself when someone becomes needy, a sense of independence and not relying on others, disregarding other people's feelings, having weak boundaries, requiring constant reassurance, being needy or clingy, becoming fixated or overly obsessed with someone, craving intimacy but struggling to trust others, and experiencing anxiety or jealousy when away from their partner. The signs may vary in different individuals (*Do Your Early Experiences Affect Your Adult Relationships?*, 2016).

It's important to note that having an anxious attachment does not nec-essarily indicate a lack of love during childhood. Instead, it suggests that the person did not receive all the emotional support and responsiveness they needed. Additionally, personality and other life experiences may con-tribute to developing anxious attachment.

Preventing Anxious Attachment From Affecting Relationships

If you have an anxious attachment style, there are specific steps you can take to navigate your relationships.

To start, learning effective communication skills can be tremendously helpful. Learning to express your emotions and ask for what you need can help you become more transparent and clear in your relationships. Additionally, understanding nonverbal cues, such as posture and gestures, can enable you to read your partner's feelings more accurately and respond sensibly. You should also be aware of your body language and how it communicates with your partner.

Another effective way to deal with an anxious attachment style is to see a therapist. A therapist can help you understand and process early childhood experiences that may have contributed to this attachment style, allowing you to recognize and resolve these negative patterns.

It may also be helpful to seek out a secure attachment in your relationships. This can be done with some guidance. While it may be uncomfortable at first, engaging in a relationship with someone who is securely attached can provide a sense of what a stable and healthy relationship feels like. Additionally, building friendships with individuals with high self-esteem, healthy boundaries, and secure attachment styles can be beneficial in shifting your attachment patterns towards a more positive direction.

Self-Assessment Tool

Here's a self-assessment tool to help you determine your anxious attachment style. Remember, this shouldn't be used as a professional diagnosis. So, let's dive in!

1)How do you typically react when someone you're dating takes longer than usual to respond to a text or call?

a) No big deal, I'm patient and understanding.

b) I worry and overanalyze their behavior, wondering if they're losing interest.

c) I feel anxious and insecure, thinking they're intentionally trying to ignore me.

2) How would you describe your approach to relationships?

a) I feel comfortable and confident expressing my needs while respecting my partner's boundaries.

b) I tend to seek reassurance from my partner and worry about their level of commitment.

c) I often feel clingy and find trusting my partner's love and affection challenging.

3) In a romantic relationship, do you often seek validation or reassurance from your partner?

a) Rarely, if ever. I'm pretty independent and secure.

b) Occasionally, especially when I'm feeling unsure or insecure.

c) Frequently, it's almost a daily necessity for me.

4) How do you usually feel when your partner spends time with friends or family without you?

a) I enjoy my alone time and trust that they value our relationship.

b) I feel uneasy but understand the importance of maintaining separate social lives.

c) I often feel anxious and worry that they might prefer the company of others over me.

5) How do you typically handle disagreements or conflicts in a relationship?

a) I communicate openly and calmly, aiming for resolution and understanding.

b) I tend to overthink and worry that any disagreement could lead to a bigger problem.

c) I feel overwhelmed and often fear that a conflict will end the relationship.

6) How do you usually feel when you are unable to spend time with your partner?

a) It's disappointing, but I understand we both have our own lives to attend to.

b) I start to miss them and may occasionally worry about the distance affecting our connection.

c) I feel incredibly anxious and fear that they might forget about me or find someone else.

Results:

Mostly A's: You lean towards a secure attachment style. You value independence and trust in your relationships while maintaining healthy emotional connections.

Mostly B's: You lean towards having an anxious attachment style. You may occasionally experience worry or insecurity in relationships, but you can overcome these challenges with awareness and communication.

Mostly C's: It seems like you have an anxious attachment. You may often feel anxious, doubt your partner's love, and seek constant reassurance. It could be helpful to work on building self-confidence and addressing underlying anxieties to establish healthier relationship patterns.

Remember, this assessment is just a tool to give you some insights into your attachment style.

Signs in Children

Various signs may indicate a child has an attachment disorder. These signs include engaging in bullying or aggressive behavior towards others, displaying extreme clinginess and attachment to caregivers, failing to smile or show positive emotions, experiencing intense outbursts of anger, avoiding eye contact, showing no fear of strangers, lacking affection towards primary caregivers, exhibiting oppositional behaviors, struggling with impulse control, engaging in self-destructive behaviors, observing others playing but choosing not to join in, and displaying withdrawn or listless moods.

It is important to note that attachment disorders that develop during childhood can persist and impact a person's relationships in adulthood. However, it should be emphasized that the specific attachment styles experienced in childhood do not always directly translate to attachment patterns in adulthood. This means that individuals with different childhood attachment experiences can still develop a variety of attachment styles in their adult relationships.

Signs in Adults

Adults with attachment issues may exhibit a range of signs and challenges related to forming and maintaining emotional bonds with others. One common manifestation is difficulty in establishing healthy boundaries. This can manifest as having weak boundaries, leading to problems asserting one's needs and maintaining personal space, or having rigid and overly strict boundaries that can hinder closeness and intimacy with others.

Additionally, adults with attachment issues may engage in risky behaviors as a way to cope with their difficulties in forming and maintaining relationships. These behaviors can include impulsivity, seeking out unhealthy or toxic relationships, or engaging in self-destructive behaviors as a means of seeking emotional connection or relief from attachment-related struggles.

Research surrounding attachment issues in adulthood is ongoing, but evidence suggests that individuals with attachment issues may face challenges in forming and maintaining romantic relationships (*Attachment Disorder in Adults: Symptoms, Causes, and More*, 2020). These individuals may struggle with trust, finding it difficult to rely on and have confidence in their partners entirely. They may also experience heightened levels of anxiety within their relationships, often feeling insecure or fearful of rejection or abandonment.

Seeking constant reassurance from their partners or engaging in behaviors to distance themselves emotionally can be common as they try to protect themselves from becoming too attached or getting hurt.

It's important to note that while these signs and challenges are commonly associated with attachment issues in adults, individual experiences and circumstances can vary.

Causes

Attachment issues can arise from various factors, but childhood experiences primarily influence them. One main factor is the presence of inconsistent or neglectful caregivers. This means that when children have caregivers who are unreliable or fail to meet their emotional and physical needs consistently, they are more likely to develop attachment disorders. These disorders can then continue into adulthood if not addressed.

It is worth noting that not all children who experience inconsistent or neglectful caregiving develop attachment disorders. However, researchers have found a clear link between attachment disorders and certain adverse experiences (Erozkan, 2016). For example, significant neglect or deprivation, frequent changes in primary caregivers, or being raised in institutional settings can all contribute to the development of attachment disorders.

Aside from these experiences, other factors may increase the risk of developing attachment disorders. One such factor is experiencing abuse, whether physical, emotional, or sexual. Children who are subjected to abuse are at a higher risk of developing attachment issues (Riggs, 2010).

Additionally, caregivers who lack proper parenting skills, struggle with anger management, or display neglectful behavior are also more likely to contribute to the development of attachment issues. Furthermore, parents who have psychiatric conditions may find it challenging to provide consistent and secure attachment experiences for their children.

Another potential risk factor that has been identified is prenatal exposure to alcohol or drugs. When a child is exposed to such substances before birth, it can impact their neurological development, which in turn can affect their ability to form healthy and secure attachment relationships (Ross et al., 2015).

Related Conditions

Children with attachment disorders often experience difficulties across various domains of life, including academics, social interactions, emotional well-being, and behavior. These struggles can have a profound impact on their overall development and functioning.

Academically, children with attachment disorders may face challenges in a classroom setting. They may have difficulty concentrating, completing tasks, or following instructions. These difficulties can lead to lower academic performance and hinder their ability to reach their full potential.

Socially, children with attachment disorders may struggle to form and maintain healthy relationships with peers and adults. They may have difficulty trusting others, interpreting social cues, or regulating their emotions within social interactions. As a result, they may experience feelings of isolation or rejection and have limited social support networks.

Emotionally, children with attachment disorders may struggle with regulating their emotions. They may experience intense mood swings, have difficulty expressing their emotions appropriately, or have a limited range of emotional responses. These challenges can contribute to problems in managing stress, anxiety, and frustration, which can further impact their overall well-being.

Behaviorally, children with attachment disorders may exhibit disruptive or challenging behaviors. They may engage in impulsive or oppositional behaviors, have difficulty following rules or boundaries, or display aggression toward others. These behavioral challenges can create additional stressors within their family, school, and community environments.

Furthermore, children with attachment disorders are at a higher risk of encountering legal issues during adolescence (National Collaborating Centre for Mental Health [UK], 2015). Their struggles with emotional regulation, impulsivity, and difficulties with authority figures can increase their likelihood of engaging in delinquent behaviors or becoming involved in criminal activities.

In addition, children with attachment disorders may have lower IQ scores compared to their peers (Schröder et al., 2019). This cognitive impact can stem from a combination of genetic factors, environmental influences, and the impact of early adverse experiences on brain development. Furthermore, language problems are more prevalent among children with attachment disorders. They may have delays in language acquisition, difficulty with expressive or receptive language skills, or struggle to articulate their thoughts and ideas effectively.

Personality Disorders

It is important to understand that attachment disorders in children do not resolve on their own over time. While the symptoms may change or manifest differently as they transition into adulthood, they are likely to continue experiencing ongoing challenges if left untreated.

One significant aspect of attachment disorders that persists into adulthood is difficulty in regulating emotions. Individuals who have experienced attachment-related issues in childhood often struggle with managing their emotions effectively. They may have intense emotional reactions, find it challenging to control or express their feelings appropriately, or have difficulty identifying and understanding their emotional states. These difficulties in emotional regulation can lead to relationship problems, difficulties in managing stress, and overall emotional instability.

Furthermore, untreated attachment disorders can impact an individual's ability to form and maintain healthy relationships in adulthood. They may struggle with trust issues, fear of rejection or abandonment, and difficulty establishing intimate connections. These challenges can hinder the development of deep and secure relationships, preventing individuals from experiencing the support, closeness, and fulfillment that come with healthy attachments.

Additionally, untreated attachment disorders may have an impact on various aspects of an individual's life, including their mental health, academic or professional achievements, and overall well-being. The unresolved issues from childhood can contribute to increased vulnerability to mental health conditions such as anxiety, depression, or personality disorders. The lack of secure attachment experiences in childhood can also affect one's self-esteem, sense of identity, and ability to navigate life's challenges effectively.

Addressing attachment disorders and providing appropriate therapeutic interventions is essential for individuals to heal and develop healthier patterns of attachment. With the help of qualified professionals, individuals can work towards improving emotional regulation skills, building trust in relationships, and developing secure attachments. Through therapy, individuals can gain insights into the impact of their early attachment experiences, process any unresolved trauma, and learn healthier ways of relating to themselves and others.

It is crucial not to underestimate the long-lasting effects of untreated attachment disorders. Early intervention and ongoing support can make a significant difference in helping individuals overcome these challenges and cultivate healthier relationships, emotional well-being, and overall life satisfaction as they move into adulthood.

Chapter Summary

- Anxious attachment is a type of insecure relationship children have with mothers or caregivers.

- The type of attachment you had with your mother or primary caregiver can affect your relationships as an adult.

- There are four main attachment styles: secure, anxious-ambivalent, anxious-avoidant, and disorganized.

- Anxious attachment can make coping with stress and change difficult, affecting romantic and other relationships.

- Prevention and improvement strategies include learning communication skills, seeking therapy, and building relationships with securely attached individuals.

Chapter 2

Anxious Attachment & Relationships

"I think about you all the time. I hear your voice in my head, I rehearse conversations with you, I talk to myself, and imagine I'm talking to you. And I wish you felt like this about me, but I know you don't and I don't think you ever will. I think you're happy giving people your scraps. I think that's easy for you, and I don't blame you, because I hate being like this, and I wish I was more like you."

Eliza Clark.

Having an anxious attachment style can present challenges in relationships. Those with this attachment style are highly sensitive to their partner's needs and perceive them well. However, they also constantly need reassurance and affection to feel secure in their romantic relationship. If they don't receive the validation they seek, they can become worried and stressed about the state of their relationship.

Individuals with an anxious attachment style tend to internalize a perceived lack of affection and intimacy as a sign that they are not deserving of love. This leads to an intense fear of rejection. To avoid being abandoned, someone with an anxious attachment style may become clingy, hypervigilant, and prone to jealousy in their relationship. The fear of being alone overwhelms them, so they do everything they can to hold on to their partner. They see their partner as the solution to their deep emotional needs.

Recognizing Patterns

Individuals with an anxious attachment style often desire deep and meaningful connections in their romantic relationships. However, they also tend to experience high levels of stress and anxiety within these relationships. While they are highly attuned to their partner's needs and willing to go above and beyond to meet them, their insecurities and doubts about their self-worth can cause them to project their uncertainties onto their partner's behaviors. This means that if their partner does not always respond in the way they expect or meet their emotional needs, they perceive it as confirmation that they do not deserve love.

For someone with an anxious attachment style, relationships can be both a source of comfort and distress. On one hand, they have a deep fear of rejection and abandonment, which leads them to be hyper-vigilant and constantly on the lookout for any potential threat to the relationship. They constantly seek validation and reassurance from their partner, needing constant confirmation that they are loved. This constant need for reassurance can be exhausting for both parties involved. On the other hand, being in the presence of their loved one can offer them a sense of comfort and soothing, temporarily alleviating their anxiety.

Signs of an anxious attachment style in relationships include being highly attuned to their partner's needs and emotions, often prioritizing their partner's needs over their own, constantly seeking validation and assurance of their worthiness, being hyper-vigilant and overly sensitive to any perceived threats to the relationship, having a deep fear of rejection and abandonment, experiencing jealousy and suspicion towards their partner's actions, displaying clingy behavior and struggling with establishing healthy boundaries, finding it difficult to express and understand their own intense emotions, and experiencing excessive anxiety and worry about the relationship.

Ultimately, the traits associated with an anxious attachment style can be detrimental to one's love life, as they can trigger avoidant strategies in their partner, causing them to withdraw and distance themselves. Therefore, individuals with an anxious attachment style must recognize and manage their attachment patterns to cultivate healthy and fulfilling relationships.

Why Does This Happen?

Deep within, individuals with an anxious attachment style harbor a belief that once their partners truly get to know them, they will lose interest and reject them. This underlying fear stems from their low self-esteem, causing them to believe they are not good enough to maintain their partner's interest in the long run.

It is important to recognize that the thoughts and behaviors of someone with an anxious attachment style are deeply rooted in their childhood experiences. If their need for affection and intimacy is not met during their early years, it may shape their beliefs about themselves and their importance. Often, their needs were brushed aside or disregarded, leading them to believe that they and their needs were unimportant. As a result, they anticipate this pattern in their romantic relationships and go to great lengths to prevent it from happening again.

The anxious attacher's constant need for reassurance and validation is driven by their deep-seated fear of being insignificant and unlovable. They may constantly seek confirmation of their partner's love, fearing that any sign of distance or indifference signifies their impending rejection. Their actions are guided by their desperate efforts to avoid abandonment, as they believe their self-worth depends entirely on their ability to sustain a partner's interest and affection.

Understanding the origins of their anxious attachment style can provide insight into why they think and act the way they do in relationships. By acknowledging and addressing these deep-rooted insecurities, individuals with an anxious attachment style can develop healthier attachment patterns, build self-esteem, and nurture more secure and fulfilling connections with their partners.

Forming Healthy Relationships

Managing an anxious attachment style in relationships can be challenging due to the deeply ingrained patterns of attachment anxiety. However, with understanding and consistent effort, navigating and overcoming the deep-rooted fears and insecurities associated with this attachment style is possible, leading to a more fulfilling and secure romantic partnership.

A crucial step in managing an anxious attachment style is understanding the events or actions that trigger attachment insecurity. By identifying these triggers, individuals with an anxious attachment style can gain insight into how their thoughts and actions are influenced, allowing them to develop strategies to counter their typical negative responses.

Common triggers for individuals with an anxious attachment style in relationships include situations where a partner acts distant or aloof, forgets important events like anniversaries, behaves in a friendly or flirtatious manner with someone else, comes home late, or fails to respond to messages and calls promptly, and fails to compliment changes such as new clothes or a new hairstyle. Any of these triggers can potentially lead the anxious attacher to feel overwhelmed by worry or fear of rejection.

When triggered, the attachment system of someone with an anxious attachment style may activate, leading them to respond to the perceived threat to the relationship by seeking as much closeness with their partner as possible, excessively worrying, and feeling emotionally depleted. Although driven by a genuine desire for security and reassurance, these behaviors can strain a relationship and even lead to a breakup.

To manage an anxious attachment style, individuals can work on developing healthier coping mechanisms and communication skills. This may involve practicing self-soothing techniques to calm anxiety, challenging negative thoughts and insecurities, setting and maintaining healthy boundaries, and expressing their needs and concerns openly and effectively to their partner. Additionally, engaging in self-care, building self-esteem, and seeking therapy or support can be beneficial in addressing the underlying issues associated with an anxious attachment style.

It is important to remember that managing an anxious attachment style in relationships is an ongoing process that requires patience, self-awareness, and consistent effort. With time and dedication, individuals with an anxious attachment style can create more secure and satisfying relationships, breaking free from the negative cycles of anxiety and insecurity.

Effective Communication

An individual with an anxious attachment style often struggles with managing their negative emotions. They may react to their partner through bursts of anger or jealousy in an attempt to regain closeness or address their insecurities. Effective communication is important in these situations, involving taking a moment to reflect on emotions before taking action. Expressing the reasons behind frustration or worry can help open a conversation with your partner.

Loving someone with an anxious attachment style means understanding their intense fear of rejection and abandonment. This fear stems from feelings of unworthiness and can lead to a hyper-focus on any perceived threats to the relationship. Anxious individuals may exhibit protest behaviors. Protest behavior is when you're seeking validation from your partner by engaging in unhealthy behavior. This leads to self-criticism and lower self-esteem. Dealing with an anxious attachment partner can be challenging, but it is important to have an open and clear discussion about their needs and boundaries in the relationship. As I move ahead in the book, I will speak more about communication and how to improve it.

Consistency is crucial for someone with an anxious attachment style. Reassure them of their importance to you and let them know you are there to support them. Allowing your partner to express their anxieties can help them recognize any irrational thought patterns. Validate their emotions and challenge the negative narratives by providing evidence to the contrary. It is important to remember that attachment styles can be changed with knowledge, understanding, and the right tools.

Individuals with an anxious attachment style can develop a "learned" secure attachment by identifying and addressing irrational thoughts about themselves and their relationships. This can be achieved through different approaches, such as therapy, discussions with a partner or trusted friend, or by using workbooks. Regardless of the approach, consistent effort is key to achieving meaningful change. It's also important to understand how your partner can help in situations like these.

How Attachment Manifests

Anxious attachment can manifest in various ways in relationships. Here are a few examples:

- **Constant need for reassurance:** Someone with an anxious attachment may constantly seek reassurance and validation from their partner. They may crave reassurances about their partner's love and commitment, often seeking verbal confirmation of their partner's feelings.

- **Overanalyzing and overthinking behaviors:** People with an anxious attachment tend to overanalyze every action and word in a relationship, attaching meaning to even the smallest details. They may often question their partner's intentions or read into their behaviors more than necessary, leading to unnecessary conflicts or misunderstandings.

- **Fear of abandonment:** Individuals with anxious attachment often have a deep-seated fear of being abandoned. They may worry excessively about their partner leaving them, even when no evidence supports such fears. This fear can lead to clingy behavior and an inability to give their partner space.

- **Overdependence on the relationship:** People with anxious attachment tend to rely heavily on their partner for their emotional well-being. They may have difficulty being independent and often struggle with their own sense of self. This can create an imbalanced dynamic where they rely on their partner for their happiness, potentially leading to feelings of neediness or codependency.

- **Jealousy and possessiveness:** Anxious attachment can also manifest as jealousy and possessiveness in relationships. Due to their insecurity and fear of losing their partner, individuals with an anxious attachment may become overly possessive or jealous when it comes to their partner's interactions with others, even if there is no reason to suspect infidelity.

Remember, attachment styles are not set in stone, and individuals may display a combination of attachment behaviors from different styles. It is important for individuals with anxious attachment to build their self-esteem, cultivate trust, and develop healthy communication skills to foster more secure and fulfilling relationships.

Overcoming Attachment Challenges

John and Mary were deeply in love with each other. However, they both struggled with anxious attachment in their relationship, which caused frequent misunderstandings, insecurities, and a constant need for reassurance.

John had grown up in a family where his parents were inconsistent in their affection and emotional availability. Consequently, he developed an anxious attachment style and always sought validation from his partners. Mary, on the other hand, had experienced a traumatic breakup in the past, leading her to become hypersensitive to any signs of rejection or abandonment.

Their anxieties often manifested in different ways. John would constantly bombard Mary with text messages and calls, seeking reassurance of her love and commitment. Mary, overwhelmed by his constant need for validation, would occasionally withdraw to protect herself from potential rejection.

One day, they decided to confront their attachment challenges head-on. They realized that their anxieties were driving them apart and hindering the growth of their relationship. With courage and determination, they embarked on a journey of healing and growth.

John and Mary sought support from a counselor who specialized in attachment styles. The counselor helped them understand the roots of their anxieties and provided them with the necessary tools to overcome them. They learned the importance of open communication, setting healthy boundaries, and building self-confidence.

As they worked together, John and Mary gradually started to weaken the grip of their anxious attachment style. They now focused on building trust, embracing vulnerability, and practicing mindfulness in their relationship. They learned to express their needs and fears without overwhelming each other, creating a safe and secure environment for growth.

In time, their relationship transformed. John's constant need for reassurance slowly waned, and Mary's fears of abandonment lessened. They began to find strength within themselves and their partnership, realizing they were both worthy of love and that their anxious attachment did not define them.

If you also feel like John or Mary and have similar things happening in your own relationship, rest assured that you are not alone. This book will equip you with tools and information to not only understand your attachment better but also help you overcome it.

Impact on Relationships

Our early relationships with our parents or primary caregivers form the foundation for how we perceive and interact with relationships as we grow older. As we transition into late childhood and adolescence, our peer relationships become increasingly important and further shape our attachment style. Eventually, these experiences with peers impact how we enter into romantic relationships, which in turn continues to shape our attachment style. However, it's important to note that while our early experiences significantly impact our attachment style, they are not the sole determinants. Other factors also contribute, and our attachment style can change over time.

In general, individuals with a secure attachment style have had their needs consistently met during infancy. They grow up with a sense of competence and are comfortable acknowledging their limitations. As adults, they have healthy boundaries, can communicate their needs effectively in their relationships, and are not afraid to end unhealthy relationships when necessary.

On the other hand, individuals with an anxious attachment style have received love and care in an inconsistent manner during infancy. They tend to have a positive view of others but a negative view of themselves. In their romantic relationships, they often idealize their partner and heavily rely on them for their self-esteem. This can lead to behaviors such as making numerous phone calls in a short period when their partner doesn't answer.

Different attachment styles tend to manifest in predictable ways within intimate relationships. Secure individuals can navigate relationships with both anxious and avoidant types. They are comfortable enough with themselves to provide the reassurance that anxious types need while also giving avoidant types the space they require without feeling threatened.

Interestingly, anxious and avoidant individuals often find themselves in relationships with each other more frequently than with their own attachment type (Mark Manson, 2021). This may seem counterintuitive, but there is a reason behind it. Avoidant types are skilled at keeping others at a distance, and it is often the persistent efforts of anxious types that lead to these avoidant individuals opening up in a relationship.

Signs of an Anxiously Attached Partner

Seeking Assurance Repeatedly

Anxiously attached partners place a great deal of importance on their relationships as a means of validating their self-worth, feeling safe and secure, and defining their identity. This preoccupation with the relationship often leads to a constant state of worry (Lebow, 2022).

To seek reassurance, individuals with an anxious attachment style may resort to behaviors such as bombarding their partner with numerous texts or voicemails if they don't receive a prompt response. They may become anxious or upset if their partner appears distant, critical, or unhappy, constantly analyzing their partner's actions and words to decipher hidden meanings.

Moreover, those with an anxious attachment style frequently seek compliments and acknowledgment, constantly requiring reassurance from their partner that they are loved and will not be abandoned. Unfortunately, this incessant need for reassurance and validation can overwhelm their partner, as it may feel like they are being burdened with excessive or unreasonable demands.

The behavior of an anxiously attached partner, driven by their need for reassurance and validation, often creates tension and strain in the relationship. Their partner may struggle to meet the constant need for reassurance, leading to frustration and being overwhelmed. It is crucial for individuals with an anxious attachment style to establish boundaries and find healthier ways to manage their anxiety and need for validation to cultivate more balanced and fulfilling relationships.

Crave Closeness

Anxiously attached partners often find it challenging to regulate and soothe their emotions. They tend to look outside themselves for solutions to their internal struggles, believing their feelings can only be resolved through their relationships. However, relying solely on external sources for emotional stability is not sustainable.

Individuals with an anxious attachment style may experience a range of concerns and anxieties within their relationships. They may constantly worry that intimacy is not genuine or that it won't last, leading to a sense of insecurity and doubt about the authenticity of the connection. Even when things are going well in the relationship, they find it difficult to fully relax or enjoy the positive moments, as there is a constant fear that the good times will eventually come to an end.

Furthermore, anxiously attached partners tend to become more anxious when times are good, as they anticipate their partner will eventually grow tired of them or lose interest. They are hyper-vigilant for any signs that their partner may be pulling away or losing affection, which further fuels their anxiety.

The impact of an anxiously attached partner's difficulty in trusting is significant. Their partner may make sincere efforts to help them build trust, offering reassurances and demonstrating their commitment. However, over time, despite their best intentions, the anxiously attached partner may come to believe that their partner's efforts will never be enough to alleviate their deep-rooted insecurities. This can create a sense of frustration and helplessness in both partners, as the anxiously attached partner's persistent doubts and fears continue to undermine the trust and stability of the relationship.

In order to develop healthier patterns within their relationships, individuals with an anxious attachment need to focus on developing trust and security within themselves. This involves learning to regulate their emotions, cultivating self-compassion, and building a sense of inner security independent of external validation. With time and deliberate effort, it is possible for anxiously attached partners to develop more secure attachment styles and establish more fulfilling and balanced relationships.

Sabotaging a Relationship

People with anxious attachment often have a deep fear of not being able to cope without their partner. This fear can manifest in various ways, and one common response is to unconsciously push their partner away to cope with the underlying fear of their partner pulling away.

Anxiously attached individuals may exhibit behaviors such as jealousy or possessiveness. They may constantly worry that their partner will be attracted to someone else or will find someone better, leading them to become excessively possessive or territorial in their relationship. This behavior stems from their deep-seated fear of abandonment and a need for constant reassurance that their partner is committed to them.

Another way anxiously attached individuals may cope with their fears is by testing their partner's love or loyalty. They may intentionally create situations that provoke their partner's reaction, looking for signs that their partner truly cares for them. This testing behavior stems from a need for constant validation and reassurance that their partner's love is genuine.

In addition, anxiously attached individuals may engage in complaining or nitpicking. They may constantly find faults in their partner or the relationship, often as a means to seek attention or reassurance. By highlighting these perceived flaws, they seek validation that their partner is committed and willing to address their concerns.

In extreme cases, anxiously attached individuals may engage in stalking or harassment behaviors. Their fear of losing their partner can lead them to monitor their partner's activities excessively or invade their privacy. These behaviors can stem from an overwhelming need to maintain control and ensure their partner is always available and committed to them.

Lastly, anxiously attached individuals may become despondent or argumentative when their partner expresses a desire for solo activities or alone time. They may feel threatened or rejected by their partner's need for independence and interpret it as a sign that their partner is pulling away. This can manifest as emotional outbursts, clinginess, or attempts to guilt trip their partner into spending more time with them.

The possessiveness exhibited by anxiously attached partners significantly impacts their relationship. Their partner may feel constantly under scrutiny and mistrusted, causing strain and a lack of emotional safety within the relationship. The anxiously attached partner's possessive behavior can create a sense of suffocation and hinder the growth of trust and intimacy in the relationship.

Working on developing secure attachment and addressing underlying fears and insecurities is crucial for individuals with anxious attachment styles. By cultivating self-confidence and practicing effective communication, anxiously attached individuals can learn to manage their fears and build healthier, more trusting relationships.

Seeking to be Perfect

Anxiously attached partners often fear not being loved or accepted for who they truly are. They believe they can only receive love and approval if they constantly act in a way considered "perfect" or "best." This means hiding their vulnerable side and only showing their partner the parts of themselves that they believe will be liked and accepted. They are afraid that if their partner sees their true selves, with all their flaws and insecurities, they will be rejected.

Because of this fear, anxiously attached partners may believe that their love and value in the relationship depends on what they do for their partner rather than who they are as a person. They may feel that as long as they can fulfill their partner's needs and desires, they will be loved. This can lead to a lot of pressure and anxiety for the anxiously attached partner, as they constantly feel the need to go above and beyond to keep the relationship intact.

Anxiously attached partners also tend to feel responsible for maintaining the relationship and preventing it from falling apart. They may feel it is solely their job to cater to their partner's needs and make them happy. This can lead to feelings of resentment towards their partner, as they may feel that their efforts are not being reciprocated. They may silently expect their partner to do as much for them as they do for their partner, but they hesitate to express these feelings directly.

In their eagerness to please their partner, anxiously attached partners often neglect their own needs. They may engage in people-pleasing behaviors, constantly putting their partner's needs before their own. They may also have loose boundaries, allowing their partner to cross personal boundaries without speaking up. They may try to be indispensable to their partner, believing that their worth in the relationship is dependent on how much they can do for their partner.

As a result of these behaviors, anxiously attached partners may find themselves accepting unhealthy treatment from their partners. They may tolerate behaviors that are harmful or disrespectful because they believe that this is what it takes to keep their partner's love and approval. They may also hesitate to ask for what they need directly, fearing that their partner will be upset or reject them for having needs of their own.

The consequence of anxiously attached partners constantly striving to appear perfect and meet their partner's every need is that their partner may assume everything is fine in the relationship. Their partner may believe that the anxiously attached partner is happy and fulfilled because they are always trying their best to please. However, when the anxiously attached partner finally can no longer bear the weight of their own suppressed needs and resentments, they may explode with complaints and grievances seemingly out of nowhere. This can be confusing and blindsiding for their partner, who may have been unaware of the anxiously attached partner's inner struggles.

Live in Emotional Turmoil

Anxiously attached partners are sensitive to their emotions, unlike avoidantly attached individuals who tend to suppress their feelings. They often experience intense emotions of loneliness, emptiness, or a lack of safety in their relationships. These emotions can be overwhelming and may lead the anxiously attached partner to exhibit certain behaviors and patterns.

As a result of their fear of abandonment, anxiously attached partners may also have frequent or dramatic emotional ups and downs. They can easily become overwhelmed by their emotions and may react exaggeratedly to seemingly small triggers. Their emotions can be intense and quickly fluctuate, making it difficult for them to maintain a sense of emotional stability. They may often feel overwhelmed by their emotions and struggle to regulate or control them.

Another characteristic of anxiously attached partners is their tendency to create drama in their relationships. This can manifest in various ways, such as starting arguments or engaging in attention-seeking behaviors. They may unconsciously create conflict in order to seek reassurance or attention from their partner. This constant drama can be exhausting for the anxiously attached partner and their partner, creating a cycle of emotional turbulence and strain in the relationship.

The consequence of an anxiously attached partner's heightened emotionality is that their partner may feel smothered or exhausted. The intense need for reassurance and constant emotional fluctuations can be overwhelming for their partner. The anxiously attached partner's fear of abandonment may result in them being overly clingy or possessive, which can feel suffocating and restrictive for their partner. The constant drama and emotional rollercoaster may drain their partner's energy and make them feel like they are always walking on eggshells.

Feeling One-Down

Individuals with an anxious attachment style often carry deep-seated insecurities and fears related to their self-worth and desirability. They may constantly question their value and worry that something inherently wrong with them pushes people away. These feelings of being unlovable, powerless, alone, and undesirable can create a constant state of anxiety and insecurity in their relationships.

As a result of these insecurities, anxiously attached partners often project their fears and doubts onto their partners. They may misinterpret innocent actions or harmless remarks from their partner as indicators that their partner doesn't truly care for them or is planning to leave. Even the smallest signs of distance or perceived rejection can trigger intense anxiety and self-doubt in the anxiously attached partner.

This tendency to misconstrue their partner's intentions and misinterpret their actions can create a significant burden for their partner. The anxiously attached partner's constant need for reassurance and validation can make their partner feel responsible for their happiness and emotional well-being. They may feel burdened by the pressure to constantly prove their love and commitment to their anxious partner, as any perceived lapse in attention or affection can be exaggerated and lead to feelings of rejection.

The anxiously attached partner's one-down stance, fueled by their fears of being unlovable and undesirable, can create a dynamic where their partner feels responsible for managing their partner's emotions and happiness (Psychology Today, n.d.). A one-down stance in a relationship refers to a position where one person consistently puts themselves in a lower or subordinate position compared to their partner. This can manifest in behaviors such as constantly checking in, praising and reassuring their partner, and making sacrifices to meet their partner's needs, even at the expense of their well-being.

Over time, this dynamic can become exhausting and overwhelming for the partner of an anxiously attached individual. They may feel constant pressure to prove their love and support, which can lead to feelings of resentment and frustration. The anxiously attached partner's dependency on their partner for validation and reassurance can leave the partner feeling emotionally drained and burdened by the weight of their partner's unhappiness.

Overinvesting in the Relationship

Individuals with an anxious attachment style have a strong desire for deep and meaningful connections in their relationships. They may enter a new partnership, hoping to finally fulfill their longing for intimacy and closeness. However, this intense longing and need for connection can manifest in various behaviors and patterns within the relationship that can strain both partners.

Anxiously attached individuals often seek rapid emotional intimacy and may try to accelerate the pace of the relationship. They may feel an urgency to establish a deep bond with their partner and may push for the relationship to progress quickly, bypassing the natural progression of getting to know each other at a more gradual pace.

To quell their anxieties and uncertainties, anxiously attached partners frequently seek reassurance and validation from their partners. They may constantly ask their partner about the state of the relationship, seeking confirmation that their partner values and cares for them. However, this constant need for reassurance can be emotionally exhausting for the partner and may create feelings of suffocation or being overwhelmed.

In addition, anxiously attached partners may overly idealize their partner or the relationship itself. They might place their partner on a pedestal and see them as perfect or view the relationship as flawless. This idealization can serve as a defense mechanism that shields them from their fears of rejection or abandonment. However, it can also create unrealistic expectations and lead to disappointment or frustration when the partner inevitably falls short of the idealized image.

The fixation on the relationship that characterizes anxiously attached individuals can consume their time and attention. They may become preoccupied with the relationship, constantly thinking about it and investing significant energy and effort into maintaining it. This intense focus on the relationship can sometimes cause them to neglect other important aspects of their life, such as personal hobbies, friendships, or career goals.

The consequence of an anxiously attached partner's overwhelming focus on the relationship is that their partner may feel burdened with responsibilities they didn't sign up for or feel capable of fulfilling. The constant need for reassurance, the rapid advancement of the relationship, and the idealization can create a heavy emotional weight on their partner's shoulders. They may feel overwhelmed by the pressure to meet the anxiously attached partner's emotional needs and live up to their expectations.

The relentless fixation on the relationship by the anxiously attached partner can leave their partner feeling trapped or suffocated, as if their own needs and desires are overshadowed by the demands of the relationship. This imbalance can lead to strain and difficulties in maintaining a healthy and fulfilling partnership for both individuals involved.

Helping Your Partner

If you find yourself in a relationship with a partner who has an anxious attachment style, it can be challenging to navigate how to provide them with the support they need while also maintaining your own independence. It is important to seek your own support during this time, but some strategies can help you support your partner with anxious attachment.

First and foremost, it is beneficial to identify your attachment style and how it may influence the dynamics of the relationship. For example, if you have an avoidant attachment style, you may find it difficult to meet your partner's needs for closeness. Understanding your attachment style can provide insight into your own behaviors and help you be more compassionate towards your partner's anxieties.

Clear and effective communication is crucial when supporting a partner with an anxious attachment. It is important to be direct and empathetic when talking to your partner about your needs and boundaries. For instance, if you are unable to message your partner during the workday, it is important to clearly communicate this to them. Being vague about your boundaries can lead to miscommunication and unnecessary worry for your partner.

Establishing consistency and connection in the relationship can also provide support to a partner with an anxious attachment. Creating routines that allow both you and your partner to feel connected and valued can be incredibly helpful. This could involve setting aside a specific night each week for a date, enjoying a cup of coffee together before work, or simply sending each other a text before going to bed. While maintaining consistency won't necessarily change your partner's attachment style, it can create a stable foundation where healing can occur.

It is important to note that attachment styles can change over time. A person with an anxious attachment style may begin to feel more secure and safe with a committed and emotionally available partner. This means that the effects of anxious attachment may become less invasive in long-term relationships. Healthy relationships that prioritize clear communication and mutual respect can help reshape your attachment style and provide you with new experiences that contradict any negative childhood experiences tied to attachment.

Dating Tips

To successfully navigate the initial stages of dating and find a healthy match for yourself, it is crucial to have self-awareness and take specific steps to manage your anxious attachment style. Alongside being aware of your attachment style, here are some tips to help you navigate dating:

Recognize when you are overly preoccupied with the relationship in your mind. This could manifest as frequently imagining a future together or constantly replaying past conversations in your head. While some level of thinking about the relationship is normal, excessive or intrusive thoughts can hinder your ability to fully engage with the present. Acknowledge when this occurs and label it for what it is: intrusive thoughts.

Redirect your attention to your immediate environment. When you notice yourself spiraling into thoughts about the relationship, deliberately shift your focus to what is happening in the present moment. Engage in activities or conversations that keep you grounded and centered. By redirecting your attention, you can break the cycle of anxious rumination and regain a sense of balance and presence.

Practice mindfulness techniques. Mindfulness involves intentionally paying attention to the present moment without judgment. It can be useful in managing anxiety and helping you stay grounded. Engage in mindfulness techniques such as deep breathing exercises, meditation, or guided imagery to bring yourself back to the present and reduce anxious thoughts.

Communicate your needs and concerns. It is important to communicate openly and honestly with your partner about your anxious attachment style and any concerns or insecurities you may have. By expressing your needs and fears, you can foster a sense of emotional safety and understanding in the relationship. Effective communication can help both partners navigate uncertainties and build a stronger foundation.

Take things at a comfortable pace. It is crucial not to rush into a committed relationship or put undue pressure on yourself or your partner. Allow the relationship to evolve naturally and take time to build trust and connection. Setting healthy boundaries and being mindful of your emotional well-being is essential. This allows you and your partner to feel secure and develop a solid foundation for a healthy relationship.

When you sense that something is not quite right in a new dating relationship, it is essential to pause before reacting. The initial instinct may be to hurry and reconnect with the person, seeking reassurance or clarification about the situation. However, it is important to step back and check in with yourself before acting impulsively.

Take a moment to acknowledge and identify your feelings. Are you feeling anxious, insecure, or uncertain about the relationship? Recognize that your emotions can be heightened by your anxious attachment style. Validate your feelings and remind yourself that it is normal to have some level of unease in the early stages of dating.

Instead of immediately seeking validation from your partner, shift your focus inward. Take steps to soothe yourself and calm your nervous system. Engage in activities that bring you comfort and relaxation, such as deep breathing, meditation, or a hobby you enjoy. This self-soothing exercise will help regulate your emotions and allow you to approach the situation with a clear and more grounded mindset.

Reframe your perspective on the need for immediate connection. Rather than feeling the urgency to reconnect with your partner right away, recognize that what you truly need is to regain a sense of calm and equilibrium within yourself. By prioritizing self-care and emotional well-being, you can approach the relationship from a place of inner strength and stability.

Remember that taking time to self-soothe and reflect does not mean neglecting the relationship or avoiding difficult conversations. It simply means recognizing that your immediate need is to center yourself before engaging with your partner. This pause can actually benefit the relationship by allowing you to respond in a more thoughtful and balanced manner.

Chapter Summary

- The Anxious attachment style is characterized by high sensitivity to a partner's needs and a constant need for reassurance and affection.

- Individuals with this attachment style internalize a lack of affection as a sign that they do not deserve love, leading to intense fear of rejection.

- To avoid abandonment, those with anxious attachment may become clingy, hypervigilant, and prone to jealousy in relationships.

- Anxious individuals see their partner as the solution to their emotional needs and fear of being alone.

- Lack of validation and reassurance can cause worry and stress for those with an anxious attachment style in their romantic relationships.

Chapter 3

Links to Your Past

"Learn from past experiences but accept them all as perfect while staying in the present. Let go of everything that doesn't serve you."

Mike Basevic.

Various factors, including genetic components and early childhood experiences, can trigger anxious attachment. Research has shown that anxiety tends to have a genetic component, with children as young as four months of age displaying behavioral disinhibition that is linked to later separation anxiety (Madrid, 2012).

However, childhood experiences can also contribute to attachment anxiety. For instance, being raised by overprotective parents, experiencing abuse or neglect can result in insecure attachment patterns. Attachment plays a critical role in ensuring a child's survival as it establishes a sense of security for the child. For instance, when a child experiences distress, their instinct is to seek comfort from their attachment figures.

If a child fails to receive comforting responses from the attachment figures, they may not develop a sense of security. This can lead to elevated levels of fear, anxiety, and distress that linger throughout life. This pattern can repeat itself in later relationships, where the individual may expect comfort from others but fail to receive it, leading to feelings of insecurity and further perpetuating negative attachment patterns.

Coping With Anxious Attachment

Individuals with attachment anxiety often resort to ineffective coping strategies, such as excessive checking on their partner, which only exacerbates their anxiety and strains their relationships. Identifying helpful and healthy coping strategies to break free from these negative patterns is crucial.

If you recognize signs of anxious attachment in your behavior, there are several strategies you can implement to manage these tendencies and improve your overall well-being:

Being mindful of your partner's attachment style can help in understanding how it affects your attachment anxiety. A partner with a secure attachment style can provide a stable and nurturing environment, fostering a more secure attachment for both individuals. Try to foster open and honest communication with your partner. Encourage them to express their feelings, fears, and needs without judgment. Create a safe space where they can share their thoughts and experiences. Also, listen attentively to your partner and try to understand their perspective. Validate their emotions and show empathy. Also, try being responsive and available to your partner's emotional needs. Offer reassurance and support when they express anxiety or insecurity.

Instead of dwelling on past negative experiences, consciously make new choices that align with your desired life. Shifting your perspective towards a positive future can help reduce attachment anxiety.

Let's look at a short story. Emma realized that she had to make new choices to create the life she truly desired. She began by looking closer at her current situation and identifying what was holding her back.

Emma discovered that fear and self-doubt were the main culprits preventing her from taking risks and pursuing her passions. But she was determined to change that. One by one, Emma started making choices that aligned with her goals. She left her unfulfilling job and pursued a career in a field she was passionate about. She made a conscious effort to surround herself with positive and supportive individuals who believed in her dreams.

Emma also prioritized her self-care. She made time for exercise, meditation, and activities that brought her joy. As her physical and mental well-being improved, so did her ability to make choices that aligned with her desired life.

Working with a therapist experienced in helping individuals transition from insecure to secure attachment can be immensely beneficial. Through therapy, you can gain insights into your attachment patterns, explore underlying causes, and learn effective strategies to develop a more secure attachment style. A counselor or therapist can help in various situations.

Writing down your thoughts, feelings, and reactions in a journal provides a valuable outlet for self-reflection. This practice can help you gain a deeper understanding of your attachment anxiety and identify patterns or triggers that contribute to it. Try doing this every day, to begin with, and eventually do it once a week.

Learn more about attachment anxiety to enhance your understanding of the issue. This knowledge can empower you to make informed choices, alter your perspective, and develop healthier coping mechanisms. This book is your companion in your healing journey. You may often come back to revisit the concepts and get ideas on what to do to reduce your relationship anxiety.

Recognize the people in your life who tend to trigger your attachment anxiety. When you interact with certain people, pay attention to how you feel. Do you feel anxious, worried, or insecure? Acknowledge these emotions and their intensity. Look for consistent patterns in your emotional responses. Are there specific people who consistently make you feel anxious or trigger your attachment anxiety? This awareness allows you to proactively manage your responses and set boundaries to minimize anxiety-inducing situations.

Coping With an Anxious Partner

If you are in a relationship with someone who has attachment anxiety, there are ways you can support and help them feel more secure:

- **Validate their feelings:** Acknowledging and validating your partner's feelings is crucial rather than minimizing or dismissing them. Don't shut them out. Rather than saying, "You're suffocating me," try saying, "I understand what you're going through, and I want to help you." Understanding that their attachment anxiety is real and significant can make a significant difference in their sense of security.

- **Communication and awareness:** Encourage open communication about how their attachment anxiety affects your relationship. By discussing this together, both partners can better understand triggers, patterns, and potential solutions. As mentioned in the previous point, speak with them and understand their feelings rather than shutting them out.

- **Consistency and reliability:** Building trust is essential for someone with attachment anxiety. Be consistent in your words and actions, honoring commitments and promises. This consistency helps reassure your partner that they can rely on you and fosters a more secure attachment. Something as simple as sharing your phone's password with your partner shows that you trust them.

- **Show care and reassurance regularly:** Make an effort to demonstrate your care and concern for your partner on a regular basis. Small gestures of love and affection, kind words, and reassurance can go a long way in alleviating their attachment anxiety.

- **Couples therapy:** Consider attending couples therapy together. This can be an effective approach to addressing attachment-related issues as a couple, improving communication and understanding, and finding constructive ways to manage attachment anxiety within the relationship. A therapist can facilitate discussions, provide tools, and help both partners develop healthier attachment patterns.

Remember to approach these strategies with empathy, patience, and understanding. Supporting a partner with attachment anxiety requires compassion, active listening, and a willingness to learn and grow together. By offering this support, you can contribute to creating a more secure and fulfilling relationship for both of you.

Getting Over Your Past

Those with an anxious attachment style often carry emotional baggage from their past, particularly from experiences with their parents or significant romantic relationships. If their parents were consistently inattentive to their emotional or physical needs or if they were let down in previous relationships, it can lead to the development of an anxious attachment style.

The lessons we learned in our formative years can shape our behavior and coping strategies in our current relationships. However, sometimes, these once-helpful strategies can become counterproductive. For example, you may attempt to protect yourself by controlling or worrying about outcomes, but such behaviors can harm your relationships.

To address this, it is necessary to heal and let go of past disappointments so that you can accurately assess and respond to the present situation. When you have an anxious attachment style, it can be challenging to differentiate between your reactions and the role your partner plays in the dynamic.

To uncover the influence of your past on your current relationships, consider whether there are any similarities between your current experiences and what you went through as a child or witnessed in your parents' relationship. This self-reflection can help shed light on how your attachment style manifests in your current interactions.

Ask yourself, "What can I learn from my past?" Reflect on the lessons or insights that your experiences have given you. Consider how it has shaped your perspective, values, or decision-making.

By acknowledging the impact of your past experiences and recognizing how they may be affecting your present relationships, you can begin the process of healing and working towards a more secure attachment style. It may be helpful to seek the support of a therapist who specializes in attachment-related issues. They can guide you on this journey of self-discovery and provide tools to develop healthier patterns in your relationships. With time, effort, and self-compassion, you can free yourself from the limitations of anxious attachment and cultivate more fulfilling and secure relationships.

Focused Exercises

To delve deeper into the link between childhood experiences and your current anxious attachment style, below are some detailed exercises you can try. Give yourself permission to take it at your own pace and be patient with yourself as you navigate this journey of understanding and healing your anxious attachment style.

- **Reflect on your early childhood experiences:** Set aside some dedicated time to reflect on your relationship with your primary caregivers during your early years. Consider aspects such as the consistency of care you received, how responsive they were to your needs, and whether you felt secure and loved. Write down any significant memories or patterns that come to mind, noting positive and challenging experiences.

- **Identify attachment-related triggers:** Pay close attention to situations or behaviors that trigger your anxious attachment style. Take note of instances where you feel a heightened need for reassurance or become overly sensitive to your partner's actions. Sensory experiences such as specific smells, tastes, sounds, or tactile sensations can trigger memories or emotions associated with the trauma. Write down these triggers and try to identify any common themes or patterns that emerge. Understanding your triggers can help you become more aware of when your anxious attachment tendencies are activated.

- **Engage in journaling exercises:** Make journaling a regular practice to explore your attachment-related emotions and thoughts.

Set aside dedicated time to write about specific incidents or conflicts that have triggered your anxious attachment style. Reflect on how you felt during those moments and explore any underlying fears or insecurities that arise. This process can help you gain insights into your emotional patterns and clarify what triggers your anxious attachments. At this step, it is recommended that you write in a physical journal, even though a digital journal is also possible. Set aside your phone, sit alone without distractions, take the time, feel the pen in your fingers, and truly focus on writing down your thoughts and feelings.

- **Practice self-compassion:** Cultivate self-compassion as a countermeasure to the negative beliefs and self-worth issues often associated with anxious attachment. When you experience feelings of anxiety or fear in your relationship, remind yourself that these emotions are natural responses rooted in your early experiences. Start by becoming aware of your thoughts, emotions, and physical sensations. Notice when you are being self-critical or judgmental towards yourself. Mindfulness helps you observe your experiences without getting caught up in them. This practice can help you challenge negative self-talk and develop a more compassionate and understanding perspective towards yourself.

Breaking Down Personal Patterns

Understanding and addressing personal patterns related to anxious attachment is a complex but crucial endeavor that can lead to personal growth and healthier relationships.

Use the knowledge from this book to learn more about anxious attachment styles and how they influence relationships. This will help you gain insights into your own patterns and behaviors. This could include identifying common triggers, reactions, or fears that tend to arise.

Anxious attachment often involves negative self-perception and a fear of abandonment. To break free from these patterns, actively work on challenging and reframing these negative thoughts and beliefs. Try using affirmations like "I deserve love and security in my relationships" or "I trust in the strength of my connections and believe in the goodness of others."

Identifying Triggers and Responses

Developing an understanding of your triggers and responses in relation to anxious attachment is a valuable process that can lead to greater self-awareness and the ability to manage your attachment style effectively.

When you experience triggers, it may feel as though you are reliving a traumatic event. However, a technique called the flashback halting protocol can help interrupt the flashback and bring you back to the present moment. This process can assist your mind and body in recognizing that the trauma is no longer happening.

Here's a detailed breakdown of the steps involved in the flashback halting protocol:

- **Recognize your current emotions:** Begin by acknowledging and labeling the emotions you are feeling at that moment. It could be fear, anxiety, panic, sadness, or any other emotion that arises during the flashback.

- **Observe the sensations in your body:** Take a moment to notice and identify any physical sensations you are experiencing. This could include shaking, sweating, dizziness, or other bodily responses associated with the triggering event.

- **Identify the trigger:** Identify the specific aspect of the traumatic event you remember or are reminded of. For instance, this could be the person involved, a particular vehicle, or a childhood-related memory.

- **Ground yourself in the present:** Shift your attention to the present by stating the current date and time. This helps remind your mind that the present moment is separate from the past trauma.

- **Recognize your environment:** Look around and identify five objects that you can see in your surroundings. Naming these objects engages your senses and brings your awareness to the present moment.

Practical Strategies for Breaking Negative Cycles

Breaking negative, anxious attachment cycles can be challenging, but with perseverance and the right strategies, it is possible to overcome them. Here are some strategies you can try to help break negative cycles. Start by focusing on your thoughts and identifying any negative, self-critical, or irrational patterns. Write them down and challenge them by asking yourself if they are based on evidence or if there are alternative perspectives to consider.

When negative thoughts arise, imagine how you would respond to a friend in a similar situation and offer yourself the same compassion. Create a list of positive affirmations or self-statements and repeat them daily. These affirmations can help counteract negative thoughts and build self-confidence.

When you catch yourself making negative assumptions or jumping to conclusions, challenge those interpretations by considering alternative explanations or seeking evidence to support or refute your assumptions. Try asking yourself, "Why did this happen?" rather than "This shouldn't have happened."

Chapter Summary

- Anxious attachment can be triggered by genetic components and early childhood experiences.

- Genes play a role in anxiety, with children displaying behavioral disinhibition at a young age that later leads to separation anxiety.

- Childhood experiences, such as overprotective parenting, abuse, and neglect, can contribute to insecure attachment patterns.

- Attachment is crucial for a child's survival as it establishes a sense of security and comfort.

- If a child does not receive comforting responses from attachment figures, they may develop elevated levels of fear, anxiety, and distress that can persist into adulthood and impact later relationships.

Chapter 4

Changing Your Mindset

"The trick is not to get hooked on the highs and lows and mistake an activated attachment system for passion or love. Don't let emotional unavailability turn you on."

Amir Levine.

A t its core, your mindset shapes your beliefs, values, and attitudes about yourself and the world you inhabit. It ultimately shapes how you perceive and experience the world. Depending on your mindset, you may either feel like life is happening to you, or it is happening for you. You may feel like you have complete control over your life or that your destiny is predetermined. You may believe strongly in personal growth, or conversely, you may be content living within the confines of your comfort zone.

People can often be described as "stuck in their ways", holding rigid beliefs that may be outdated or no longer serve them. Others may be seen as pessimistic, whereas some may be labeled optimists. These different labels are all indicative of the different types of mindsets people hold.

The good news is that it is possible to change your mindset. The ability to shift one's mindset is a key trait shared by successful people who have achieved their goals. Everyone is capable of changing their mindset, which can improve the quality of their life and even propel them towards their desired success. There are several ways to shift your mindset, and taking concrete steps toward cultivating a more positive and productive mindset can profoundly impact your personal and professional life.

Stop Gossiping

Have you ever found yourself venting about your partner's behavior to a friend or family member? While this may seem like a natural response to a frustrating situation, it is important to be mindful of the impact of negative talk on your relationships.

One reason why it's not ideal to talk about your partner negatively with others is that it can create a cycle of negative energy. As the saying goes, "What goes around comes around." If you engage in negative gossip about your partner, you are confirming to yourself that there is something fundamentally wrong in your relationship. By focusing on their flaws and making them the central topic of conversation, you are inadvertently amplifying their negative qualities in your mind.

It's important to remember that energy flows where focus goes. If all your energy is focused on the negative aspects of your relationship, it can be difficult to see the positive aspects. This can lead to further dissatisfaction and disappointment in your relationship, which can then be expressed through more negative talk.

Of course, it is understandable to want to share your frustrations with others from time to time. The key is to be mindful of how often you do it and to balance out the negative talk with positive talk. Rather than focusing solely on your partner's flaws, try to devote equal energy to discussing the positive aspects of your relationship. This can help shift your focus towards the positives and cultivate more positivity in your mind.

Adjusting to Your Partner's Mood

Let me illustrate a situation that you might find familiar. It's the weekend, and you've been excitedly looking forward to spending quality time with your partner. However, when the weekend arrives, your partner is in a bad mood due to a rough week and doesn't feel up for doing anything. In this scenario, it's easy to feel upset or annoyed.

But here's an alternative perspective: You can choose not to allow your partner's negative mood to affect your own emotions. This doesn't mean that you ignore or dismiss your partner's feelings; it simply means that you don't take on their mood as your own. By adopting this mindset, you can relieve the pressure on your relationship.

When you expect your partner to always be in a cheerful mood, it implies their role is to "make you happy." However, it's important to recognize that happiness is not solely your partner's responsibility—it is ultimately your own. This realization highlights the importance of taking ownership of your happiness.

By acknowledging that you have the power to cultivate happiness within yourself, you can relieve your partner of the burden of constantly ensuring your happiness. This shift in mindset allows you to approach your relationship from a place of understanding and support rather than harboring unrealistic expectations.

Be There for Yourself

Taking responsibility for your happiness is crucial not only in romantic relationships but in all aspects of life. We often have the desire for others to show up for us, meet our expectations, and make our lives easier. However, it is important to acknowledge that life is a journey of growth, and sometimes, people may not always do what we expect them to.

In the scenario mentioned earlier, where your partner doesn't want to participate in the activities you planned for the weekend, you have the opportunity to show up for yourself. Not showing up for yourself could involve feeling annoyed and spending the entire weekend on the sofa, indulging in popcorn and chocolate. However, showing up for yourself could look different. It might involve reaching out to friends to see what they're up to, enjoying a good book, or taking a peaceful solo walk.

You may wonder how this relates to the longevity of your relationship. When you allow yourself to stay sour and dwell in negative thoughts for the entire weekend, it can significantly impact your perception of your partner. Your thoughts about them are likely to be negative, and this can strain the relationship. On the other hand, when you show up for yourself and maintain a positive attitude, you can approach the situation with the understanding that everyone has bad days. By choosing to have a good time regardless of your partner's mood, you can move forward and nurture a healthier relationship.

Inner Wounds

We all carry inner wounds from our past experiences, whether from childhood or previous relationships. Unfortunately, these unresolved issues can often impact our current partnerships when we project our triggers onto our significant other.

It's common to fall into the belief that our partner shouldn't have behaved in a certain way or said certain things. However, it's essential to recognize that we have a choice in how we interpret and react to a situation. Our past experiences tend to condition us to think in a specific way, but it's crucial to challenge and explore these patterns. By doing so, we can let go of our emotional baggage and cultivate a more relaxed and open-minded attitude in our relationship.

Exploring and releasing our inner wounds not only allows us to heal and grow individually but also has a positive impact on our partnership. By addressing our baggage, we become more self-aware and less likely to blame our partner for triggering our old wounds. This newfound clarity and understanding create a healthier dynamic in the relationship.

When we let go of the limitations imposed by our past, we can approach our partners and situations with a fresh perspective. We understand they are not responsible for our past hurts, and we become more compassionate and empathetic towards them. This shift in mindset fosters better communication, trust, and overall harmony in the relationship.

Taking the time to work on ourselves and heal our inner wounds ultimately benefits not only our well-being but also the longevity and strength of our partnership. By embracing self-reflection and letting go of emotional baggage, we create space for growth, understanding, and a deeper connection with our significant other.

Don't Compare

Your thoughts have a significant impact on the relationship you have or desire to have. It may seem obvious, but it's worth emphasizing that creating the relationship of your dreams starts and continues with the thoughts you cultivate. Comparing your relationship to others, indulging in thoughts like "Why doesn't my partner do this like someone else's partner?" or even fantasizing about someone else can hinder the growth of your relationship.

When you find yourself thinking about others or making comparisons, you divert your attention and energy away from nurturing your relationship. As humans, we can only hold one thought at a time. So, by focusing on someone else's garden, you neglect the cultivation of your own. Instead of spending time and effort on your relationship, you're directing your energy towards something that isn't within your control.

If there are specific actions or behaviors that you desire from your partner but aren't currently receiving, it's important to take a proactive approach. Rather than dwelling on what your partner isn't doing, shift your mindset and water your garden. In other words, take actions that foster love and affection within your relationship. Show your partner acts of kindness and love that make them feel valued and cherished. By doing so, you redirect your focus towards love instead of dwelling on its absence. As a result, not only does your partner feel loved and appreciated, but you also cultivate a sense of love within yourself.

By continuously nourishing your relationship with positive thoughts and actions, you create an environment conducive to the growth and development of the relationship you desire. Remember, the grass may appear greener on the other side, but investing time and energy into your garden will yield a more fulfilling, authentic, and loving relationship.

Boundaries

In the past, I used to believe that it was only necessary to set boundaries for everyone except my romantic partner. However, I have come to realize just how mistaken I was. Boundaries are crucial for every person in our lives, especially our partners. Our significant others have a greater potential to unintentionally violate our boundaries simply because they are the closest to us and have more access to our personal space.

A key factor that played a role in my liberation was the realization that not establishing healthy boundaries is detrimental not only to myself but also to the other person involved. Looking back, I now recognize that I may have unknowingly crossed the emotional boundaries of others before I fully grasped the concept. Due to my lack of knowledge on how to safeguard myself through healthy boundaries, I allowed people to harm me emotionally. This lack of self-protection not only resulted in my suffering but also contributed to a negative impact on those around me.

Often, we only become aware of the need to establish boundaries when one of our boundaries is violated, which we may not have even known about. In such situations, we can choose to address the issue through open and honest communication or, depending on the circumstances, make a commitment to behave differently in the future. Boundaries primarily concern how we present ourselves and what we allow in our lives. Once we gain a deeper understanding of ourselves, we become better equipped to align our actions and behaviors with our true selves. This ultimately benefits our relationship, as when we remain true to ourselves, there is no need to place blame on others. I will speak more about boundaries later in the book.

Unconditional Love

It's essential to recognize that being in a relationship is a choice, and it's not always an easy one. However, we always have the option to leave if we are not happy or satisfied with where we are. I mention this because some of us tend to continually criticize our partners, even though we have no intention of ending the relationship.

Whether it's their eating habits or forgetfulness, when we constantly criticize our partners for their flaws, it indicates that we do not fully love and accept them as they are. While we may claim that we love them, our partners may not feel truly loved and accepted for who they are. This point is significant because we all yearn to be loved and accepted for our authentic selves. If we fail to fulfill our part by showing unconditional love and acceptance, tension in the relationship will likely build over time.

Cultivating Self-Compassion

Self-kindness and embracing our common humanity are two interconnected concepts that can greatly impact our well-being. They remind us of the following:

1. We are all human beings,

2. It is perfectly okay to be imperfect.

Instead of defining ourselves solely by our thoughts, feelings, and behaviors, we can practice self-compassion by giving ourselves the same leniency and understanding that we would extend to others.

For instance, if a friend neglects to answer your phone call out of laziness, you are unlikely to jump to the conclusion that they are a bad person. By permitting ourselves to be human, we can acknowledge and accept our flaws. This realization allows us to recognize that we are not alone in experiencing imperfections; it is a common aspect of the human condition.

Abigail grappled with deep-seated feelings of inadequacy and self-doubt. Seeking therapy, she confronted these issues head-on. Through self-reflection, she learned to challenge negative thoughts and treat herself with kindness.

Abigail embraced the idea of being a work in progress, understanding that mistakes are opportunities for growth. Instead of harsh self-criticism, she adopted a compassionate mindset. For instance, when she makes a mistake at work, Abigail reframes it as a chance to learn and improve.

By practicing self-compassion, Abigail found a balance between self-improvement and self-acceptance. She acknowledged her strengths and weaknesses without judgment, fostering inner peace.

An important aspect of self-compassion is treating ourselves with the same care and empathy we would offer to a friend in need. When a friend is feeling down, hurt, or upset, we may offer physical gestures of comfort, such as patting them on the back or holding their hand. Similarly, using gentle and forgiving language, including terms of endearment like "darling" or "sweetheart," can help cultivate self-kindness, even if it feels initially unfamiliar or awkward.

Becoming Self-Aware

If you find positive affirmations to be ineffective or unnatural, an alternative approach you can try is using "releasing statements." Releasing statements can be considered exercises in self-forgiveness and are closely related to the concept of detached non-judgment in mindfulness (Moore, 2019). Instead of engaging with negative thoughts, like "I'm such a horrible person for getting upset," you can turn it around and consciously "release" yourself from that negative feeling. For instance, you can say to yourself, "It's okay that I felt upset." This practice allows you to acknowledge and accept your emotions without attaching negative judgments to them.

Another important aspect of self-compassion is self-acceptance, which involves embracing your perceived weaknesses and character strengths. It's essential to avoid over-inflating or defining yourself solely based on these shortcomings. Instead, recognize that thoughts and feelings are simply behaviors and states, and they do not fully define who you are as a person.

Practicing mindfulness can be valuable in cultivating self-compassion. Mindfulness exercises help you stay present in the moment and can serve as a grounding technique. Not only is mindfulness one of the key components of self-compassion, but activities like yoga and deep breathing can be practiced anywhere and at any time, making them accessible tools for promoting self-care and self-acceptance.

Gaining Perspective

One way to cultivate self-kindness is by letting go of the need for outside validation. Often, when we berate ourselves for our choices, such as eating something indulgent, it is because we internalize societal pressures related to appearance and weight. By consciously deciding not to tie our happiness and self-worth to external influences, we can demonstrate self-compassion and positively impact our overall well-being. This act of self-kindness can have a ripple effect, allowing us to break free from the cycle of seeking validation from others and instead focus on nurturing our inner contentment.

Additionally, reaching out to others can be a valuable strategy for cultivating self-compassion. It may seem contradictory to the previous point, but this technique is about gaining perspective and placing our feelings within a larger context. When we engage in conversations with others and open up about our experiences, we often discover that we are not alone in experiencing pain or self-criticism. This realization reaffirms our sense of connectedness and helps us reframe our perceived problems within the bigger picture of shared human experiences. Moreover, reaching out creates an opportunity to build social support networks that play a crucial role in our overall well-being, providing understanding, empathy, and encouragement along our self-compassion journey.

Practical Exercises for Building Self-Love

Building self-love is a powerful practice that can significantly improve your overall well-being and relationships. Here are a few practical exercises you can incorporate into your daily routine to cultivate self-love:

Begin your day by stating positive affirmations about yourself. Repeat statements such as "I am worthy," "I am enough," and "I love and accept myself unconditionally." This helps rewire your thoughts towards self-compassion and strengthens self-love.

Whenever you find yourself being self-critical or experiencing difficult emotions, take a moment to pause. Acknowledge your feelings and remind yourself that it's okay to struggle. Then, offer yourself words of comfort and support, similar to what you would say to a close friend in a challenging situation.

Set aside a few minutes each day to write down things you appreciate and are grateful for about yourself. It could be your strengths, achievements, or qualities. Focusing on gratitude for your attributes can help cultivate self-love and appreciation.

Develop regular self-care practices that nurture your physical, emotional, and mental well-being. This could include activities like taking a hot bath, enjoying a cup of tea, practicing mindfulness or meditation, engaging in your favorite hobbies, or spending time in nature. Prioritize self-care as a way of showing love and care for yourself.

Set aside some time each week for self-reflection. Ask yourself how you're feeling, what you need in the moment, and any areas where you need to offer yourself more compassion. Listen to your intuition and be kind and gentle with yourself.

Surround yourself with people who support and uplift you. Seek out positive role models, inspiring books, podcasts, or online communities that promote self-love and personal growth.

Strategies for Overcoming Self-Critical Thoughts

Here are some strategies for overcoming self-critical thoughts:

Start by becoming aware of your self-critical thoughts. When you notice negative self-talk, challenge it by asking yourself if it's rooted in reality or a distorted perception. Look for evidence that supports or contradicts the negative thoughts and try to reframe them in a more realistic and compassionate light.

Pay attention to when and why self-critical thoughts appear. Is there a specific trigger or situation that tends to activate them? By understanding the patterns and underlying causes, you can better address and challenge these thoughts. Mindfulness practices, such as meditation or journaling, can help cultivate self-awareness and reduce self-critical thinking.

Instead of viewing mistakes as personal failures, reframe them as valuable learning experiences. Embrace the opportunity to grow, develop new skills, and gain wisdom from your experiences. Remember that nobody is perfect, and growth comes from embracing and learning from failures.

Create a list of your achievements and review it regularly. Celebrate even the small victories and acts of self-improvement. You can treat yourself to some pizza or ice cream. With time, this practice can help rewire your brain to focus on your strengths and foster self-appreciation rather than self-criticism.

Reframing Negative Thought Patterns

The way we think, feel, and behave are intricately connected and continuously impact each other. Sometimes, however, we develop patterns of thoughts or behaviors that are unhelpful and detrimental to our well-being. This can create a vicious cycle where these negative patterns influence our emotions, which then further impact our thoughts and behaviors.

Unfortunately, many of us are unaware that we have the power to influence and improve this process, ultimately enhancing our mental health. One effective method is to challenge and replace these unhelpful thoughts. By doing so, we can effectively address stress and anxiety, improve our sleep patterns, and significantly elevate our overall mood. This, in turn, can have a transformative effect on our mental health and overall sense of well-being.

To accomplish this, it is essential to learn how to take a step back and examine our thoughts critically. By questioning the evidence that supports these negative thoughts, we can gradually shift them towards more positive and constructive ones. With practice and dedication, it is possible to reshape our thought patterns and cultivate a more optimistic and resilient mindset. This shift in thinking can have a profound and lasting impact on our mental health, leading to improved well-being and a more fulfilling life.

Here are a few examples:

Example 1:

- **Negative Thought:** "I made a mistake. I'm so stupid."

- **Reframed Thought:** "Making mistakes is part of being human. This mistake is an opportunity for me to learn and grow. I can take this experience as a chance to improve my skills and be more careful in the future."

Example 2:

- **Negative Thought:** "I failed my exam. I'm a complete failure."

- **Reframed Thought:** "Failing an exam doesn't define my worth. It's an indication that I need to adjust my studying approach or seek help if necessary. This setback is an opportunity for me to reflect, regroup, and approach future exams more effectively."

Example 3:

- **Negative Thought:** "I was rejected when I asked someone out. I'm unlovable."

- **Reframed Thought:** "Rejection is a normal part of life, and it doesn't reflect my worth as a person. This experience means that I had the courage to take a chance, and it's simply an opportunity to find someone who appreciates and reciprocates my feelings."

When reframing negative thoughts, you can ask yourself questions like:

- Is this thought based on factual evidence, or is it a distortion?

- How would I respond if a friend or loved one had the same experience or thought?

- How can I reframe this thought in a more compassionate and realistic way?

- What can I learn from this situation? What opportunities for growth does it present?

- How can I view this experience from a different perspective or with greater understanding?

You can certainly add these reframed thoughts and the questions you ask yourself to your journal. Writing down negative thoughts and challenging them with reframed thoughts and questions can help you gain clarity, develop self-awareness, and foster a more positive and compassionate mindset.

Steps and Strategies

It is often the case that we are unaware when we engage in unhelpful thinking patterns. This can make it hard to recognize these thoughts in the first place. However, we can learn to identify what sort of thoughts are unhelpful in making the spotting process easier.

Unhelpful thoughts come in different forms, such as always expecting the worst from any situation, only focusing on the negative sides of a situation, seeing things as either good or bad with nothing in between, and considering oneself the sole cause behind unfortunate events.

Being aware of these categories of negative thoughts is essential, and if you have an unhelpful thought throughout your day, you can identify which category it belongs to. Although it may seem difficult to tune into these thoughts initially, being familiar with the types of unhelpful thoughts can help you recognize and reduce the frequency of them. With practice, this skill of reflecting on your thoughts will become more natural, and you will be able to spot them instantly.

Once you have identified an unhelpful thought, the next step is to assess it fully. You can do this by taking a step back and reviewing the situation. For instance, you may be worried about failing a significant task at work and believing everyone calls you a failure for it.

Rather than accepting this thought, take a quantifiable amount of time to check it. Ask yourself some questions surrounding the thought, such as how likely the outcome of the task is, whether there is good proof to support the thought, whether there are other possibilities, whether there are alternative ways to approach the situation, and what you say to a friend suffering from similar thoughts.

When you have successfully identified and examined your negative thoughts, strive to reframe them to more positive or neutral ones. Reflect on your questions when assessing the thought and see how you can approach the situation differently.

If you can't turn the negative thought into a positive one, don't worry. This process isn't about having right or wrong answers. It is about developing flexibility in your thinking patterns and gaining control over your thoughts. Learning to distinguish helpful and unhelpful thoughts, as well as finding a new perspective, can break the cycle of negative thoughts and bring about a fresh outlook, often making the situation less intense than you initially thought. I will discuss this further later in the book.

Additional Tips to Change Unhelpful Thinking

Negative thinking patterns can have a significant impact on our well-being and overall mindset. It is important to recognize these patterns in order to replace them with more helpful and positive thoughts. Some commonly observed negative thinking patterns include:

- **Black and white thinking:** This is when we see things as either completely right or completely wrong, with no room for shades of gray or alternative perspectives. It limits our ability to see different possibilities and can lead to extreme judgments.

- **Personalizing:** In this thinking pattern, we tend to take personal responsibility for everything that goes wrong, disregarding external factors or circumstances that may have contributed to the outcome. This can be self-blaming and put unnecessary pressure on ourselves.

- **Filter thinking:** This occurs when we selectively focus only on the negative aspects of a situation or person, ignoring any positive aspects. It can create a distorted perception and prevent us from seeing the whole picture.

- **Catastrophizing:** This involves constantly imagining and assuming the worst-case scenarios, even when there is little evidence to support such catastrophic outcomes. It often leads to unnecessary anxiety and stress.

Recognizing these negative thinking patterns is the first step towards replacing them with more helpful thoughts. Mindfulness practices, such as meditation, can assist in redirecting our focus to the present moment and distancing ourselves from depressive thoughts and emotions. By detaching ourselves, we can view our negative thoughts objectively and challenge them more easily.

Keeping a thought diary is another effective technique to interrupt negative thoughts. By writing down our negative thinking styles, we gain a better understanding of their impact on our emotional reactions. This self-reflection helps us identify patterns and provides an opportunity for us to reframe our thoughts more positively and realistically.

Focusing on gratitude is also a powerful tool to counteract negative thinking. Even during challenging times, make an effort to think about three things you are grateful for each day, even if they are small. Shifting our attention to what we appreciate helps cultivate a more positive mindset.

However, if negative thoughts persist or become overwhelming, seeking professional help from a therapist is highly recommended. While friends and family can provide support and perspective, a mental health professional can offer specialized guidance and provide additional tools and strategies to effectively change our thinking patterns. It is essential to prioritize our mental well-being and seek appropriate support when needed.

Overcoming Self-Doubt

Self-doubt can arise from various sources, such as past negative experiences or anxious attachment style issues. Individuals with insecure attachment styles may have been subjected to criticism, which can later contribute to self-doubt. Such individuals may find it challenging to trust their abilities or judgment. Furthermore, negative experiences in the past, such as being discouraged or told that they are not good enough, can create a lasting impact on their self-worth and increase self-doubt.

In addition to personal experiences, societal pressure to achieve can be another source of self-doubt. The constant pressure to be successful and meet unreasonable standards can lead to fears of failure and inadequacy. Instead of motivating individuals, this pressure can create additional insecurities and amplify self-doubt.

If left unaddressed, self-doubt can have significant consequences. It can lead to anxiety, depression, procrastination, emotional instability, low self-esteem, and difficulty making decisions. These negative effects can be detrimental to an individual's overall well-being and prevent them from reaching their full potential.

Therefore, recognizing and addressing self-doubt is crucial for promoting emotional and mental health. Seeking support from a therapist, adopting self-care strategies, and challenging negative thoughts are effective methods of reducing self-doubt. By developing self-compassion and practicing positivity and mindfulness, individuals can improve their self-confidence and reduce self-doubt. Taking action to address self-doubt can help individuals overcome obstacles and achieve their goals.

Start by becoming aware of the self-doubting thoughts that arise in your mind. Pay attention to the negative statements you tell yourself and challenge them by asking for evidence that supports or contradicts those thoughts. Replace self-doubt with more compassionate and realistic self-talk. For example, if you catch yourself thinking, "I can't do this," remind yourself of times when you have overcome challenges in the past and reframe the thought to "I may face challenges, but I am capable and have what it takes to succeed."

Surround yourself with positive and supportive people who believe in your abilities. Seek out friends, mentors, or a supportive community who can offer encouragement and provide constructive feedback. Share your goals and aspirations with them, and allow their belief in you to strengthen your self-belief.

Also, break down your goals into smaller, achievable steps. By setting realistic goals and taking action, you build momentum and gain confidence in your abilities. Celebrate each small success along the way, reinforcing your belief in yourself and your capabilities. It would help if you also used visualization techniques to imagine yourself successfully accomplishing your goals. Visualizing positive outcomes can help rewire your brain and build confidence in your abilities. Practice visualizing yourself confidently overcoming challenges, and achieving the things you desire.

Overcoming self-doubt is an ongoing process. Be patient with yourself and commit to these exercises regularly. With persistence and practice, you can gradually build self-belief and overcome self-doubt.

Imposter Syndrome

Imposter syndrome is a psychological phenomenon that often accompanies self-doubt. It refers to the overwhelming feeling of being a fraud or an imposter despite evidence of achievements and accomplishments. Imposter syndrome is commonly experienced, particularly among women and minority groups, who may face additional societal pressure and stereotypes ("Rising above the Imposter Syndrome Trap on Women & Minorities," n.d.).

The impact of imposter syndrome is profound. It can hinder individuals from taking risks, pursuing new opportunities, or fully showcasing their abilities. The fear of being exposed as inadequate or unworthy can prevent individuals from putting themselves out there in a meaningful way. Even though they have accomplished great things, imposter syndrome causes them to doubt their qualifications, performance, and overall competence. This self-doubt can manifest in various areas of life, including work, relationships, friendships, parenting, and other activities.

The negative effect of self-doubt and imposter syndrome on self-esteem cannot be underestimated. Constantly questioning one's abilities and feeling like an imposter diminishes a person's confidence and belief in their worth. It can lead to feelings of inadequacy, anxiety, and fear of failure.

Fortunately, there are strategies that can help combat self-doubt and imposter syndrome and cultivate self-confidence. One powerful approach is to reframe negative thoughts and challenge the imposter syndrome narrative. Recognizing and acknowledging achievements, skills, and successes can help rewire the belief that one is a fraud. It is important to celebrate and internalize accomplishments, giving oneself credit for the hard work and effort put into achieving those goals.

Building a support network of trusted individuals who provide encouragement and validation can also be instrumental in combating self-doubt. Surrounding oneself with people who believe in their abilities and provide constructive feedback can help counteract feelings of being an imposter. Seeking mentorship and guidance from successful individuals who have faced similar challenges can provide inspiration and guidance.

Practicing self-care and self-compassion is another key component of overcoming self-doubt. Taking time for personal well-being, engaging in activities that bring joy and fulfillment, and acknowledging one's strengths and value is crucial in building self-confidence and combating imposter syndrome.

It is important to remember that self-doubt and imposter syndrome are common experiences, and many successful individuals have dealt with them. Seeking professional help from a therapist or counselor can provide further guidance and support in navigating these feelings and developing strategies to overcome self-doubt.

Chapter Summary

- Mindset shapes beliefs, values, and attitudes about oneself and the world.

- Different mindsets may result in different perceptions of life.

- People can change their mindset to improve their quality of life and achieve success.

- Being able to shift one's mindset is a key trait of successful people.

- Cultivating a positive and productive mindset can have a profound impact on personal and professional life.

Chapter 5

Communication and Connection

"**Communication is the solvent of all problems and is the foundation for personal development.**"
Peter Shepherd.

E ffective communication is vital for positive social interaction and overcoming anxious attachment. However, it can be challenging to have a healthy conversation and avoid over-communicating. This is especially important in romantic relationships.

A common communication model involves a sender, a receiver, and a message that is encoded by the sender and decoded by the receiver. This model also includes feedback from the receiver and any noise that could disrupt the communication process.

Encoding refers to the sender transforming their thoughts into communicable messages while the receiver interprets the message they receive, both verbally and nonverbally. However, this process is not as straightforward as it seems, as some personal filters and biases can influence how the message is decoded.

In addition, messages are not purely factual information. According to Friedemann Schulz von Thun's Four-Sides model of communication, every message has four facets: the factual aspect, self-revelation, the relationship aspect, and an appeal (Domendos, 2021). The emphasis placed on each facet can vary, and the intended meaning may differ from the perceived meaning. For example, a wife saying "the sugar jar is empty" may be less about the fact itself and more of a hint for her husband to refill the jar.

Furthermore, as receivers, we often have one facet that we are more attuned to, such as focusing on the factual aspect, the relationship aspect, self-revelation, or the appeal. This can further complicate communication, as misinterpretations can occur when the emphasis placed on each facet varies between the sender and receiver.

This type of breakdown in communication can lead to misunderstandings and conflicts. It is essential to recognize that what we hear may not accurately reflect what the other person intended to convey. It is important to be aware of our own biases and tendencies in order to engage in healthy communication.

To improve communication, it is crucial to understand and consider all four facets of the message. For instance, when feeling questioned or misunderstood, it can be helpful to go back to the original statement and assess the various aspects. By focusing on factual information and using questions to clarify understanding, we can better grasp the intended message and avoid unnecessary conflicts or misunderstandings.

Relationships With No Communication

If there is a lack of communication in a relationship, it is possible that both parties are not truly listening to each other. Instead, they may be more focused on proving themselves right or engaging in simultaneous tasks that distract from active listening.

Several common listening mistakes can hinder effective communication:

- Daydreaming or allowing thoughts to wander while the other person is speaking, even if it's something as mundane as thinking about a grocery list.

- Preparing a response in your mind instead of fully engaging with what the other person is saying.

- Judging or critiquing the other person's words instead of trying to understand their perspective.

- Listening with a specific goal or desired outcome in mind can limit the ability to truly hear and comprehend the other person.

However, active listening encompasses much more than simply refraining from talking. It is an art that requires a genuine interest in the other person and a curiosity rather than a preoccupied mindset. Active listening involves:

- Demonstrating nonverbal involvement to show attention, such as making eye contact and nodding.

- Focusing on the person in front of you rather than your thoughts.

- Avoiding judgment and creating a safe space for open expression.

- Being comfortable with moments of silence can allow for deeper understanding and reflection.

One practical exercise to revive communication in a relationship is called "The Listening Exercise." Set aside a specific time for both partners to participate in this exercise, free from distractions. Decide who will go first and who will be the listener. The speaker will have 10-15 minutes to talk about their thoughts, feelings, and concerns without interruption from the listener (Freed, 2023).

The listener's role is listening actively without offering advice, judgment, or solution. After the speaker has finished, the listener will summarize what they heard, focusing on the speaker's emotions and main points. When the listener has summarized, the roles will be reversed, and the other partner will have their turn to speak while the first partner listens.

Repeat this exercise regularly, for example, every weekend, allowing both partners equal time to speak and be heard. This exercise helps to improve communication by providing a safe space for each partner to express themselves fully while the other partner practices active listening. It promotes understanding, empathy, and a deeper connection between partners.

Better Communication

When it comes to addressing a situation like your date arriving late, it's important to communicate your observations without adding labels or interpretations. Instead of assuming that their lateness reflects a lack of interest or prioritization, stick to the facts. Simply acknowledge, "I noticed you were late for our date." This statement highlights your observation without any evaluation or judgment.

Effective communication involves more than just sharing observations; it also requires expressing emotions. When emotions are left unexpressed, they can build up and eventually lead to arguments, misunderstandings, and resentment. Therefore, it is important to take the time to understand and communicate your feelings.

Understanding your emotions is a crucial first step in expressing them effectively. Take the time to reflect on what you are feeling and why you feel that way. Identify the specific emotions you are experiencing, whether it's annoyance, frustration, sadness, or any other feeling. This self-awareness will help you articulate your emotions more clearly.

Once you have identified your emotions, express them to your partner in a non-judgmental manner. Avoid attacking or blaming your partner, as this can escalate the situation. Instead, use "I" statements to take ownership of your emotions and communicate how you are feeling. For example, instead of saying, "You always make me angry," you could say, "I am feeling annoyed right now."

When expressing your emotions, try to provide context and explain why you feel the way you do. Help your partner understand the impact their actions or words have had on you. For instance, you could say, "I am bothered by this because it makes me wonder whether you are looking forward to spending time with me."

By openly sharing your emotions, you provide your partner with insight into your emotional state and foster a better understanding of your perspective. This can lead to more empathetic and constructive communication. It allows both you and your partner to have a deeper connection and work towards resolving any issues or conflicts that may arise.

Furthermore, it's essential to understand and communicate your needs. Expressing your needs allows your partner to evaluate if they can fulfill them while also giving them an opportunity to prioritize your relationship. This also helps alleviate anxious attachment fears. For example, you might say, "I would like to be treated with consideration, and I want to feel important to you." By articulating your needs, you establish a clear framework for what you expect from the relationship.

The final step is to make a direct request. Clearly communicate what your partner needs to do in order for your needs to be met. In this case, you could say something like, "That is why I ask you to arrive at the agreed-upon time." By making a specific request, you outline the concrete action that would address your needs and improve the situation

Active Listening Techniques

Maintaining appropriate eye contact is crucial in face-to-face conversations. However, it's important to find a balance, as excessive eye contact can be intimidating. To adapt to the situation, consider breaking eye contact every five seconds or so. Additionally, to show active listening, focus on one eye for five seconds, switch to the other eye for another five seconds, and then shift your gaze towards their mouth. If you need to look away, it's better to look to the side or up rather than down, as looking downwards can indicate disinterest and a desire to end the conversation. Do this as many times as you want. The more you do it, the better it helps improve your techniques.

In addition to actively listening and engaging in verbal communication, it is important to pay attention to your posture and be aware of non-verbal cues during conversations. Posture plays a significant role in conveying openness and attentiveness.

To create an open posture, make sure to avoid crossing your arms or legs, as this can give off a closed-off or defensive vibe. Instead, keep your arms relaxed at your sides or place them comfortably on your lap. Similarly, avoid slouching or leaning back too far, as this may indicate disinterest. Instead, aim to sit upright or lean slightly forward or sideways, as this demonstrates that you are actively listening and engaged in the conversation.

Non-verbal cues such as a slight tilt of your head or resting your head on your hand can also indicate attentiveness. These cues signal to the speaker that you are interested in what they have to say and that you are actively processing their words.

Developing a habit of maintaining an open posture can greatly enhance your communication skills. By consistently practicing open body language, it will become more natural and effortless for you to maintain an open and engaged posture during conversations.

Effective listening involves not only paying attention to verbal communication but also being attentive to non-verbal cues. Facial expressions, tone of voice, and gestures can provide valuable information about a person's emotions and thoughts.

Observing the other person's body language can give you insight into their level of engagement and comfort. Are they smiling and maintaining eye contact, indicating that they are responsive and interested, or are they crossing their arms defensively, suggesting they may be guarded or disengaged? Paying attention to these cues allows you to better understand the underlying emotions and thoughts behind their words.

Even during phone conversations where visual cues are absent, it is essential to be mindful of the tone of the person's voice. The tone can convey subtle nuances and emotions that may not be explicitly expressed in their words. Listen for changes in pitch, volume, and pacing, as these can provide insights into their emotional state or attitude.

Avoid jumping in and interrupting the other person. Interrupting can be frustrating for them and gives the impression that you consider your thoughts or time more important. If you tend to be a quick thinker or speaker, make a conscious effort to slow down and allow the other person to express themselves fully. Remember, it's not necessary to jump in immediately during pauses or moments of silence.

One practical exercise to improve active listening skills is "Reflective Listening." Choose a topic or scenario to practice active listening. One partner will be the speaker, and the other will be the listener. The speaker will share their thoughts, feelings, or experiences about the chosen topic for two to three minutes. The listener's role is to actively listen and refrain from interrupting or responding verbally (UNSW Teaching Staff Gateway, n.d.).

After the speaker has finished speaking, the listener will then reflect on what they heard, using phrases such as, "It sounds like you're saying..." or "I hear you saying..." The speaker will confirm whether the reflection is accurate or provide clarification.

Switch roles, where the speaker becomes the listener and vice versa. Repeat the exercise with different topics or scenarios to continue practicing active listening. This exercise helps improve active listening by encouraging individuals to focus on what the speaker is saying without immediately offering their thoughts or opinions. It also allows the listener to demonstrate understanding and empathy by reflecting on what they heard, which can enhance effective communication and foster deeper connections in relationships.

Demonstrate active listening through non-verbal cues. Nod your head, smile, and make small verbal affirmations like "yes" and "uh huh" to show that you're engaged and encourage the speaker to continue. Avoid looking at your watch, fidgeting, or playing with your hair or fingernails, as these behaviors can be distracting and indicate disinterest.

Resist the urge to impose your opinions or solutions. Instead, provide a listening and supportive ear. Listening attentively can be much more rewarding for the other person than receiving unsolicited advice. For example, when a loved one is facing health problems, they often want to express their feelings and talk about their experiences rather than receiving an abundance of advice on what they should do. In other areas of life, most individuals prefer to come to their solutions. If you feel compelled to share your ideas, ask first if they would like to hear them. For instance, say something like, "Would you like to hear my suggestions?"

Asking relevant questions can demonstrate that you've been actively listening and help clarify information. If you're unsure whether you've understood something correctly, wait until the speaker pauses and then ask for clarification, such as saying, "Did you mean that x..." or "I'm not sure if I understood what you were saying about..."

Incorporating open-ended questions, when appropriate, can also be beneficial. These questions, like "How did that make you feel?" or "What did you do next?" can encourage the person to share more about their experiences and thoughts.

Expressing Your Needs and Setting Boundaries

Effective communication is crucial when it comes to expressing your needs to others, especially loved ones. Rushed conversations, unclear language, and vague requests can make it difficult for others to understand and respect your boundaries.

One important factor to consider is timing. It is best to establish boundaries with your partner when both of you are relaxed and able to focus on the conversation. If you find yourselves in the midst of an argument, it may be beneficial to take a step back and revisit the topic once both of you have calmed down.

Being prepared can also contribute to effective communication. If you feel nervous about discussing your needs, it may be helpful to write down your points before the conversation. This way, you can articulate your needs clearly and concisely.

Let's look at the story of Mike and Emily. They had been together for a few years and deeply loved each other. However, over time, they started feeling overwhelmed and noticed a decline in their well-being.

Emily, a hardworking woman, felt drained and exhausted at the end of each day. Mike, on the other hand, struggled with anxiety and constantly worried about the future. They both realized that they needed to set boundaries in their relationship to maintain balance and preserve their mental and emotional health.

One evening, after a particularly stressful day, Emily gathered her courage and approached Mike to discuss their boundaries. She expressed her need for some personal time after work to decompress and engage in activities that rejuvenate her. Emily explained that this didn't mean she loved Mike any less; she just needed space to recharge and care for herself.

Initially taken aback, Mike slowly started to understand and appreciate Emily's perspective. He realized that her well-being was crucial for the overall health of their relationship. Inspired by Emily's courage, he also shared his need for open communication and reassurance when his anxiety spiked, without feeling judged or overwhelmed.

They agreed to support each other in asserting and respecting these boundaries. Emily began setting aside time in the evenings for self-care, whether reading, taking walks, or enjoying her hobbies. Mike, in turn, initiated open conversations with Emily whenever he felt overwhelmed, allowing them to address his anxiety together.

As both partners started prioritizing their needs and respecting each other's boundaries, their relationship flourished. They felt more connected, understood, and balanced. By establishing boundaries, they protected their mental and emotional well-being and nurtured a healthier, more fulfilling relationship.

From that point forward, Mike and Emily continued to communicate openly about their boundaries, adapting as needed, and their relationship grew stronger with each passing day. They had learned the valuable lesson that setting and respecting boundaries was a sign of love and respect not only for themselves but also for their partner.

When communicating your boundaries, try to use "I" statements to express how you feel. Avoid using "you" statements, as they can come across as accusing or confrontational. For example, instead of saying, "You never help around the house," you could say, "I feel overwhelmed with the amount of work I have to do when you're away." Expressing your emotions in a non-confrontational manner can lay the groundwork for establishing boundaries in a relationship.

Clarity is key when expressing your needs. While a vague request may get the message across, it is better to be as specific as possible to avoid confusion. For instance, instead of saying, "I'd like more personal space," you could say, "I feel disrespected and uncomfortable when you come into my room without knocking. Please knock before entering." Using a calm but firm tone conveys that you are serious about your boundaries while still being respectful.

It is important to address any feedback or questions your partner may have about your boundary. While you are not obligated to justify your needs or explain yourself, doing so can help the other person understand where you are coming from. You may even ask follow-up questions to ensure your message is effectively conveyed.

In romantic relationships, it is especially important to ask your partner how they feel about a request instead of assuming their reaction. Ask if they find your request unfair or unusual. Inquire whether it conflicts with their own needs or wants. Each person in the relationship has their thoughts and feelings, and it is each individual's responsibility to communicate them clearly in order to be understood.

Remember that you are not responsible for how the other person reacts to your boundary. While it is natural to care about the other person's feelings and reactions, you should not disregard your own needs. For example, if the other person feels upset or disagrees with your request for more "me time," it is important to remind yourself why you are setting this boundary in the first place. You want some time alone to pursue your hobbies and avoid feeling emotionally overwhelmed. You should not feel guilty or selfish for prioritizing your own needs in this situation.

Enforcing Boundaries

It is important to acknowledge that not everyone in your life will always respect your boundaries. In some cases, a partner may accidentally cross a boundary, while difficult family members may intentionally do so.

When someone crosses a boundary, it can be helpful to restate your needs. It is possible that the other person didn't fully understand your original request or may have forgotten it. In this situation, it is important to remain calm, firm, and clear about what you need. Clearly articulate the boundary that was crossed and express how it made you feel. For example, you might say, "I feel disrespected when you talk over me. It is important to me that we have equal opportunity to express ourselves in our conversations."

Establishing clear and reasonable consequences for crossing a boundary can also be effective. For example, if someone has a habit of talking over you, you might communicate a consequence by saying, "If you talk over me again, I will have to end the conversation." This communicates the seriousness of the issue and demonstrates that there will be consequences for crossing the boundary.

However, it is important to only state the consequences you are willing to enforce. If you are not willing to follow through on a consequence, the other person may feel empowered to continue crossing your boundaries in the future. For instance, if you tell your partner that you will take a break from the relationship if they keep lying to you, it is crucial to actually follow through on that consequence if the boundary continues to be crossed. This reinforces the importance of setting boundaries and maintaining their integrity.

Setting and enforcing consequences can be challenging, especially in close relationships. However, doing so is essential for establishing and maintaining healthy boundaries. By consistently reinforcing your boundaries and the consequences for crossing them, you send a clear message that your needs must be respected.

Responding When Others Set Boundaries

It is important to remember that boundaries are not only established by you but by others in your life as well. When someone sets a boundary, it may trigger negative emotions such as shame or frustration. However, it is essential to approach these conversations with an open mind and willingness to understand.

When faced with boundaries that trigger negative emotions, taking the time to breathe and actively listen can be helpful. Deep breathing can help calm your nervous system's response, enabling you to be more receptive to the information being shared.

It is important to remember that the person setting the boundary knows what is best for themselves. While you may have your thoughts and preferences, expressing your needs in order to find a compromise that works for both parties is crucial.

Respecting boundaries means giving your partner the space to voice their needs without jumping to conclusions or making assumptions. Each person processes and experiences emotions differently, so it is important to allow them the opportunity to express themselves without judgment or interruption.

Apologizing when necessary is crucial in respecting boundaries. If you inadvertently overstep a boundary, it is important to be humble and apologize for your mistake. Additionally, if there is any confusion, ask for clarity to ensure you fully understand the boundary and how to respect it moving forward.

By accepting and acknowledging the boundaries set by others, you can improve your connections and relationships with those around you. Effective boundaries create a sense of empowerment for both parties involved and contribute to a healthier and more fulfilling relationship overall.

Guidelines and Examples for Assertive Communication

When practicing assertive communication, it is important to use "I" statements to express your thoughts and feelings. This helps take ownership of your perspective and avoids blaming or accusing the other person. By saying "I feel" or "I need," you are clearly conveying your own experiences and requirements.

In addition, it is crucial to be clear and specific when communicating your needs, thoughts, or concerns. Avoid using vague or ambiguous statements that can lead to misunderstandings. Instead, be explicit about what you want or expect. This allows the other person to better understand your request or concern and respond accordingly.

Projecting confidence and assertiveness through your body language is also key. This includes standing tall, maintaining eye contact, and speaking in a clear and firm voice. Avoid defensive postures like crossing your arms or avoiding eye contact, as these may convey a lack of confidence. By displaying assertive body language, you are more likely to be taken seriously and have your message heard.

Practicing active listening is another important aspect of assertive communication. This involves giving complete attention to the speaker and showing that you understand by summarizing or paraphrasing what they have said. Active listening demonstrates respect and helps prevent misunderstandings or misinterpretations.

Keeping a calm and composed demeanor throughout the conversation is essential, even if it becomes emotional or intense. Take deep breaths and pause when necessary to collect your thoughts. Respond thoughtfully rather than reacting impulsively. Remaining calm allows for a more constructive and productive dialogue.

Here are some examples of assertive communication:

- **Requesting a change:** Instead of blaming or demanding, clearly state your needs and expectations. For example, "I need you to complete the report by tomorrow as agreed upon so we can meet the deadline and avoid any delays."

- **Expressing boundaries:** It is important to assert your boundaries and communicate what makes you comfortable. For instance, "I am not comfortable sharing personal information at work. I prefer to keep my personal life separate from my professional life."

- **Giving feedback:** Provide constructive feedback by acknowledging effort and suggesting improvements. For example, "I appreciate your effort on this project, but I think there are areas that could be improved. Can we discuss potential solutions to enhance the quality?"

- **Saying no:** It is okay to say no when you are overwhelmed or unable to take on additional tasks. Be clear and assertive in expressing your limitations. For instance, "I have a lot on my plate at the moment, and I won't be able to take on any additional tasks right now. I encourage you to look for alternative resources."

- **Disagreeing respectfully:** When you have a different perspective, it is important to express it respectfully. You can say, "I see your point of view, but I have a different perspective on this matter. Can we explore both sides and find a middle ground?"

Navigating Conflict

Falling in love is undoubtedly a beautiful experience filled with excitement, joy, and an almost euphoric feeling. However, as time goes by, the initial romantic bliss may fade, and you may find yourself facing challenging issues in your relationship. Misunderstandings, heated arguments, placing blame, or growing apart due to differences can all lead to a strained relationship. To prevent this from happening and ensure a healthy, lasting relationship, it is important to learn effective conflict resolution skills. Here are some tips to help you navigate through conflicts and positively resolve them.

Express Yourself

There might be times when you choose to hold back your grievances with your partner, thinking that you will address them later. However, if left unresolved, these unspoken grievances can accumulate and gain emotional momentum, leading to a destructive outcome, much like a tornado. It is crucial for the health of your relationship that both you and your partner openly and directly express your concerns in a firm, honest, and compassionate manner.

To initiate these discussions, it is important to start by showing consideration for your partner's feelings. You can say something like, "I deeply care about our relationship," or "I know you don't intend to upset me." This will help create a foundation for open and respectful communication. Next, clearly describe the behavior or action that is bothering you, providing specific details. It is important to express the feelings that arise within you, whether it be anger, hurt, irritation, frustration, or confusion. By sharing these emotions, you allow your partner to understand the impact of their actions on you.

After expressing your concerns, it is essential to ask for a specific change you would like to see. For example, you could say, "I would prefer it if you spoke to me in a calm and gentle tone," or "I would appreciate it if you could wait until I finish speaking before responding." By clearly stating your desired change, you give your partner a tangible action they can work on.

Finally, it is important to ask for an agreement at the end of your request. This gives your partner the opportunity to respond and discuss whether they are willing to make the change you have asked for. For instance, you can ask, "Are you willing to agree to this request?" By seeking agreement, you promote a sense of teamwork and collaboration in finding a resolution.

Take a moment to reflect on how effectively you express yourself in various aspects of your life. Consider your communication skills, ability to share your thoughts and feelings, and how comfortable you are expressing yourself. Rate yourself on a scale of 1-5, with 1 being low and 5 being high, for each statement below:

- I am able to convey my opinions and ideas clearly and confidently.

- I am at ease when it comes to expressing my emotions and vulnerability to others.

- I pay close attention when others speak and show empathy and understanding.

- I am able to communicate my needs and boundaries assertively without being aggressive.

- I am open to constructive feedback and willing to engage in productive conversations.

- I adjust my communication style depending on the situation and the needs of others.

- I actively seek opportunities to improve my communication skills through learning and practice.

- I am mindful of nonverbal communication cues and use them to my advantage.

- I am able to handle conflicts and disagreements in a respectful and positive way.

- I recognize my strengths and areas in which I need to improve in terms of communication.

Once you have rated yourself for each statement, take a moment to reflect on your answers. Identify areas where you feel strong and confident in expressing yourself and where you could benefit from growth or improvement. Consider setting specific goals or actions to enhance your ability to express yourself effectively in those areas.

This self-assessment is a tool for self-reflection and can help guide personal development. It is not meant to be an evaluation or judgment but rather an opportunity to understand yourself better and improve your communication skills.

Avoid the Blame Game

In relationships, it is common to feel tempted to blame our partners for various problems that arise. Whether it is something they said, did, or didn't do, the reasons for assigning blame can seem endless. However, engaging in the blame game rarely leads to positive outcomes. When one person is blamed, they often feel attacked, which triggers a defensive response rather than addressing the actual issue at hand. For example, if a partner says, "You're crazy for thinking that!" in response to a fear of infidelity, the blame instantly shifts away from the real issue. The other partner will likely react defensively, saying, "I'm crazy? You're the one who's crazy!"

Instead of engaging in the blame game, it is important to use "I feel" statements to handle conflicts in a relationship. This approach keeps the focus on the specific issue and avoids attacking the other person. By using "I feel" statements, you communicate your emotions and concerns without putting your partner down. This approach encourages better communication and leads to more constructive results.

By avoiding blame and focusing on expressing your feelings, you create a safe space for open dialogue and problem-solving. It also recognizes and honors the emotions of your partner, fostering a sense of empathy and understanding. Remember, conflicts are an opportunity for growth and strengthening your relationship when handled with care and respect.

One Argument at a Time

It is common for an argument to start with a specific topic and then unexpectedly spiral into various other related issues. This can be compared to a car losing control on black ice during winter. In order to maintain a healthy and productive argument, it is important to be aware of this tendency and stay focused on one topic at a time.

Let's look at a short story. Sarah and John had been together for several years. They were generally happy and loved each other deeply. However, like any couple, they occasionally had disagreements.

One day, Sarah came home from work feeling exhausted and stressed. She noticed that John had left his dirty clothes on the bedroom floor. Though minor, it irritated her because they had previously discussed the importance of tidiness in their home. Without thinking much, Sarah confronted John about the clothes and asked him to pick them up. Preoccupied with a project at work, John responded with a sigh and said he'd do it later.

Feeling unheard, Sarah's frustration grew. She couldn't understand why John wouldn't simply pick up after himself. The conversation quickly escalated into an argument as Sarah accused John of not caring about their home or her feelings. In his turmoil, John's stress from work mixed with the argument, and he lashed out defensively, saying that Sarah was overreacting and being unreasonable.

As their voices grew louder, the argument escalated further. Past resentments and unrelated issues began creeping into their exchange. They started bringing up old wounds and frustrations, attempting to prove who was more in the wrong.

What had started as a seemingly trivial argument over dirty clothes quickly spiraled into something bigger. Their pent-up frustrations and unexpressed grievances took center stage, overshadowing the initial issue.

Finally, Sarah and John realized how far they had strayed from the original disagreement. The room fell silent as they caught their breaths and took a moment to reflect on the hurtful words that had been exchanged.

With heavy hearts, Sarah and John embraced, realizing their love for each other was stronger than this trivial disagreement and the unnecessary pain they had caused themselves. They vowed to communicate better, to address concerns promptly, and to approach conflict with empathy and understanding.

From that point forward, they committed to actively listening, expressing their needs and emotions honestly, and resolving conflicts before they spiraled into something bigger. They learned that true growth within a relationship comes from recognizing and addressing underlying issues instead of getting caught up in trivial matters.

When an argument shifts away from the original idea, it becomes easy to get overwhelmed and confused by the array of different issues being brought up. This can hinder the progress of finding a resolution as the main problem gets lost in the midst of these unrelated matters. By sticking to one argument, you increase the chances of finding a specific solution to the issue at hand rather than trying to solve multiple problems simultaneously.

Staying committed to addressing one argument also allows both partners to process their emotions and thoughts with patience and understanding. By giving each other the necessary time to fully comprehend and express their feelings, it becomes easier to reach a resolution before moving on to a new topic.

To prevent an argument from going nowhere, it is essential to navigate through the slippery road conditions of the conversation by focusing on one topic at a time. This approach significantly increases the chances of finding a solution that satisfies both partners and contributes to a healthier and more effective communication dynamic.

Communication

Healthy communication is a timeless and essential component of a successful relationship. Active listening is one of the key elements of healthy communication. It involves giving your undivided attention to your partner, making eye contact, and genuinely absorbing what they are saying. By actively listening, you demonstrate respect and show that you value their perspective and opinions.

Furthermore, healthy communication includes responding appropriately to your partner's thoughts and feelings. It is crucial to maintain a conversational tone, ensuring that your responses are respectful, engaged, and open. Non-verbal cues, such as maintaining open body language, can also help convey that you are receptive and attentive to their message.

Using "I" statements is another significant aspect of healthy communication. By expressing your feelings and experiences, rather than assigning blame or making accusatory statements, you create a space for understanding and empathy. This approach encourages your partner to do the same, fostering a safe environment where both individuals feel heard and validated.

Additionally, healthy communication requires the willingness to acknowledge when you are wrong. It takes humility and self-reflection to admit faults and take responsibility for your actions. By being accountable for your mistakes, you demonstrate maturity and a commitment to growth within the relationship.

By incorporating all of these ingredients into your communication, you lay the foundation for a relationship built on love and harmony. Effective communication nurtures understanding, resolves conflict more effectively and cultivates a deeper connection between partners. It is the bedrock upon which a strong and successful relationship can be built, fostering trust, intimacy, and shared growth.

Be Open-Minded

When it comes to resolving conflicts in relationships, one effective technique is to maintain an open-minded attitude throughout disagreements. It is natural to become entrenched in our perspectives and cling to our viewpoints during arguments. However, this narrow-minded approach hinders our ability to be flexible and empathize with our partner's concerns.

In order to foster productive conflict resolution, couples must set aside their egos and approach the situation objectively. This means actively considering both sides of the argument without bias or personal agendas. By adopting this mindset, the door is opened for a reasonable and respectful discussion, where each partner can express their thoughts and feelings without fear of judgment.

Remaining open-minded and objective not only allows for a deeper understanding of our partner's perspective but also increases the likelihood of accepting their viewpoint as valid. This acceptance does not mean agreeing at all times but rather acknowledging and respecting the experiences and feelings that have shaped their viewpoint. By doing so, partners lay the foundation for compromise and finding common ground rather than engaging in a power struggle or escalating conflicts.

When couples consistently practice open-mindedness and objectivity, they are equipping themselves with essential skills for handling the challenges that life inevitably presents. By fostering a climate of understanding and respectful communication, couples are better equipped to navigate disagreements and conflicts, leading to a stronger and more harmonious relationship overall.

Partner's Intentions

It is common to leap to negative conclusions about your partner's behavior in situations where they fall short of your expectations. When your partner forgets to take out the trash, shows up late, or fails to promptly reply to your text, it can be easy to generate a negative interpretation of their actions and respond accordingly.

However, jumping to negative conclusions is not a constructive way to foster a harmonious home environment. Instead, it is essential to take a step back, pause, and reflect on your assumptions. Ask yourself, "What am I assuming here?" and "Is it time to reframe?"

Reframing refers to the ability to consider alternative perspectives and explanations after your mind has defaulted to a negative interpretation. By reframing the situation, you can create space for alternative possibilities and interpretations of your partner's behavior that are positive or neutral rather than negative.

Here's another story to illustrate this for you. Anna and David had been married for many years. They loved each other deeply but often found themselves entangled in confrontations that left them feeling frustrated and disconnected.

One day, after a particularly heated argument over household chores, Anna and David felt exhausted and discouraged. They realized that their confrontations were becoming a pattern, and they wanted to find a way to break free from it.

They decided to seek guidance from a therapist who introduced them to reframing. The therapist explained that reframing involved looking at a situation from a different perspective, with the intention of shifting one's mindset and reactions.

Excited and hopeful, Anna and David decided to apply this idea to their next disagreement. A few days later, they found themselves in a similar situation, arguing over a dispute about finances. But this time, they consciously chose to reframe the situation.

Instead of viewing it as an opportunity to prove who was right, Anna and David took a step back and reminded themselves of their love for each other. They realized that the real issue wasn't about money but their fears and concerns regarding their financial stability and future.

With this newfound perspective, they decided to approach the conversation with empathy and curiosity. They listened to each other's fears and worries, acknowledging that their emotions were valid and deserving of understanding.

They discovered that by reframing the situation and focusing on their shared goals and values, they could collaborate as a team instead of opposing each other. Together, they brainstormed potential solutions and compromises to address their concerns while considering their needs.

As they continued to reframe their confrontations, Anna and David felt a shift in their relationship. Their arguments became less frequent and more constructive. They no longer viewed disagreements as threats to their connection but as opportunities for growth and understanding.

Consider whether there are justifiable reasons for your partner's behavior, such as exhaustion or distraction. Search for positive explanations that put your partner's actions in a more favorable light. Additionally, if you are uncertain about your partner's motives, it is always helpful to seek clarification and ask for their perspective.

By adopting a more positive and open-minded perspective, you can create a healthier and more productive communication dynamic between you and your partner. Avoid jumping to unjustified conclusions and provide space for deeper understanding and empathy to flourish. Ultimately, this will promote a more harmonious and loving relationship.

Chapter Summary

- Effective communication is crucial for positive social interaction and happiness, especially in romantic relationships.

- The communication process involves a sender encoding a message and a receiver decoding it, with feedback and noise affecting the process.

- Personal filters and biases can influence how messages are decoded, making communication more complex.

- According to the Four-Sides model of communication, messages have four facets: factual, self-revelation, relationship, and appeal.

- Individuals may be more attuned to one facet, leading to potential misinterpretations and breakdowns in communication. Understanding and considering all four facets can help improve communication and avoid conflicts.

Chapter 6
Building Lasting Change

"To improve is to change; to be perfect is to change often."

Winston Churchill.

In any relationship, whether it's new or you've been together for years, there are steps you can take to build a healthy and fulfilling connection with your partner. It's important to remember that all relationships go through ups and downs, and they require work, commitment, and a willingness to adapt and grow together.

If you've had past relationship failures or struggled to reignite romance in your current relationship, don't lose hope. Staying connected, finding fulfillment, and experiencing lasting happiness can be achieved through various ways. It all starts with acknowledging that every relationship is unique, and people come together for different reasons. A significant element of a healthy relationship is having a shared objective for what you desire your relationship to be and where you want it to go. This comprehension can only be attained by engaging in profound and truthful conversations with your partner.

One practical exercise to reignite romance in your relationship is to plan a surprise date night. Choose a specific day and time when both of you are free and can dedicate quality time to each other. Pick a theme for your date night that resonates with both your interests or a special memory. It could be a movie night, a picnic in the park, a candlelit dinner at home, or even recreating your first date.

Take the lead and plan all the details for the evening. Arrange for any necessary reservations, buy supplies or ingredients for your chosen activity, and ensure everything is ready. Leave subtle hints or clues for your partner to discover throughout the day leading to the surprise date night. It could be small notes with romantic messages, sending them sweet texts, or leaving a small gift for them to find.

On the day of your surprise date, try to dress up nicely and set a romantic atmosphere. Light candles, play soft music, or decorate your chosen space to create a cozy and intimate ambiance. Once your partner is surprised and you both are on your date, focus on being fully present and enjoying each other's company. Put away distractions, such as phones or work-related thoughts, and enjoy the moment together.

The key to reigniting romance is putting in effort and making your partner feel special. Surprise date nights can help create new memories, strengthen your bond, and remind each other of the love you share.

There are certain characteristics that most healthy relationships have in common, and knowing these principles can help you maintain a meaningful, fulfilling, and exciting connection with your partner, regardless of the challenges you may face. One of these principles is maintaining a meaningful emotional connection with each other. It's not just about being loved, but also feeling loved and emotionally fulfilled. Feeling accepted, valued, and understood by your partner is crucial in creating a strong bond. It's important to avoid getting stuck in a state of peaceful coexistence without truly relating to each other emotionally, as this can create distance in the relationship.

In a healthy relationship, you should not be afraid of respectful disagreement. Every couple handles conflict differently; some prefer calm discussions, while others may express their disagreements more passionately. The key is not to fear conflict but rather to feel safe in expressing your concerns without the fear of backlash. Resolving conflict without resorting to humiliation, degradation, or the desire to always be right is essential.

Maintaining outside relationships and interests is also important in a healthy relationship. It's unrealistic to expect one person to fulfill all your needs. Putting too much pressure on your partner can strain the relationship. It's necessary to sustain your own identity outside of the relationship, maintain connections with friends and family, and nurture your hobbies and interests. Stimulating and enriching your romantic relationship can be achieved with this.

Having open and honest communication is a crucial element of a healthy relationship. Effective communication serves as the basis for any fruitful relationship. When both partners have a clear understanding of what they expect from the relationship and feel at ease expressing their wants and needs, it creates a sense of trust and reinforces the bond. This transparent communication enables growth and facilitates finding ways to tackle challenges and make necessary changes together.

Keep in mind that developing and maintaining a strong relationship is a continuous journey that demands commitment and contribution from both sides. By focusing on maintaining emotional connection, not fearing disagreement, nurturing outside relationships and interests, and communicating openly and honestly, you can create a meaningful and fulfilling partnership with your loved one. This chapter will look at making changes and how to approach it.

Spending Quality Time

When you first fall in love with someone, there is an undeniable connection that comes from looking at and listening to each other. The early stages of a relationship are filled with excitement and new experiences. You likely spent hours talking and finding new things to do together. However, as time goes on and the responsibilities of life start to pile up, finding quality time for each other can become more challenging.

Many couples find that the face-to-face contact they had during the early days of dating is replaced by quick texts, emails, and instant messages. While digital communication has its benefits, it does not have the same positive impact on your brain and nervous system as face-to-face communication. Simply sending a text or a voice message saying "I love you" is nice, but if you rarely make an effort to look at your partner or spend dedicated time together, they may feel that you don't truly understand or appreciate them.

Constantly looking at your partner and giving them undivided attention shows you value and cherish their presence. It demonstrates that you are willing to invest time and energy into nurturing the relationship. Conversely, if you rarely see and engage with your partner, they may feel neglected, unimportant, or misunderstood.

Dedicated time together allows couples to deepen their emotional connection, share experiences, and strengthen their bond. It creates opportunities for meaningful conversations, laughter, physical affection, and creating new memories together. It also helps in reducing anxious attachment in relationships.

To sustain that feeling of falling in love over the long term:

- Make a commitment to spend quality time together on a regular basis.

- Even if you have a busy schedule, take a few minutes each day to put aside your electronic devices and distractions.

- Make a conscious effort to focus on and connect with your partner.

- This could involve having meaningful conversations, sharing your experiences and feelings, or simply enjoying each other's presence.

Additionally, find something that you both enjoy doing together. It could be a shared hobby, taking a dance class, going for a daily walk, or simply sitting down over a cup of coffee in the morning. The activity itself is not as important as the fact that you are doing it together and creating shared experiences. This will strengthen your bond and create lasting memories.

Trying new things together is also important. Doing new activities as a couple can infuse excitement and keep things interesting. It does not have to be extravagant; it can be as simple as trying a new restaurant or going on a day trip to a place you have never been before. The key is to step out of your comfort zone and explore new things together. This will bring a sense of novelty and adventure to your relationship.

Lastly, do not forget to prioritize having fun together. In the early stages of a relationship, couples often have a playful attitude, but as challenges and resentments build up, that playfulness can fade away. Maintaining a sense of humor can help you navigate tough times, reduce stress, and work through issues more easily. Find playful ways to surprise your partner unexpectedly, such as bringing home flowers or booking a table at their favorite restaurant. Playing with pets or spending time with small children can also help you reconnect with your playful side and bring joy into your relationship.

Nurturing your connection and keeping the love alive requires effort, intentional actions, and a commitment to prioritize each other. By consistently looking and listening to each other, spending quality time together, trying new things, and embracing a sense of playfulness, you can keep your relationship strong and thriving.

Do Things Together

One of the most powerful ways to maintain a strong and healthy relationship is to jointly engage in activities that hold meaning and value for both partners outside of the relationship. This could include volunteering for a shared cause, participating in a project together, or engaging in community work that benefits others. By focusing on something that has meaning for both individuals, couples can keep their relationship fresh and interesting while also deepening their bond.

Additionally, engaging in activities to benefit others has been shown to have significant mental health benefits, including reducing stress, anxiety, and depression. Humans have an innate desire to help others, and doing so can bring immense pleasure and fulfillment to individuals and couples alike. Through engaging in community service and other philanthropic activities, couples can not only strengthen their relationship and support a valuable cause but also positively impact the world around them.

Stay Connected

Effective communication is essential for building and maintaining a healthy relationship. When you and your partner have a positive emotional connection and communicate well, you both feel safe, understood, and happy. However, a breakdown in communication can lead to a disconnect, especially during times of change or stress. The good news is that as long as you continue to communicate, you have the ability to work through any challenges you may face.

Expressing your needs to your partner is crucial. It may not always be easy to talk about what you need in the relationship. Many people don't take the time to truly reflect on what is important to them. Furthermore, discussing your needs can make you feel vulnerable, embarrassed, or even ashamed. However, it's important to consider your partner's perspective. Providing comfort and understanding to someone you love should be a pleasure, not a burden.

Even if you have been together for a long time, it's important to remember that your partner is not a mind-reader. While they may have some understanding of your thoughts and needs, it is healthier to express your needs directly to avoid any confusion.

Recognize and pay attention to your partner's nonverbal cues. Much of our communication is conveyed through nonverbal cues such as eye contact, tone of voice, posture, and gestures. These cues often communicate more than words alone. By being attuned to your partner's nonverbal cues, you can better understand their true feelings and respond accordingly. Both you and your partner need to understand each other's nonverbal cues, as people's responses and interpretations may differ. For example, one person may find a hug comforting after a stressful day, while another may prefer to take a walk or have a conversation.

Ensure that your words align with your body language. If you say, "I'm fine," but your clenched teeth and avoided eye contact indicate otherwise, there is a clear mismatch between your verbal and nonverbal communication.

Positive emotional cues play a significant role in fostering a loving and happy relationship. When you show interest in your own and your partner's emotions, you strengthen the connection between you. It is important not to lose sight of emotions, especially during stressful times, as neglecting emotions can strain communication and weaken the relationship.

Being a good listener is just as important as being able to express yourself. By actively listening and making your partner feel valued and understood, you can deepen your connection. Listening goes beyond simply hearing the words spoken. It involves being fully engaged and attentive to your partner's tone of voice, subtle intonations, and the emotions they are trying to convey. Being a good listener does not mean you have to agree with everything your partner says. However, it allows you to find common ground and resolve conflicts more effectively.

During times of stress or emotional overwhelm, it is easy to misinterpret your partner's words or unintentionally send negative nonverbal signals. It can also lead to reactive behaviors that you may later regret. Learning how to manage stress and return to a calm state quickly is crucial not only for avoiding regrets but also for preventing conflicts and misunderstandings. By staying calm, you can also help your partner de-escalate tensions during heated moments.

Physical Intimacy

Touch is an essential aspect of our human experience. Research conducted on infants has highlighted the critical role of regular, affectionate contact in the development of their brains (*CEDARS News*, n.d.). Interestingly, the benefits of touch extend beyond childhood. Affectionate physical contact actually increases the body's production of oxytocin, a hormone that plays a significant role in bonding and attachment.

While sex often holds a central position in committed relationships, it is crucial to recognize that physical intimacy goes beyond sexual encounters. Regular displays of affectionate touches, such as holding hands, hugging, and kissing, are equally important for maintaining a healthy relationship.

However, it is essential to be attentive and considerate of your partner's preferences when it comes to touch. Unwanted or inappropriate touching can cause discomfort and lead the other person to withdraw, which is the opposite effect you aim for. Communication becomes vital in these circumstances, and expressing your needs and intentions clearly to your partner is crucial, just like in other aspects of a healthy relationship.

Even if you and your partner are burdened with hectic work schedules or the demands of raising young children, it is still possible to nurture and prioritize physical intimacy. Setting aside dedicated time for just the two of you can help keep the flame of physical intimacy alive. Whether this takes the form of a regular date night or simply an hour at the end of the day for meaningful conversation or hand-holding, carving out this time demonstrates your commitment to maintaining a deeply connected, intimate relationship.

Give and Take

Understanding and honoring your partner's priorities is a key component of a healthy relationship. Similarly, your partner needs to acknowledge and respect your desires, which must be clearly communicated. Continuously sacrificing your own needs for the sake of others will only breed resentment and anger.

Approaching your partner with an ultimatum mindset, where things must be done your way or else, will hinder the ability to reach a compromise. Such an attitude often stems from unmet needs during childhood or accumulated resentment in the relationship that has reached a breaking point. While it's acceptable to hold strong convictions, it is also crucial to listen to and respect your partner's perspective. Each person should be treated with respect, and their viewpoint should be acknowledged.

Peter and Sally had been together for many years. Despite their love for each other, they often argued over small things and became frustrated with each other's points of view.

One day, Peter came home from work and immediately started complaining about a colleague who had taken credit for his work. Sally listened to his story and sympathized with him but then shared her perspective, saying that maybe the colleague hadn't intended to take credit and it might be worth giving them the benefit of the doubt.

Peter immediately became defensive, believing Sally was taking the colleague's side. He accused her of not trusting him and suggested that she had never supported him in his career. Sally was hurt by this. She had always been his biggest cheerleader and didn't understand why he was attacking her. They went to bed that night feeling angry and distant.

The next day, Peter could see the hurt in Sally's eyes, making him realize he had not been listening to her perspective. He realized she was only trying to help, not to attack or hurt him. He took a deep breath, apologized for his behavior, and asked his wife to explain her point of view again. This time, he listened, respected her perspective, and even saw her point of view. He felt grateful for the fresh perspective and realized his initial reaction had been rash and unfair.

Learning to resolve conflicts respectfully is an important skill in maintaining a strong relationship. Conflict is inevitable, but both individuals must feel heard and understood for the relationship to thrive. The objective should not be to win the argument but rather to preserve and strengthen the connection.

Ensure that fair fighting practices are followed. Keep the focus on the specific issue at hand and maintain respect for the other person. Avoid starting arguments over matters that cannot be changed or resolved.

Instead of directly attacking someone, use "I" statements to express your feelings. For instance, replace "You make me feel bad" with "I feel bad when you do that." Avoid bringing up past arguments or harboring grudges. Instead, focus on finding solutions to the current problem and consider what actions can be taken in the present.

Be willing to forgive. Conflict resolution becomes impossible if you are unwilling or unable to forgive others. Forgiveness allows for healing and moving forward in the relationship.

If emotions become heated, it is important to take a break. Step away for a few minutes to reduce stress and regain composure before saying or doing anything that may be regretted. Always remember that you are arguing with someone you love, and it is essential to handle disagreements with care.

Recognize when it is necessary to let go of an issue. If an agreement cannot be reached, it may be best to agree to disagree. It takes two individuals to prolong an argument, and if it becomes unproductive, disengaging and moving on can be a healthier option.

Ups and Downs

In every relationship, it's important to acknowledge that there will be ups and downs. There will be moments when you and your partner are not on the same page. These differences can stem from various factors, such as individual struggles with personal issues like the loss of a loved one, job loss, or health problems. Additionally, disagreements may arise regarding financial management or parenting styles.

It's crucial to recognize that people cope with stress differently. Misunderstandings that aren't effectively addressed can quickly escalate into frustration and anger.

When dealing with your problems, it's important not to take them out on your partner. Life's stresses can make us short-tempered, and it might seem convenient to vent and even snap at your partner. Fighting in this manner may provide temporary relief, but it gradually poisons the relationship. Instead, seek healthier ways to manage stress, anger, and frustration.

Trying to force a solution can often lead to more problems. Each person uniquely approaches problems and issues. Remember that you are a team, and working together and moving forward can help you overcome challenging times.

Reflecting on the early stages of your relationship can be beneficial. Take the time to revisit the moments that brought you together, identify when you may have started to drift apart, and determine how you can work together to reignite that feeling of falling in love.

Remaining open to change is vital. Change is an inevitable part of life, and it will happen whether you resist or embrace it. Being flexible allows you to adapt to the ongoing changes in any relationship and enables you to grow together during the good and the challenging times.

If you find that your relationship requires external assistance, don't hesitate to seek help together. Sometimes, issues in a relationship can become complex or overwhelming, and it may be beneficial to seek couples therapy or speak with a trusted friend or religious figure who can provide guidance and support. Remember, seeking help is a sign of strength, and it can offer valuable insights and tools for navigating relationship challenges.

Implementing Daily Changes

In life, one often finds happiness in significant events or achievements, such as the joyous occasion of welcoming a new baby into the world, the exhilaration of receiving a well-deserved promotion, or the thrill of winning the lottery and realizing our dreams. These significant milestones undoubtedly bring immense happiness and contentment to our lives.

However, there are also moments when happiness comes from the little things, the seemingly insignificant occurrences that have the power to uplift our spirits. Picture yourself walking to work, engrossed in your thoughts and suddenly you stumble upon a breathtakingly beautiful flower garden. As you stop to take in the vibrant colors and delicate petals, you can't help but feel a profound sense of joy and gratitude. Likewise, imagine meeting up with a friend you haven't seen in ages, and as you embrace each other tightly, a wave of warmth and happiness washes over you.

These small yet meaningful moments of happiness are what we are focusing on here. I believe that incorporating certain adjustments and improvements into your daily routine can have a remarkable impact on your overall well-being, allowing you to experience greater happiness, improved health, and heightened productivity.

By consciously making little changes to your day-to-day activities, you can create opportunities for these happiness boosters to occur more frequently. Whether practicing gratitude, engaging in acts of kindness, taking a few minutes to connect with nature, or simply savoring a delicious meal, these seemingly minor adjustments can make a significant difference in your overall happiness and well-being.

Set Your Daily Ritual

Creating a morning ritual can have a powerful impact on how you start your day. Whether going for a run, meditating, or enjoying a healthy breakfast, engaging in a meaningful activity that energizes you sets a positive and proactive tone for the rest of the day. By establishing a structured start to your day, you can eliminate stress and mental fatigue and enhance your productivity.

A structured start to the day can help set a positive tone and increase productivity. Set a consistent wake-up time that gives you enough hours of sleep for optimal rest. Avoid hitting the snooze button. When your alarm goes off, get out of bed to start your day.

Drink a glass of water or have a cup of warm lemon water to rehydrate your body after a night's sleep. This will also help kickstart your metabolism. Engage in some light stretching or exercise to wake up your body and get the blood flowing. This can be a short yoga routine, a brisk walk, or any form of exercise that suits you.

Practice mindfulness or meditation for a while. You can find a calm and peaceful place, sit in a comfortable position, and concentrate on your breath. Alternatively, you can use a guided meditation app to help you clear your mind and set positive intentions for the day. Take a few minutes to go through your schedule and to-do list. Sort out your tasks in order of priority, and set practical goals for the day. This will help you stay focused and organized.

Remember to allocate time for a breakfast that includes a balance of protein, healthy fats, and carbohydrates. Doing so will help you stay energized throughout the day and maintain your focus. Spend some time engaging in activities that promote personal growth. This could be reading a book, listening to a podcast or audiobook, or learning a new skill or hobby.

Take a moment to reflect on the things you are grateful for in your life. Write down three things you appreciate or say them out loud. This can help shift your mindset towards positivity and create an optimistic outlook for the day. Following this structured routine can set you up for a productive and fulfilling day. Adjust the timings and activities to suit your preferences and commitments, but include activities that promote physical and mental well-being and personal growth.

Surrounding yourself with positive people can significantly impact your happiness. As the saying goes, "You are the average of the five people you spend the most time with." Choose to spend time with individuals who uplift and support you while letting go of toxic relationships. Surrounding yourself with positive influences can create a ripple effect of happiness and positivity in your life.

Regular exercise not only benefits your physical health but also boosts creativity, cognitive abilities, and mood. Exercise releases endorphins, natural chemicals that act as mood boosters and natural anti-depressants. Making time for exercise can be an effective way to energize yourself and improve your overall well-being.

Mastering the art of listening is crucial for effective communication in both personal and professional relationships. Paying attention to others and truly listening not only makes them feel valued but also helps you understand them better and gain new perspectives. Active listening involves being genuinely present, avoiding distractions, and observing non-verbal cues.

Taking a break from social media can have a positive impact on your mental health ("Social Media Breaks: Benefits and Tips to Consider," 2022). With the average person spending a significant amount of time on social media, studies have linked excessive social media usage to higher rates of depression. A social media detox, where you intentionally disconnect from digital platforms for a certain period each day, can reduce stress and mental clutter, allowing you to reconnect with the world around you.

Investing in self-care and taking time to unwind is essential for your overall well-being. Engaging in activities that make you feel good, such as listening to music, learning a new skill, indulging in a relaxing bath, or preparing a delicious meal, can have a significant impact on your mood, mental health, and self-esteem.

Actionable Steps for Immediate Improvement

To start making immediate improvements in your life or work, it's important to first identify and prioritize the areas that need attention. Take some time to reflect on what specific aspects could benefit from improvement.

Once you have identified these key areas, it's important to set clear and realistic goals for each one. Ensure that your goals are specific, measurable, attainable, relevant, and time-bound (Mind Tools, n.d.).

Next, break down each goal into smaller, actionable steps. These steps should be specific actions you can take to work towards accomplishing the goal. For example, if your goal is to improve communication skills, a step could be to enroll in a public speaking course, practice active listening in your regular conversations, or engage in communication exercises with your partner, as described in the last chapter.

Start by identifying your long-term and short-term goals for your personal and professional life. Write them down to keep them at the forefront of your mind. Prioritize your goals based on their importance and urgency. This will help you focus on what needs to be done first.

Plan your day or week in advance and allocate specific times to work on tasks that align with your goals. Use a planner or time management app to help you stay organized. Avoid distractions such as social media, personal phone calls, or unnecessary meetings. Use time blocking to focus on specific tasks and avoid multitasking, often resulting in poorer quality work.

Take strategic breaks between work times to reset and avoid burnout. This could be a short yoga routine, reading a chapter from a book, or simply taking a short walk. Reevaluate your goals and progress regularly and adjust your plans accordingly. This allows you to stay flexible and adapt to changing circumstances.

Once you have your actionable steps, create a plan or schedule to implement them. Assign specific actions to each day, week, or month, depending on your timeline. This will ensure you have a clear roadmap to follow and help establish a routine.

Taking immediate action is key to making immediate improvements. Don't wait for the perfect moment or for everything to be in place. Start implementing your plan and executing the actionable steps as soon as possible. The sooner you start, the sooner you'll see results.

Don't hesitate to seek support from others. Share your goals and action plan with someone who can hold you accountable and provide guidance or feedback when needed. This could be a mentor, coach, colleague, or friend. Having someone to support and encourage you can help keep you motivated and focused.

Practice self-reflection and continuous improvement. Take time to reflect on your actions, achievements, and areas that still need improvement. Learn from your experiences, adjust your approach if necessary, and keep striving for growth and improvement. This ongoing self-reflection will help you maintain a mindset of continuous learning and development.

Seeking Support

Seeking support is a valuable step towards bringing about lasting change. Here are some actionable steps to help you find the support you need:

- **Identify your support network:** Make a list of individuals or groups who could potentially offer the support you need. This could include friends, family members, mentors, colleagues, or professionals in the field you are looking to improve.

- **Share your goals and aspirations:** Reach out to the people in your support network and explain your goals and aspirations. Be open and honest about what you are trying to achieve and the kind of support you are seeking. This will help them understand how they can best support you.

- **Seek guidance from mentors or coaches:** If you have specific areas of improvement in mind, consider finding a mentor or coach who specializes in those areas. They can provide targeted guidance, share expertise, and offer personalized strategies for lasting change.

- **Join communities or groups with similar interests:** Look for communities or groups focused on the area you want to improve. This could be an online community, a local meetup, or a professional organization. Engaging with like-minded individuals can provide support, encouragement, and new perspectives.

- **Attend workshops or training programs:** Seek out workshops or training programs that align with your goals for lasting change. These can be valuable opportunities to learn new skills, gain insights, and connect with others who share similar aspirations. Take advantage of these resources to strengthen your support network and deepen your understanding.

- **Build accountability partnerships:** Find an accountability partner or form a small group of individuals striving for lasting change. Regularly meet or check in with each other to review progress, share challenges, and provide support and encouragement.

- **Be open to feedback and advice:** When seeking support, be open to receiving feedback and advice from others. Sometimes, outside perspectives can provide valuable insights and help you see blind spots or areas for improvement you may have overlooked.

Seeking support is not a sign of weakness but rather a sign of strength and an acknowledgment that you are committed to making lasting changes. By reaching out, leveraging your support network, and being open to guidance, you can enhance your chances of bringing about the change you desire and then recovering from anxious attachment.

The Role of Friends and Family in the Recovery Process

Friends and family play a crucial role in the recovery process of an individual facing anxious attachment or undergoing a personal struggle. Here are some ways in which friends and family can support someone in their recovery:

- **Emotional support:** Friends and family provide emotional support by offering empathy, understanding, and compassion. They can be a safe space for the individual to express their feelings, frustrations, and fears. By actively listening and validating their emotions, friends and family contribute to the person's overall well-being, self-esteem, and motivation to recover.

- **Encouragement and motivation:** Friends and family can serve as a source of encouragement and motivation throughout the recovery process. They can remind the person of their progress, praise their achievements, and provide positive reinforcement. This support can help bolster the individual's confidence and belief in their ability to overcome challenges.

- **Practical assistance:** Friends and family can offer practical assistance by helping with daily tasks or responsibilities that the person may struggle with during recovery. This can include cooking meals, running errands, attending appointments together, or providing transportation. By alleviating some practical burdens, they enable the person to focus on their recovery.

- **Accountability and structure:** Friends and family can play a role in keeping the individual accountable to their recovery goals. They can check in regularly, ask about progress, and gently remind them of their commitments. By providing structure and holding the person accountable, friends and family contribute to maintaining a sense of discipline and commitment.

- **Providing a supportive environment:** Creating a supportive and nurturing environment is crucial for a successful recovery process. Friends and family can help establish boundaries, set a positive atmosphere, and support the person's healthy choices. They may also remove triggers or unhealthy influences from the person's surroundings, making it easier for them to stay on track.

- **Education and research:** Friends and family can educate themselves about the specific challenges the person is facing. By learning about the condition, treatment options, and recovery strategies, they can better understand the person's experiences and provide more informed support. This knowledge allows them to communicate effectively and assist in finding appropriate resources.

- **Seeking professional help together:** Friends and family can actively participate in the recovery process by attending therapy sessions or support groups together with the person. This shows solidarity and signals their commitment to supporting the individual's recovery. In some cases, family therapy or counseling can help address underlying family dynamics or communication patterns that may impact the person's recovery.

It's important to note that supportive friends and family members should also take care of their well-being to avoid burnout. Seeking support from other sources, such as support groups or therapy, can be beneficial for them, too.

Overall, friends and family contribute significantly to a person's recovery process by providing emotional support, encouragement, practical assistance, accountability, and a nurturing environment. Their involvement can greatly enhance the individual's chances of successfully overcoming challenges and achieving long-term recovery.

Celebrating Progress

Recognizing and celebrating progress is a fundamental aspect of the journey towards healing from anxious attachment. In the pursuit of a more secure attachment style, it becomes essential to applaud the incremental steps taken, both big and small. These celebratory moments play a pivotal role in boosting confidence and sustaining the motivation required to continue cultivating a healthier attachment style.

Breaking down the recovery journey into manageable milestones provides a clear roadmap for personal growth. Each milestone achieved signifies a triumph over anxious attachment patterns, marking a positive shift towards greater emotional security. By acknowledging these steps, individuals can reinforce their commitment to change and build a foundation for a more fulfilling connection with others.

To enhance the celebratory aspect of progress, incorporating a reward system can be both motivating and enjoyable. Establishing a range of rewards, from simple treats like indulging in a favorite dessert or treating yourself to a movie to more substantial rewards such as a weekend getaway or a coveted purchase, creates a tangible connection between achievement and positive reinforcement.

The choice of rewards should align with personal preferences and aspirations, making each milestone a personalized and meaningful victory. This not only adds an element of excitement to the journey but also serves as a reminder of the progress made and the resilience demonstrated in overcoming anxious attachment tendencies.

Crucially, amidst the celebration of achievements, it is paramount to maintain a compassionate and gentle approach towards oneself. Recognizing that the journey towards a more secure attachment style is a process of growth and self-discovery allows for a kinder perspective. Embracing both the big and small victories fosters a nurturing environment for personal transformation.

In summary, the practice of celebrating progress in the journey towards healing from anxious attachment contributes significantly to building resilience and fortifying the commitment to change. By breaking the recovery process into small, achievable milestones and attaching meaningful rewards to these accomplishments, individuals can create a positive feedback loop that fuels motivation and reinforces the pursuit of a healthier attachment style. Remembering to be gentle with oneself throughout this journey ensures that each step forward is not only acknowledged but cherished as a significant victory on the path to emotional well-being.

Chapter Summary

- Building a healthy relationship takes work, commitment, and a willingness to adapt and change with your partner, regardless of the length of the relationship or past relationship failures.

- Communication with your partner regarding shared goals and understanding the basic principles of healthy relationships are essential to keep the relationship meaningful, fulfilling, and exciting.

- Successful couples maintain a meaningful emotional connection with each other and are unafraid of respectful disagreement.

- Couples keep outside relationships and interests alive as no single person can meet all their needs.

- Open and honest communication is key in any successful relationship as it increases trust and strengthens the bond between
  two people.

Conclusion

"Anxious attachment stems from a deep sense of inner
instability where old wounds make people anticipate
that they will be abandoned again and again."

Jessica Baum.

I n conclusion, *Anxious Attachment Recovery* is a comprehensive guide-
book that provides valuable insights and practical strategies for individuals seeking to heal from anxious attachment patterns and build
healthier, more secure relationships. The book's main ideas revolve around
understanding the origins and impacts of anxious attachment, identifying
and challenging anxious thoughts and behaviors, and developing new patterns of secure attachment.

I introduced the concept of attachment theory, explaining how early childhood experiences shape our attachment styles. I emphasized that anxious
attachment often stems from inconsistent or unpredictable caregiving
during childhood, leading to a deep-seated fear of abandonment and a
constant need for reassurance and validation in relationships.

One of the key takeaways is the importance of recognizing and understanding one's attachment style. By becoming aware of the patterns and
triggers associated with anxious attachment, individuals can begin to un-
ravel the root causes of their anxiety. I also provided various self-assessment

exercises and reflective prompts to help you gain insight into your attachment style and how it manifests in your relationships.

I also highlighted the significance of self-compassion and self-care in the recovery process. Anxious individuals often tend to blame themselves for their attachment anxieties, which only reinforces the cycle of insecurity. I also encourage you to practice self-compassion and develop healthy self-care routines that prioritize your emotional well-being.

Another central theme was the need for clear and effective communication. Anxious individuals often struggle with expressing their needs and boundaries for fear of pushing their partners away. I provided practical tips and scripts for initiating difficult conversations, setting boundaries, and expressing needs in a non-accusatory and assertive manner.

Furthermore, I delved into the importance of establishing trust and security in relationships. I explored strategies and techniques for building trust with a partner and creating a safe emotional space where both partners feel valued and understood. I emphasized the importance of consistent and reliable behavior and guided how to foster open and honest communication.

I also offered a range of techniques to help individuals manage their anxious thoughts and reduce their emotional reactivity. By learning to observe and challenge your anxious thoughts, you can gain a sense of control over your emotions and develop more constructive responses in your relationships.

I also spoke about the concept of boundaries and emphasized their role in cultivating healthier relationships. I stressed the importance of setting clear boundaries and assertively communicating them to one's partner. Additionally, I explored the significance of boundaries in managing expectations, promoting self-worth, and maintaining individual autonomy within the relationship.

An important aspect of *Anxious Attachment Recovery* is developing new patterns of secure attachment. It guides how to cultivate and nurture secure attachment styles, which involve consistently meeting one's own emotional needs and fostering a sense of security and trust within oneself. It offered strategies for building self-confidence, developing emotional resilience, and embracing vulnerability in relationships.

Overall, *Anxious Attachment Recovery* offered a wealth of information and practical tools for individuals seeking to heal from anxious attachment patterns. By gaining insight into their attachment style, practicing self-compassion, improving communication skills, and cultivating secure attachment within themselves, readers can work towards building healthier and more fulfilling relationships. Recovery is a gradual and ongoing process and encourages individuals to be patient and persistent in their journey toward healing and growth.

Now that you have gained valuable insights and practical strategies, it's time to take action and apply what you've learned to your own life and relationships. Here are a few tips to help you get started:

- **Reflect on your attachment style:** Take some time to reflect on your attachment style and how it manifests in your relationships. Consider the patterns and triggers that contribute to your anxious attachment. This self-awareness is the first step towards healing and growth.

- **Practice self-compassion and self-care:** Recognize that anxious attachment is not your fault. Be gentle with yourself and practice self-compassion. Implement self-care routines that prioritize your emotional well-being. Prioritizing your own needs will help you build a stronger sense of self and create a more secure foundation for your relationships.

- **Communicate effectively:** Work on improving your communication skills by being clear and assertive about your needs and boundaries. Use the techniques and scripts provided in the book to initiate difficult conversations and express yourself in a constructive and non-accusatory manner. Effective communication is essential for building trust and understanding in your relationships.

- **Challenge anxious thoughts:** Practice mindfulness and cognitive restructuring exercises to observe and challenge your anxious thoughts. By questioning the validity of these thoughts and replacing them with more realistic and positive ones, you can reduce your emotional reactivity and gain a sense of control over your emotions.

- **Set clear boundaries:** Take the time to identify your boundaries and communicate them to your partner. Boundaries are crucial for maintaining a healthy balance in a relationship and establishing a sense of safety and respect. Be assertive in setting and enforcing your boundaries, ensuring that your needs are met and that you maintain your autonomy.

- **Build secure attachment within yourself:** Focus on nurturing a sense of security and trust within yourself. Practice self-reliance, build self-confidence, and cultivate emotional resilience. Embrace vulnerability in your relationships, as vulnerability is a key ingredient in deepening emotional connections and building secure attachment bonds.

Remember, applying the knowledge and strategies outlined in this book will require patience, persistence, and a commitment to personal growth.

Be prepared for setbacks and obstacles along the way, but stay focused on your intention to heal and build healthier relationships.

By taking action and applying what you've learned, you have the opportunity to break free from anxious attachment patterns and create a more secure and fulfilling future for yourself and your relationships. Begin your journey of transformation today and experience the positive impact it can have on your life.

With knowledge and commitment, I am pretty sure you will achieve your goals!

Glossary

- **Anxious Attachment:** A style of attachment characterized by a deep-seated fear of abandonment, a constant need for reassurance and validation, and a tendency to be overly sensitive to relationship cues.

- **Secure Attachment:** A style of attachment characterized by trust, emotional security, and a healthy balance of independence and interdependence in relationships.

- **Reflective Prompts:** Questions or statements designed to encourage self-reflection and deeper exploration of one's thoughts, emotions, and behaviors.

- **Blame:** The act of attributing fault or responsibility to oneself or others. Anxious individuals often engage in self-blame, holding themselves accountable for their attachment anxieties.

- **Self-Compassion:** The practice of extending kindness, understanding, and forgiveness to oneself when facing difficulties or setbacks.

- **Emotional Reactivity:** The tendency to have intense emotional responses to certain triggers or situations, often resulting in impulsive or heightened reactions.

- **Mindfulness:** The practice of cultivating present-moment awareness and non-judgmental acceptance of one's thoughts, feelings, and sensations.

- **Cognitive Restructuring:** A technique that involves identifying and challenging negative or irrational thought patterns and replacing them with more realistic and positive ones.

- **Grounding Techniques:** Strategies that help individuals connect with the present moment, such as deep breathing, sensory awareness, or focusing on physical sensations.

- **Boundaries:** The limits and guidelines one sets for themselves and their relationships to establish healthy emotional and physical boundaries.

- **Effective Communication:** Clear and open communication that fosters understanding, empathy, and connection in relationships.

- **Self-Reliance:** The ability to meet one's emotional needs and have a sense of independence and self-sufficiency.

- **Emotional Resilience:** The ability to adapt, cope with, and recover from emotional challenges and stressful situations.

- **Vulnerability:** The willingness to be open, sincere, and exposed in relationships, allowing for deeper emotional connections and trust.

- **Trust:** The process of developing trust and creating a safe emotional space in relationships through consistent and reliable behavior.

References

Amir Levine Quotes (Author of Attached). (n.d.). www.goodreads.com. Retrieved December 9, 2023, from https://www.goodreads.com/author/quotes/4417525.Amir_Levine

Anxious Attachment Quotes (6 quotes). (n.d.). www.goodreads.com. Retrieved December 1, 2023, from https://www.goodreads.com/quotes/tag/anxious-attachment#:~:text=Don

Anxious Attachment Quotes (6 quotes). (n.d.-b). www.goodreads.com. Retrieved December 8, 2023, from https://www.goodreads.com/quotes/tag/anxious-attachment#:~:text=%E2%80%9CI%20think%20about

Anxiously Attached Quotes by Jessica Baum. (n.d.). www.goodreads.com. Retrieved November 28, 2023, from https://www.goodreads.com/work/quotes/94317849-anxiously-attached-becoming-more-secure-in-life-and-love#:~:text=If%20you%20are%20in%20love

Attachment disorder in adults: Symptoms, causes, and more. (2020, October 30). www.medicalnewstoday.com. https://www.medicalnewstoday.com/articles/attachment-disorder-in-adults#relationships

Brennan, D. (2021, April 8). What is anxious attachment? WebMD. https://www.webmd.com/mental-health/what-is-anxious-attachment

Cherry, K. (2022, May 26). *The different types of attachment styles. Very-well Mind.* https://www.verywellmind.com/attachment-styles-2795344

Do your early experiences affect your adult relationships? (2016, March 12). Psych Central. https://psychcentral.com/blog/how-childhood-trauma-affects-adult-relationships#:~:text=Trust%20challenges

Domendos. (2021, May 28). *4 Sides model of communication. Projectman agement.guide.* https://projectmanagement.guide/4-sides-model-of-commu nication/

Erozkan, A. (2016). *The link between types of attachment and childhood trauma. Universal Journal of Educational Research, 4(5), 1071–1079.* ht tps://doi.org/10.13189/ujer.2016.040517

Freed, M. (2023, June 12). *10 Ways to improve communication in your marriage and strengthen your relationship. Freed Marcroft LLC.* https://freedmarcroft.com/10-ways-to-improve-communication-in-yo ur-marriage-and-strengthen-your-relationship/

Gorlick, A. (2016, April 16). *Media multitaskers pay mental price, Stanford study shows. Stanford News; Stanford University.* https://news.stanford.ed u/2009/08/24/multitask-research-study-082409/

Lebow, H. I. (2022, June 22). *Anxious attachment style: What it looks like in adult relationships. Psych Central.* https://psychcentral.com/health/anxi ous-attachment-style-signs

Madrid, E. (2012). Facebook.com. https://www.facebook.com/verywell

Mark Manson. (2021, January 13). *Attachment Theory. Mark Manson.* https://markmanson.net/attachment-styles

Mikulincer, M., & Shaver, P. R. (2009). An attachment and behavioral systems perspective on social support. Journal of Social and Personal Relationships, 26(1), 7–19. https://doi.org/10.1177/0265407509105518

Mind Tools. (n.d.). SMART Goals. Mind Tools. https://www.mindtools.com/a4wo118/smart-goals

Moore, C. (2019, June 2). How to practice self-compassion: 8 Techniques and tips. Positive Psychology. https://positivepsychology.com/how-to-practice-self-compassion/

National Collaborating Centre for Mental Health (UK). (2015). Introduction to children's attachment. Nih.gov; National Institute for Health and Care Excellence (UK). https://www.ncbi.nlm.nih.gov/books/NBK356196/

News from CEDARS. (n.d.). Cedarskids.org. Retrieved December 26, 2023, from https://cedarskids.org/news/news.html/article/2021/08/11/hold-me-close-physical-touch-and-brain-development#:~:text=In%20this%20way%2C%20nurturing%20physical

Past Experiences Quotes (13 quotes). (n.d.). www.goodreads.com. Retrieved December 8, 2023, from https://www.goodreads.com/quotes/tag/past-experiences#:~:text=%E2%80%9CLearn%20from%20past%20experiences%20but%20accept%20them%20all%20as%20perfect%20while%20staying%20in%20the%20present.%20Let%20go%20of%20everything%20that%20doesn%27t%20serve%20you.%E2%80%9D

Reflective Listening | UNSW Teaching Staff Gateway. (n.d.). www.teaching.unsw.edu.au. Retrieved December 26, 2023, from https://www.teaching.unsw.edu.au/group-work-reflective-listening#:~:text=Reflective%20listening%20appears%20deceptively%20easy

Riggs, S. A. (2010). Childhood emotional abuse and the attachment system across the life cycle: What theory and research tell us. Journal of Aggression, Maltreatment & Trauma, 19(1), 5–51. https://doi.org/10.1080/10926770 903475968

Rising above the Imposter Syndrome trap on women & minorities. (n.d.). Hospitalityinsights.ehl.edu. https://hospitalityinsights.ehl.edu/imposter-syn drome-women-minorities

Ross, E. J., Graham, D. L., Money, K. M., & Stanwood, G. D. (2015). Developmental consequences of fetal exposure to drugs: What we know and what we still must learn. Neuropsychopharmacology, 40(1), 61–87. https://doi.org/10.1038/npp.2014.147

Schröder, M., Lüdtke, J., Fux, E., Izat, Y., Bolten, M., Gloger-Tippelt, G., Suess, G. J., & Schmid, M. (2019). Attachment disorder and attachment theory–Two sides of one medal or two different coins? Comprehensive Psychiatry, 95(95), 152139. https://doi.org/10.1016/j.comppsych.2019.152139

7 Telltale signs of an anxiously attached partner | Psychology Today. (n.d.). www.psychologytoday.com. Retrieved December 26, 2023, from https://www.psychologytoday.com/intl/blog/narcissism-demystified/202306/ 7-telltale-signs-of-an-anxiously-attached-partner#:~:text=6.%20Anxiously %20attached%20partners%20feel%20one%2Ddown%20in%20a%20relation ship.

Social media breaks: Benefits and tips to consider. (2022, May 12). Www.medicalnewstoday.com . https://www.medicalnewstoday.com/articles/social-media-breaks#:~:text =Eases%20anxiety&text=Social%20media%20use%20can%20cause

35 Quotes about communication for inspiring team collaboration | Vibe. (n.d.). Vibe.us. https://vibe.us/blog/35-quotes-about-communication/#:~:text=%E2%80%9CCommunication%20is%20the%20solvent%20of

Winston Churchill Quotes. (n.d.). BrainyQuote. https://www.brainyquote.com/quotes/winston_churchill_138235

Work less and do more by applying the Pareto Principle to your task list. (2012, June 1). Lifehacker. https://lifehacker.com/work-less-and-do-more-by-applying-the-pareto-principle-5914877

Avoidant Attachment Recovery

5 Steps to Overcome Fear of Intimacy, Strengthen Connections and Transition from Avoidant to Secure Attachment

Amy Harper

Introduction

Understanding Attachment Styles

> "There are two philosophies when it comes to getting young children to sleep. There is 'sleep training,' which basically involves putting your kids to bed and listening to them scream all night; or there is 'attachment parenting,' which essentially involves lying down with your kids, cuddling them, and then listening to them scream all night."
>
> Jim Gaffigan

Have you ever felt a confusing mix of wanting connection and pushing people away? It is more common than you may think. Do you see yourself in Amanda? This character's story will deeply resonate with anyone experiencing avoidant attachment.

Amanda is an independent woman in her mid-thirties who came to the big city and made a name for herself with sheer hard work. But now she finds herself alone in the bustling streets of Manhattan and yearns for meaningful connections.

At first glance, Amanda's life appears idyllic. Her bustling café overflows with customers each evening, her boyfriend of two years just proposed, and a vibrant social circle, filled with seemingly close friends, surrounds her.

Yet she isn't the epitome of female empowerment and self-sufficiency as people think. You may look at her to find a lively, confident, and composed businesswoman. But a subtle ache lingers deep within her soul – a longing for intimacy keeps her up at night. Even in the company of her best buddies and would-be husband, she can almost feel a hole in herself.

How did Amanda grow up to be so afraid of intimacy? What makes her a closed book when it comes to expressing emotions? For that, we have to go 20 years in the past. We have to look back at her childhood. As the daughter of an absent father and a negligent mother, Amanda learned to become self-reliant.

She learned how to navigate life's challenges on her own. But this independence came at a price. As a grown-up, she suffers from severe avoidant attachment. As a result, she:

- Is emotionally distant.

- Doesn't let her guard down easily.

- Isn't comfortable seeking help.

- Doesn't like to rely on someone else.

- Is afraid of vulnerability.

- Approach relationships with caution.

- Is apprehensive of intimacy.

- Doesn't express her emotions openly.

Now, she's afraid. Afraid she might push her loved ones away. Afraid that one day, the mask would come off and everyone would see the real Amanda. This fear of losing control manifests in a terrifying possibility - calling off the wedding, severing ties, and running away, repeating the cycle of emotional isolation. What do you think she did next?

Amanda realized she needed to be brave and open up to someone. She sought therapy, talked to a mental health professional, and told her girlfriends about her condition. They were very supportive and told her about a unique new way for people like her to get better.

Unveiling the Secrets of the 5-Step Journey

What did you say? Are you interested in the 5-step program too? Good for you, then! Just like this program worked for Amanda and helped her rediscover her emotional self, it'll do wonders for you, too. Here's a brief overview of the 5 steps and what they cover.

Step One – Self-Discovery and Understanding: Avoidant attachment often works in mysterious ways. It's a pattern that shapes your attachment style over time. Do you avoid intimacy? Do you avoid making long-lasting relationships with other people? All of this might be happening in your subconscious. Well, this phase will be the stepping stone in a long-winded journey in which we'll lay down the much-needed groundwork for change. You'll reflect on your childhood history, previous relationships, and attachment patterns. This stage is for introspection – to look deep into your heart and bury the seed of self-awareness that will bloom into the flower of self-transformation. A few self-assessment exercises will be your tools to make the necessary changes.

Step Two – Emotional Attunement: How much do you understand your emotional landscape? How in touch are you with your emotional side? This stage will help you recognize, validate, and get control of your emotions. Some types of avoidant behaviors stem from these complex feelings that make you bad at emotional regulation. But don't fret; this step will include some fantastic tips to handle your emotions in a healthy way. Is detachment your default mode? Well, this stage will change that, and you'll be more emotionally expressive.

Step Three – Communicating Needs and Embracing Vulnerability: Do you find it difficult to express your needs and desires openly? Does it make you feel bad, abashed, or uncomfortable to open talk about what you need? Because you don't want to be seen as vulnerable, needy, or someone who relies on others? Learn how to embrace vulnerability as your strong suit rather than a weakness. In this stage, we'll tear down the walls that make intimacy an alien concept to you. You will learn practical communication tips so you can be more outspoken about your needs. Find out how to talk to others about your boundaries. It'll help you forge deeper connections with people.

Step Four – Creating Lasting Connections: Now you know how to open up about your feelings. Once people know you're vulnerable, you can move to have a stronger bond with them – a bond of trust, friendship, and mutual reliance. So, this part of the book will cover fantastic tips on nurturing this bond. How do you keep a friendship? How do you make a connection last for months or years? How do you never lose a friend again? Remember, the secret of lasting connections lies not in forging them but in cherishing them. Involve your partner in the process. I'll be there every step of the way to provide unparalleled guidance.

Step Five – Creating Growth and Security: Even newly acquired habits fizzle out and die after a while. How do you avoid relapse? How do you solidify the habits you've picked in the previous four steps? The fifth stage aims to make these new behavior patterns long-lasting and permanent. You will learn to be healthy for good and keep implementing the lessons learned here for the rest of your life. Create an attachment style that stays with you forever. How else are you going to develop lasting and fulfilling relationships? This chapter shows you that overcoming avoidant attachment isn't about following a few processes; it's a lifelong procedure that requires constant effort.

There you have it! You just learned in very brief detail why the 5-step program is helpful to you. How does it help you grow as a person? How does it reveal the hidden side of your personality that you've been suppressing since childhood? In broad strokes, what is the purpose of these five steps?

- Find out what past events make you emotionally detached.

- How to get in touch with your "emotionality" (a pun on sexuality)?

- Tips to make vulnerability your strength and use it to create lasting bonds.

- Nurturing these bonds and making them last for life.

- Growing yourself under the shadow of secure attachment.

The beauty of this program lies in its simplicity and effectiveness. Imagine a powerful roadmap to transformation distilled into just five clear steps, easily remembered and readily implemented. Does this approach resonate with you? Integrating this structured program into your daily routine can become the key to promoting lasting change.

In the next section, you'll learn the reasoning behind these five steps. Find out why a systematic approach always works and helps people easily embrace the lessons of self-recovery.

Why Are We in Love with a Systematic Approach?

There's a fundamental reason why I'm using a systematic approach here. It's a powerful method for change that leads to lasting transformations. Check out these reasons why this approach is ideal for this guide:

- It makes it easier to identify your attachment patterns.

- It gives you a sense of guidance and direction, making the healing process manageable.

- Instead of expecting drastic changes, you will make gradual changes over time, leading to a more sustainable approach to recovery.

- You'll apply self-healing tips chapter by chapter and then apply these skills in the real world. So, don't forget the previous chapter when reading the next one.

- This system makes you reflect on your actions and behaviors. So, you understand how your attachment pattern has affected your romantic life. Self-reflection is the key to permanent healing, right?

- Incremental learning is also great for personal growth. It helps you take control of the healing process. You'll notice an increase in your self-confidence, and soon, it'll be much easier to bring lasting changes.

Just like learning to ride a bike, overcoming avoidant attachment takes practice and a supportive guide. Initially, you might feel a little unsteady and unsure of yourself. But don't worry: I'll be there with you every step of the way, offering support and encouragement. Gradually, as you gain confidence, we can slowly decrease that support. This will allow you to feel more empowered and in control. Soon, you'll be cruising along on your own, navigating your journey with newfound confidence.

A structured program, similar to learning a new skill, equips you with the tools you need to overcome your fear of intimacy and navigate your path to secure attachment.

Do you still think this book doesn't address your needs and concerns? Don't worry; I'll soon explain why this book was written with you in mind. This book is like a novel; you're the main character, my dear reader.

Who am I, and who is This Book for?

Are you wondering if avoidant attachment might be impacting your relationships? Do you want to improve your love life? Be more successful romantically? Reciprocate your partner's feelings for you? Or does your partner sometimes struggle with emotional intimacy, perhaps exhibiting signs of avoidant attachment?

In all cases, this is the perfect book for you. Does keeping your partner at arm's length sound familiar? Avoidant attachment could be the reason. Learn how to create a closer bond.

My name is Amy Harper, and I am your guide and companion throughout this journey of healing and recovery. I'm here to support you on your journey to overcome avoidant attachment. Please think of me as your guide and cheerleader, helping you conquer those intimacy fears and build the relationships you deserve.

Throughout my career as a counselor, I've encountered many individuals with a variety of behavioral challenges. Among them, I've observed a significant number who experience avoidant attachment. In fact, research suggests it affects roughly 30% of the global population, which highlights its prevalence. My deep understanding of this condition has led me to write this book.

In this book, Avoidant Attachment Recovery, I'll discuss this condition in detail. So, don't lose hope; your quest toward secure attachment is only a few pages away. But first, you have to keep a few principles in mind to speed up the healing process.

Setting the Tone - A Journey of Change

You may wonder how this book will help you become a changed person. Well, let's set the tone for the whole book here in this small section. When you're reading this book, keep these three principles in your mind – like a charm that'll help you heal faster:

1. You'll overcome avoidant attachment one day; we'll keep this hope alive.

2. Let healing come from a place of empathy, understanding, and compassion.

3. This book is your judgment-free zone for exploring your emotions. Let your guard down and discover a path to greater intimacy.

Never forget that the seedling of healing and growth lies deep within your heart. You are in control and possess the power to change yourself. With little effort, you can push that seed to grow into a small plant of self-realization that will soon bloom into a huge plant of permanent healing. Positive changes lie ahead, and this book is the road to recovery. You are the driver, so have faith in your skills. I believe you can do it. Do you?

This journey is a team effort. While this book offers valuable tools, your active participation unlocks its full potential.

Read the following section carefully and find the key that makes this book work.

What do I Want from You?

If you want to make this healing process work, cooperate with me. Here's what I want you to do while reading this guide:

- Open yourself up to the contents of this book. The more actively you participate, the greater the rewards.

- Engage emotionally with the tips mentioned here.

- Approach each chapter with an open mind and the desire to change.

- Always be prepared to reflect on what you've read, grow with it, and make healing part of your daily routine.

Let's embark on this incredible journey of healing and self-discovery. Whether you want to revitalize your romantic life or get back the one who got away, this guide will help you through and through. From Chapter 1, the healing process begins!

Chapter 1 - Step 1

The Fundamentals of Self-Discovery & Understanding

"I think self-discovery is the greatest achievement in life because once you discover yourself and accept who you are, you can fulfill your true potential and be happy."

Marco Pierre White

I see that you're reading Chapter 1 now. The bravest thing a person could do is to step on the road of self-discovery. That's when your transformation begins, and you slowly become a better person. It isn't easy to confront your fears and vulnerabilities head-on or even acknowledge that they exist. It takes courage to say, "I have this flaw and need help."

As your fingers keep turning these pages and your eyes glance upon these words, you shouldn't forget that you're not alone in this journey. Many have walked this path before and will do after you. Surveys show that over 14% of kids in America have an avoidant attachment (Ocklenburg, 2023). These kids will likely grow up to walk the path you're walking right now.

So, are you willing to explore your attachment style? Do you wish to bring everlasting changes in your life? I should warn you that the journey you're about to undertake isn't that easy. No, sir! You may have to face ugly truths about yourself, face the aspects of your personality you've always avoided, and shatter the beliefs that affected your romantic life. But remember this: every step you take will bring you closer to self-awareness and a more fulfilling life.

You'll learn some crucial answers on this quest, such as:

- What are the signs of avoidant attachment?

- How does it affect your relationships?

- How do you embrace a secure attachment style?

So, embrace this journey with an open heart and mind. Don't forget our shared goal is not perfection but progress. So, let's make this progress together, my friend!

Avoidant Attachment - Recognizing the Telltale Signs

I've been providing counseling to people with behavior issues. Many of my clients struggle with avoidant attachment and similar conditions. One of my clients was Jessica, a 25-year-old schoolteacher married to her high school sweetheart. Her story can help you recognize the telltale signs of avoidant attachment.

Now, Jessica wasn't an introvert; she liked to hang around with friends and partying with them. At her job (I knew her because she taught one of my kids), she was every kid's favorite teacher. But there was still something missing in her life.

Sometimes, she used to choose to stay at home and do nothing. She told me she sometimes spent hours watching movies on her tablet and didn't respond to her friends. They wanted to go shopping – and Jessica loved shopping – but she used to say no. Or even left her best friend on read without even bothering to respond.

Even her husband had to suffer because of her emotionally distant attitude; he wanted to spend time with her, but she didn't reciprocate the same warmth and love. Even when they were out – like watching a movie or having a double date with mutual friends – she was always miles away in her own thoughts. In any social gathering, she was the least talkative person.

And Jessica was aware of all that. She just didn't know how to start connecting with people and stop ghosting her childhood friends. Even her work productivity began to decline due to her condition. She stopped showing up for team-building exercises or helping new teachers adjust to the environment. "I am afraid to rely on others, and I also don't want anyone else counting on me."

Then Jessica shared the thing she was terrified of the most. She was afraid that if she kept pushing people away, she might end up ending things with her husband, the man whom she very much loved. It was a thought that kept her awake at night, but she didn't know what she could do about it.

After reading Jessica's story, you can see interesting parallels. You want to behave like her in real life, don't you? Honestly answer these simple questions:

- Do you choose to be alone even if you want to be with friends?

- Do you cut your friends off and struggle to respond to them?

- Do you refuse to socialize with your coworkers?

- Do you try to do things by yourself all the time?

- Do you pull away when your partner wants to be close to you?

As the saying goes (or my kids made it up and told it to me), "Name the beast to tame the beast." Realizing your flaws and recognizing your symptoms are the very first stepping stones toward healing. If you wish to start your journey toward the secure shores of secure attachment, evaluate your attachment pattern.

Self-Assessment - How Well Do You Know Your Attachment Style?

Let's start with a brief session of self-assessment. We must ensure you understand your current attachment style and avoidant tendencies very well.

Below, you'll find a list of the key avoidant tendencies often exhibited by avoidantly attached people. Please read each question carefully and then honestly assess your current level of proficiency on a scale of 1 to 5. The self-assessment in this book is designed for self-reflection and isn't an official diagnosis. It's a helpful way to gauge your tendency for avoidant behaviors, but it's important to consult with a professional for a proper evaluation and advice.

- "1" means a strong "Yes" (indicating Strong Avoidance).

- "2" means a mild "Yes" (indicating Mild Avoidance).

- "3" means neutrality, i.e., neither "Yes" nor "No."

- "4" means a mild "No" (indicating Mild Security).

- "5" means a strong "No" (indicating Strong Security).

1- Do you feel emotionally distant from your partner, family, and friends?

☐1   ☐2   ☐3   ☐4   ☐5

2- Do you always try to do things on your own and don't like accepting help?

☐1   ☐2   ☐3   ☐4   ☐5

3- Do you approach new relationships with caution and are suspicious of men/women seeking your companionship?

☐1   ☐2   ☐3   ☐4   ☐5

4- Does intimacy seem like a scary concept to you? Does it make you uncomfortable or wear you down?

☐1   ☐2   ☐3   ☐4   ☐5

5- Does self-expression make you embarrassed? Do you not like showing emotions?

☐1   ☐2   ☐3   ☐4   ☐5

6- Are you the kind of person who doesn't want to rely on others and doesn't want others to rely on you?

☐1   ☐2   ☐3   ☐4   ☐5

7- Is it hard for you to respond to your friends, leading to unread chats and unseen messages?

☐1   ☐2   ☐3   ☐4   ☐5

8- Is it hard for you to socialize with your coworkers since you don't want to be too attached to them?

☐1   ☐2   ☐3   ☐4   ☐5

9- Do you choose to be a loner despite your strong desire for intimacy and hanging out with friends?

☐1   ☐2   ☐3   ☐4   ☐5

10- Does it make you mad when people try to be close to you, and you think they are being too clingy?

☐1   ☐2   ☐3   ☐4   ☐5

11- Do you sometimes think you're not worthy of your partner's love or that he/she deserves someone better?

☐1   ☐2   ☐3   ☐4   ☐5

12- Does criticism make you too depressed? It makes you think low of yourself?

☐1   ☐2   ☐3   ☐4   ☐5

13- Do you try to keep a poker face (show-no-emotion face) when dealing with tough times?

☐1   ☐2   ☐3   ☐4   ☐5

14- Do you refuse to give or take emotional support? Do you expect others to be just as emotionally distant as you are?

☐1   ☐2   ☐3   ☐4   ☐5

15- Do you spend or want to spend most of your time alone? Do you describe yourself as a loner?

☐1   ☐2   ☐3   ☐4   ☐5

16- Do you think you're not 100% invested in your current relationship? Do you keep suspecting, "Something will go wrong in this relationship?"

☐1   ☐2   ☐3   ☐4   ☐5

17- Are you always suspicious of your partner? Do you think they might cheat on you, dump you, or disappoint you some other way?

☐1   ☐2   ☐3   ☐4   ☐5

18- Do you stay away from intimacy because you are afraid of being rejected by your partner?

☐1   ☐2   ☐3   ☐4   ☐5

19- Are you always the one to prematurely end the relationship?

☐1   ☐2   ☐3   ☐4   ☐5

20- Are you commitment-shy? Are you afraid to make a commitment or invest in a relationship?

☐1   ☐2   ☐3   ☐4   ☐5

21- Are you bad at reading emotions? Do you have a hard time recognizing people's emotions or understanding how they feel?

☐1   ☐2   ☐3   ☐4   ☐5

22- Do you fantasize about a relationship after it ends? Do you muse over your exes?

☐1   ☐2   ☐3   ☐4   ☐5

23- Do you deliberately or accidentally sabotage your own relationship?

☐1   ☐2   ☐3   ☐4   ☐5

24- Do you believe intimacy is the same as vulnerability?

☐1　　☐2　　☐3　　☐4　　☐5

25- Do you try to get out of a relationship when it gets more serious?

☐1　　☐2　　☐3　　☐4　　☐5

26- Are you unwilling to open up to your partner about your personal life?

☐1　　☐2　　☐3　　☐4　　☐5

27- Do you avoid difficult conversations and try to stay miles away from hard-to-handle topics?

☐1　　☐2　　☐3　　☐4　　☐5

28- Do you get visibly disturbed when your partner brings up delicate topics?

☐1　　☐2　　☐3　　☐4　　☐5

29- Do you feel like you always have to be perfect and give your 100% to everything?

☐1　　☐2　　☐3　　☐4　　☐5

30- Does sharing too much information embarrass you? Does it make you feel naked and wounded?

☐1　　☐2　　☐3　　☐4　　☐5

31- Do you ruminate over bygone events and bad experiences of the past?

☐1　　☐2　　☐3　　☐4　　☐5

32- Do you easily get offended when someone judges or condemns you?

☐1   ☐2   ☐3   ☐4   ☐5

33- Do you keep changing sexual partners?

☐1   ☐2   ☐3   ☐4   ☐5

34- Do you prefer to engage sexually with someone you're not romantically attached to?

☐1   ☐2   ☐3   ☐4   ☐5

35- Do you think negatively of people who are securely attached to their partners?

☐1   ☐2   ☐3   ☐4   ☐5

36- Are you estranged from your parents, siblings, or children?

☐1   ☐2   ☐3   ☐4   ☐5

37- Do you blame yourself for your avoidant tendencies?

☐1   ☐2   ☐3   ☐4   ☐5

38- Do you think therapy or counseling isn't something for you?

☐1   ☐2   ☐3   ☐4   ☐5

39- Do you prefer being with yourself over shared activities with your partner?

☐1   ☐2   ☐3   ☐4   ☐5

40- Do you end friendships or refrain from making new ones due to your fear of intimacy?

☐1   ☐2   ☐3   ☐4   ☐5

Please take a moment to reflect on your responses and consider areas where you may want to focus your efforts for improvement. I encourage you to read the book and try out what you will learn in your own life. Then come back and re-do this assessment to see where you improved and where you still need to focus on.

It's Ancient History - Tracing the Roots of Avoidance

How do we trace the roots of avoidant attachment? For that, we've got to plunge deep into the memory lane and peek into our childhood. Consider Amanda's example and how a childhood filled with unrealized wants and unmet desires made her the woman she later became.

Can you recall anything from your past that made you the way you are now? Remember, there's no judgment here. We're merely doing this exercise to understand what makes you "you."

Some studies have pointed out that three major factors are responsible for avoidant attachment in adults (Wardecker et al., 2020), namely:

1. Your personality traits (e.g., are you an introvert or extrovert?).

2. Significant life events (e.g., a sick sibling getting all the attention from parents).

3. Cultural influences (e.g., do you come from a culture where boys are preferred by parents and girls get the crumbs?).

Research also shows that a person's experience with their earliest caregivers influences her attachment style (Riggio et al., 2020). In most cases, these caregivers were your parents. You may develop avoidant attachment if your parents:

- Criticized you too much when you were a kid.

- Didn't look after your medical needs if you were sick.

- Didn't feed you enough to worry about your well-being.

- Made fun of you or didn't pay you enough attention.

- Weren't there for you when you were stressed out.

Do you remember the very first quote? Jim Gaffigan says that parents can either put their kids to bed and listen to them scream all night or lie in bed with them and then listen to them scream. You can see that the second approach is obviously excellent parenting. But it's the first approach that sows the oats of avoidant tendencies in kids.

We have to look into the type of care you received in your childhood. So, I need you to go back in the past and look at various stages of your life – childhood, teenage years, and adulthood. What do you see?

Do you see a pattern? A pattern of neglect, contempt, and emotional unavailability? Recognize these patterns, and you're golden!

Check out these questions, and they might help you remember something from your past – a memory you were keeping hidden deep inside:

- Did your parents save you from bullies at school?

- Did your parents or caregivers attend parent-teacher meetings?

- Were your caregivers there for you when you needed them the most?

- Were you and your siblings equally loved and valued?

- Did your caregivers spend time with you after coming back from work?

- Did any of your caregivers have a substance use disorder?

- Did your parents have a divorce? If yes, then how did it affect you?

The kind of care and treatment you received as a kid may have evolved you into a more emotionally distant person. Your childhood experiences are impacting your love life and reshaping your relationship dynamics. Hopefully, you can see the constituents of your present-day avoidant tendencies. Now, we can work toward progress and healing.

The key idea here is understanding what causes avoidant attachment and how it impacts your overall well-being. Only then we'll be able to do something about it. For now, here's what I recommend you do:

- How do you process these feelings about your childhood? Write them down. Pick journaling as a hobby. Keep a diary where you write about how the neglect you've been subjected to in the past keeps haunting you even today.

- It'll help you find a very prominent link between your childhood experiences and current behavior patterns. You'll realize how those memories are responsible for your current avoidant tendencies.

- Most importantly, don't blame your caregivers. Let sleeping dogs lie. Let bygones be bygones. This exercise is only meant to help you understand your trauma. So, learn to forgive but not forget.

Don't worry, dear reader. Soon, we'll explore how much your upbringing impacts your attachment style. It'll help you begin a journey of healing.

Avoidant attachment can leave you feeling isolated, longing for connection, yet hesitant to pursue it. But fear not! This book will be your guiding light, helping you navigate the challenges and illuminate a path to secure attachment. Next, let's explore some common behavior patterns associated with this condition.

Avoidance Decoded - Recognizing Behavior Patterns

You can now quickly recognize the telltale behavior patterns associated with avoidant attachment. In simple words, this is what avoidant attachment looks like (Lampe et al., 2018):

- You yearn for intimacy.

- But you also fear rejection.

- You don't trust your partner fully.

Does it ring a bell? Do you often display a sense of emotional detachment? Are you afraid of connecting with people intimately? Do you prefer to keep to yourself most of the time? It suggests you may have an avoidant attachment style (Wardecker et al., 2020).

If you still need more help recognizing the behavior patterns of avoidance, we can get help from a well-known character – a person we all love.

Do You Remember Chandler Bing from Friends?

Who doesn't remember Chandler's humor and sarcasm? But have you ever noticed how he shows clear signs of avoidant tendencies? The neglect he faced as a kid from his parents made him fearful of commitment to such an extent that he sabotaged his relationships to avoid getting too close to his girlfriends.

He leans on sarcasm to deflect serious conversations, especially when the topic touches his emotions. And what else? He's married to someone even more avoidant than him.

Yes, Monica Geller is another classic example of avoidant tendencies that stem from past trauma. All Friends fans know how Monica always lived in Ross's shadow, who was preferred by her parents for being a "medical marvel," while Monica stayed under heavy scrutiny by a picky mother. So, she develops a protective shell around herself, engages in obsessive-compulsive behavior, and can be quite controlling of herself.

These two examples will help you understand the telltale signs of avoidant tendencies. If you still have trouble determining these very obvious behavior patterns, then I suggest you check these everyday examples and see if they fit you:

- Try to recall all the relationships you've had in the past. Do you have a history of always being the one who ends a relationship? How many romantic partners have you pushed away by breaking up with them?

- Are you commitment-shy? Suppose your partner proposes to go on a vacation or plans a quick weekend getaway. But you never show any interest in doing these activities with them even though you love spending time with your partner?

- Do you think you're worthy of love? Suppose your partner tries to make big gestures of love – as they do in movies, such as hiring-a-Mariachi-band-to-serenade-you kind of gestures – and it makes you uncomfortable.

- Have you ever sabotaged a relationship like Chandler? Nitpicking a relationship is yet another example of avoidant attachment.

- Do you have trouble reading emotions? A study shows that avoidant individuals aren't very good at reading emotions and can't determine why their partner is mad at them (Schumann et al., 2019).

- Do you fantasize about someone who got away? Suppose a past boyfriend seems to you like an ideal partner now. Since you've been obsessed with that relationship for the past, you're emotionally unavailable to your current partner.

- What words do you use when talking to your partner? Suppose your partner asks you, "Where do you see this relationship going?" And then you start talking about freedom, independence, and self-reliance. If your philosophy is "I'm all I've got," it might be a problem.

- We've already talked about how avoidant individuals don't trust anyone and are always suspicious of their romantic partners. Do you think your partner is always trying to take advantage of you or take away your freedom? This paranoia may be a sign of avoidant attachment.

- Has your partner ever told you that you send them mixed messages? Showering them with love one day and then pushing them away? Do you tell your partner you want to spend more time with them, but then you cram your schedule with other tasks? Yes, these mixed messages aren't healthy at all.

- Do you always have an exit strategy to weasel out of social obligations or escape a social gathering? Especially when you had promised your boyfriend that you would show up for that thing?

These are ten telltale signs of avoidant attachment in people. Review these behavior patterns and try to see parallels in your own behavior or your loved one's behavior. Wait a second. Pick up your pen and start writing any instances where your avoidant tendencies appeared. Journaling – as mentioned earlier – improves self-understanding. So, you can easily change your behavior and progress toward secure attachment.

Don't forget that avoidant attachment also impacts your mental health. It leads to stress, anxiety, depression, and social withdrawal (Momeni et al., 2022). Moreover, keep in mind that your partner also suffers with you. When you don't connect with your partner emotionally, they feel:

- Irritated

- Insecure

- Disgruntled

If you value your partner and want to continue your romantic journey successfully, follow the healing exercises mentioned in this book.

I'll introduce some of these exercises in the next section. That's how you can begin your journey toward healing and romantic bliss.

Healing Old Wounds - How to Reprocess Trauma?

As Marco Pierre White beautifully puts it, the train bound to happiness leaves the station of self-discovery. You can't move forward without burying the skeletons in your closet. Unless you heal old wounds, new ones will keep appearing. That's why it's very, very important to reprocess your trauma to start all over.

Do you know how bad unresolved trauma can be? Research says that unresolved trauma can be hereditary; it'll pass from mothers to kids, affecting entire generations (Iyengar et al., 2014). As a result, kids are born with insecure attachments already coded in their genes. You can see how past trauma – even if it goes back to your ancestors – can affect your love life in the 21st century (and, if not addressed promptly, your grandkids' lives in the 22nd century!). So, here's what you have to do (Karantzas et al., 2023):

- Embrace your vulnerability and acknowledge there are demons in your past.

- Engage in self-awareness training to become more in tune with your true self.

- Question your dysfunctional beliefs and challenge your long-held notions about romantic relationships.

Don't forget that your avoidant behaviors likely stem from your childhood trauma. In fact, your avoidant tendencies are a natural response to the pain you suffered in the past. It is like Chandler's sarcasm or Monica's OCD – these are defense mechanisms that allow your brain to deal with trauma while keeping you functional in everyday life. They will:

- Change your entire thought process.

- Make it difficult to trust other people.

- Reinforce your avoidant tendencies.

- Leave your isolated, frustrated, and angry inside.

- Make you feel "dead inside" or emotionally distant from others.

As a result, you will feel defensive whenever your partner even mildly taunts you. Their words or actions may startle you. You will feel disconnected from them and less excited to engage in intimate or sexual activities with them. What's worse – in some cases – you may even begin questioning, "Do I even love them anymore?"

That's why trauma-induced avoidant attachment leads to conflicts in your relationship. A person with avoidant tendencies will feel alienated from her lover. It seems okay to go deeper into the concept of trauma. I promise I won't bore you with medical details. I will keep it simple and digestible.

What Is Trauma, and What Causes It?

Don't get confused by the word "trauma" being used in different medical fields. We are talking about psychological trauma, a stressful event that you lack the emotions to deal with. This event will shatter your sense of security, make you feel helpless in the world, and overwhelm your ability to cope (Wang et al., 2023). It leads to the resurfacing of past experiences that can impact your daily routines.

From being in a war zone and facing police brutality to suffering from childhood abuse and being in a traffic accident – trauma has many sources:

- Domestic abuse.

- Sexual violence.

- Harassment and bullying.

- Abandonment and neglect.

- Being kidnapped.

- Caught in the middle of a natural disaster.

- Experiencing complications during childbirth.

But don't think of your trauma as an insurmountable monster, a dragon nobody can slay. Trauma can be defeated. Check out these fantastic evidence-based techniques to deal with your trauma. Overcoming your trauma will also help you take back control of your romantic life and reverse the effects of avoidant attachment.

- **Journaling:** Once, my husband introduced me to a friend of his, a veteran who was struggling with PTSD. I asked him how he managed to overcome this serious condition. He smiled and showed me a small notebook he carried everywhere. It was his "trauma journal," where he wrote his thoughts and feelings. Research has shown that expressive writing is a great way to cope with your trauma and reduce the intensity of its symptoms (Tull et al., 2020).

- **Guided Visualization:** I call it guided visualization, but you may have heard of it as guided imagery. A therapist will help shift your thoughts toward peaceful scenes or events. This meditative technique is fantastic for folks dealing with trauma. It'll keep you in the present and help you regain mental peace.

- **Controlled Exposure:** Remember how they say to face your fears? Well, that's what therapists do in this practice. You're brought face to face with the things you fear in a controlled environment. It's like building up a tolerance, similar to that ancient king who supposedly ingested small doses of poison to become immune. We can gradually expose ourselves to challenging situations safely to build resilience. In a safe space, you learn to be strong, face your fears, and overpower them. It's a great way to beat your trauma and slowly become resistant to its harmful effects.

Traumatic memories can have a lot of power over you. But you can't let them dictate your romantic relationships, can you? Use these techniques to manage the effects of trauma and build healthy, fulfilling partnerships. Most importantly – be compassionate to yourself. Don't give yourself a tough time. What would you do if your best bud has trauma and asks for your help in his healing journey? Approach your trauma with the same kindness you would offer that friend.

Don't let your attachment style dictate your love life. It's time to take back control and start the process of healing. We're making progress here, dear reader. Now, let's move on to the next phase of our quest for recovery.

Key Takeaways

- Recognize the telltale signs of avoidant tendencies, such as obsessing over "me time," hating being touched, or thinking your partner is too clingy.

- The roots of avoidance may lie in childhood, e.g., your caregivers criticized, mocked, insulted, or neglected you excessively.

- If you have unprocessed and traumatic feelings about your childhood, they can explain your avoidant behavior as an adult.

- Some signs of avoidant attachment are being commitment-shy, bad at reading emotions and being the first to end relationships.

- Reprocess your trauma with techniques like guided visualization and controlled exposure to overcome avoidant tendencies.

Sneak Peak: What's in Chapter 2?

Congratulations – you've completed the preliminary phase of the quest. What lies ahead? This is what awaits you in the next chapter:

- What is emotional attunement?

- Tips to bolster your emotional awareness.

- Mindful and its role in honing your emotional well-being.

- How do you regulate your emotions and keep them stable?

- Tackling the reasons why you are afraid of intimacy.

This exciting journey into the depths of avoidant attachment will not stop anytime soon. We've just covered the first step of the journey. Four more pit stops are up ahead in our adventure.

Chapter 2 - Step 2

Emotional Attunement - The Fast-Track to Self-Healing

"Just like children, emotions heal when they are heard and validated."

Jill Bolte Taylor

Welcome to the second phase of your journey. The hardest part of the quest is over as you've pinpointed the past trauma responsible for your avoidant tendencies. In this chapter, you'll learn how to start the healing process and open up to people emotionally.

Throughout this book, you'll realize that true strength comes from opening up to others. You become weak when you refuse to entertain other people's emotions. Sadly for our girl Mina, she learned this lesson the hard way.

As the daughter of neglectful parents who were preoccupied with their own problems, Mina learned to be self-sufficient. As a result, she has avoidant tendencies now. She is unwilling and unable to recognize other people's emotions.

Her worst nightmare is people trying to open up to her. When someone – a coworker or a seemingly lovely guy at a bar – tries to connect with her emotionally, she withdraws. She practically screams at these people in their mind, saying: "Get away from me. Don't you see I'm the wrong person to have a heart-to-heart with?"

She always keeps her distance from people, whether they're close friends or not, afraid to get too close.

It all changes when she meets the girl of her dreams. Her partner gently encourages her to regulate her emotions and be mindful of other people's feelings. With time, our sweet Mina learns to trust people and practice emotional attunement. She actively listens to what a person has to say – especially if that person is her girlfriend – and expresses her own feelings openly. Mina says the best lesson she ever learned was never to trivialize other people's emotions.

Emotions can be damaged and hurt badly when they are trivialized and ignored. But the best way to heal emotions is to hear them, validate them, and nurture them in a supportive environment.

That's the power of emotional attunement. It did miracles for Mina and her soon-to-be wife. It can do magic for your romantic life as well.

Emotional Attunement and Your Attachment Style

Let's get to the brass tacks. What on God's green Earth is emotional attunement? What does it have to do with your attachment style and romantic setbacks? In simple terms, it means to do the following:

- Understand your partner's feelings.

- Recognize the way they feel about you.

- Respect their emotions and complaints.

- Validate their experiences with you.

- Fully engage with their emotional state.

Remember when we learned about avoidant individuals in Chapter 1? They are bad at reading people's emotions, so emotional attunement is Greek to them. Reading people's emotions can also be challenging because not everyone opens up about their feelings via spoken words. No, sir! You also have to read gestures, facial cues, and body language to understand what your partner is going through.

However, once you get in tune with your significant other's emotional state, it will boost your relationship. Emotional attunement will make your partner feel (Webb et al., 2023):

- Seen

- Heard

- Known

- Accepted

- Acknowledged

The best way to tell your partner, "I care about you and love you," is to recognize, accept, and validate their emotions. You may wonder how it's done. To be honest, it's not that hard. You just have to sit down and listen to your partner.

I admire what John M. Gottman writes about emotional attunement. Do read his book The Science of Trust if you can. He suggests you and your partner sit down for an hour to process your negative emotions and build trust in each other. Here's how it is done:

- Spend an hour every week talking about your relationship.

- Take turns as speaker and listener.

- Write down your thoughts when the other person is speaking.

- Talk about what's going right in your relationship.

- Mention 5 to 10 things you like about your partner.

- Discuss if you feel there's something you'd like to change in this relationship.

- Don't judge, blame, or criticize your partner.

- State your feelings in a neutral way.

- Instead of "you" statements, use "I" statements.

- Validate your partner's feelings and emotions.

Did you see what happened here? This brief exercise helped you get in touch with not just your partner's emotions but also your own. This is the fantastic thing about emotional attunement, i.e., it makes you self-aware. A person who is in touch with their emotions and recognizes other people's feelings in a snap is on the fast track to secure attachment.

Here's how avoidant and secure attachment styles differ when it comes to emotional attunement:

- **Secure Attachment:** These people are open to emotional experiences.

- **Avoidant Attachment:** As illustrated in Mina's example, these people dislike emotional openness and disconnect from emotions as a defense mechanism.

As a result, your interpersonal skills suffer. So:

- You don't communicate well.

- You don't do well with conflicts.

- You can't be a team with your partner.

For example, if your partner is having a bad day, what will you do? Will you listen to their complaints about their unproductive day? Will you make them feel heard? Will you offer a word of sympathy, a shoulder to cry on?

In avoidant attachment, you may end up doing nothing, shutting yourself in a shell of emotional disconnection. Just imagine how your partner will feel if you are unwilling to even indulge in their experiences.

So, do the Gottman exercise to hone your emotional attunement skills.

Next, we'll check excellent exercises to make you more emotionally aware. That's how you can overcome your avoidant tendencies by the end of this book.

Six Ways to Enhance Emotional Awareness

How well do you understand your emotions? Can you easily make sense of your thoughts and innermost feelings? Developing emotional awareness is a crucial step on the journey to secure attachment.

Studies show that women—especially mothers—can move faster toward full recovery if they perform emotional awareness exercises (Monti et al., 2014). But how do you become more emotionally aware?

Harnessing the hidden powers of emotional awareness isn't tricky. When you're upset, do you take time to figure out what you're actually feeling? Do you try to work out why you feel suspicious of your partner? Asking simple questions is the proper way to connect with your emotional side.

These detailed and practical exercises will help you tune into your emotional states and be more wary of your inner feelings:

1: Emotional Check-ins

Check-in with your emotions at least once a day. Ask yourself, "How am I doing? What do I feel?" Be your own mini-therapist and maintain a record of your emotions. Here's what you should do:

- Get a notebook app or pick your journal.

- Record your emotions every night before sleeping.

- Write about the intensity of these emotions and what caused them.

- Keep reviewing this diary to determine the common triggers of your anxiety.

There you go! Now you know what disturbs your emotional peace so that you can stay away from these triggers.

2: Full-Body Scanning

Some emotions aren't that easily noticeable. You may have to dig deeper into your emotional state via a process called full-body scanning. This meditative exercise helps redirect your attention to your body.

As a result, you'll see your anxiety and stress melting away (Kogan et al., 2021). I love doing this exercise with the family-favorite golden retriever sitting by my side. Here's how it's done:

- Set in a meditative yoga pose.

- Scan your body from head to toe.

- Do you notice any physical sensations?

- Do you notice any emotional cues when scanning your body parts?

You're now more aware of your bodily sensations and feelings.

3: Label Your Emotions

Emotions are like people; once you know their names, they're easier to recognize. That's why you should label your emotions as they arise to acknowledge. It's a fantastic way to reduce the intensity of negative emotions and cope with them effectively.

Get on a first-name basis with your emotions; you'll find them easy to control. Do keep these tips in mind when performing this exercise, however:

- Don't just name your emotions "good," "bad," "happy," "angry," or "sad."

- Identify the specific nature of your emotions. How exactly do they make you feel?

- Give them names like "envy," "suspicion," "kindness," "jealousy," "calmness," and "admiration."

4: The Five Whys of Emotions

In this exercise, you ask yourself a single question "Why?" five times. It helps you get to the root cause of your emotional distress. Learn the deeper reasons why you feel the way you do. Explore your anxiety layer by layer to discover the underlying causes (Taibbi, 2014).

The roots of the "Five Whys" technique lie in a curious concept labeled as "emotional granularity," or the ability to experience your emotions in a particular manner (Tan et al., 2022). Granularity helps you tell different emotions apart as well as label the more discrete ones. As you ask yourself the question "Why?" several times, you can understand your emotional experiences better and be "granular" in this understanding.

Consider the example of a person suspicious of her partner all the time. She will ask herself five times "Why?"

- Why am I suspicious? Because I think my partner wants to usurp my freedom.

- Why does that make me afraid? Because I value my freedom above all.

- Why do I value it so much? Because I'm afraid to rely on others.

- Why am I afraid? Because I don't trust people easily.

- Why don't I trust people? Because I have been betrayed before.

5: Emotion Pairing

Emotional pairing is a simple technique where you deliberately connect challenging emotions to positive ones. The goal is to balance out tough feelings by focusing on a positive counterpart. You may have heard there are 34,000 emotions for humans to experience. Sounds kind of overwhelming, right? Don't worry; psychologist Robert Plutchik says there are merely eight basic emotions, namely (Semeraro et al., 2021):

- Joy

- Fear

- Trust

- Anger

- Disgust

- Sadness

- Surprise

- Anticipation

So, here's what you should do: Identify the emotions that are difficult for you to handle and match them with positive emotions that can help balance your mood. For instance, if anger is something you struggle with, try pairing it with confidence to counteract its effects. This way, you won't feel overwhelmed by negative emotions. This exercise is also great for improving emotional regulation.

6: Emotion Pacing

Remember controlled exposure? This one's similar to that exercise. In this highly effective routine, you slowly bring yourself face to face with the emotions you usually avoid. But you do this in a controlled environment, in your safe space.

Use guided visualization to approach these undesirable emotions little by little. It'll help you get familiar with experiencing them and, ultimately, defeating them.

It is facing your fears all over again, but this time, you're doing it on your own.

Use these simple tools in your everyday life. Whether you're communicating with your partner, tackling friendships, or dealing with coworkers – these exercises will always come in handy. Self-awareness will lead to better progress in our joint efforts to alter your attachment style.

Keep practicing until you master the subtle art of self-awareness. You may wonder what's next in this quest. In the next section, we'll focus on emotional regulation and share a step-by-step guide to keep your emotions in check. So, don't let your feelings get the best of you.

Emotional Regulation - The Key to Secure Attachment

Do you want to manage your intense emotions and reactionary behaviors? It is the best way to understand what emotional regulation is. What does it entail? How does a person stabilize emotions?

Trust me; emotional regulation is one of the main building blocks of secure attachment. People who are in control of their emotional side can form healthy, long-lasting romantic connections.

So, let's check out some tips to tame your emotions.

What is Emotional Regulation?

Have you ever felt a sudden surge of rage and didn't know how to suppress it? Have you said very insensitive things to your partner and later regretted it? You may often find yourself in a cataclysm of conflicting emotions – rage filled with uncertainty, suspicion with denial – and you don't know how to get over these weird feelings.

Emotional regulation is the ability to control and influence your emotions. It helps you make sense of the following dilemmas (Kozubal et al., 2023):

- What kind of emotions will you have?

- When and where will you experience these emotions?

- How will you experience these emotions and express them?

Learning emotional regulation will prevent embarrassment, angry outbursts in public, grieving conflicts with your partner, and the constant feeling of detachment from your lover. Here are a few tips – presented in the form of interrelated questions – to help you regulate your emotions:

- What are your emotional or psychological triggers?

- What triggers strong emotional responses in you?

- Are there people, events, or situations that trigger your emotional outbursts?

- In what situations do you normally stay emotionally stable?

- Which triggers are easy to ignore, and which ones are hard to let go of?

But these simple suggestions are like the tip of the iceberg. We'll soon see more fantastic tips on emotional regulation. So, stay tuned, and keep reading. You've made progress in the past few pages. Don't let the success train get off track.

How to Regulate Your Emotions Like a Boss

Don't forget that the purpose of emotional regulation is not to suppress your emotions. Having emotions is normal – they are a natural reaction to different life events. We only need emotional regulation to:

- Understand our emotions.

- Trace what causes them.

- Respond to them appropriately.

Here are four tried-and-trusted exercises to help regulate your emotions:

1. **Breathing Exercises:** I always recommend breathing exercises to my clients. They're a fantastic way to release tension and bring greater balance to your emotional state. You can do them by controlling your breathing, i.e., inhale for 4 seconds, hold it for 7, and exhale for 8. Whenever you feel like your stress is beyond your control, use this exercise to be in charge of your emotional self.

2. **Cognitive Reframing:** If you ever find yourself wallowing in the bottomless pit of self-blame and low self-esteem, use this method to shift your negative thoughts and replace them with positive ideas (Mueser et al., 2015). Use phrases, mantras, and positive sentences to shift your perspective. Say things like "I'm doing great," "I'm worthy of love,""Remember why I started this journey," and others to alter your negative mindset.

3. **Muscle Relaxation:** Do you know that anxiety and stress man-

ifest as physical tension in your muscles? Progressive Muscle Relaxation (PMR) can cure this very troublesome issue by tensing and releasing each muscle group. The idea is that a relaxed body isn't easily stressed out. So, get massage therapy to calm your mind and make it immune to the effects of emotional upheavals.

4. **Timeouts:** Are you dealing with a stressful situation? Are you on the verge of breaking up with the love of your life? Don't know how to say yes to your gal's marriage proposal? If a stressful event gives you anxiety, take a timeout instead of doing something impulsive. Use this timeout to regroup your thoughts and decide how you want to tackle this situation. It'll help you respond more attentively to that situation.

Creating an Emotional First Aid Kit

Remember, there's no one-size-fits-all approach to emotional regulation. An exercise may work for one person but doesn't benefit others in any way. So, create a personalized emotional first aid kit, including all your favorite activities and techniques to help you be in control of your emotional rollercoaster. For instance, you can add:

- Positive affirmations to boost your self-esteem (e.g., "I can do it" statements).

- Physical activities like walking, dancing, biking, yoga, and others.

- Comfort items like childhood toys, photos, blankets, or lucky charms.

- Distraction tools like your favorite movie, book, video game, or puzzle.

- Write down the things you're thankful for, and remember to be kind to yourself.

Feel free to add more items or remove the existing ones if they don't help. Only add activities that help you heal and bring your emotions under control.

These simple exercises will make you an emotionally stabilized person. Regulating your emotions is imperative if you're looking for secure attachment. Next, you'll use all these techniques to tackle your fear of intimacy and improve your inner romantic.

Closeness and Fear - A Paradoxical Relationship

How do you feel about your relationship? Do you desire intimacy and closeness with the love of your life, yet simultaneously, you're afraid of it? Your heart is like a beautiful but delicate fortress; you want to share it with the man or woman of your dreams, but you also wonder if it's big enough for the two of you.

This conflicting desire for closeness and freedom is prevalent in folks with avoidant tendencies. In avoidant attachment, you feel (Mohammadi et al., 2016):

- Anxious about intimacy.

- Unresponsive to their partner's needs.

- Not too sensitive to their partner's feelings.

- Suffering from marital problems frequently.

Can there be a romantic relationship without the grains of love? Unfortunately, people with avoidant tendencies are looking for exactly this kind of relationship. So, let's see how a love-and-hate relationship with intimacy leads to relationship conflicts.

A Love and Hate Relationship with Intimacy: An Annoying Paradox

Imagine your partner is head over heels in love with you. They think the world of you and expect you to reciprocate similar feelings. How would they feel if you kept pulling away, pushing them out, acting all closed-off, and never being vulnerable with them?

They – quite reasonably – feel betrayed, confused, and distressed. They'll feel like you're sending them mixed messages, desiring their companionship but shutting them out.

Here's a simple exercise to see if you're sending your partner mixed signals. On a scale of 1 to 10, how do you rate your current relationship? Are you satisfied?

- You're afraid to be intimate.

- You can't recognize your or someone else's emotions.

- Your mind thinks intimacy equals vulnerability.

- You don't like making long-term commitments.

- You think you don't deserve to be loved.

- When a relationship gets serious, you get anxious.

- You don't respond well to negative emotions (we tackled this beast).

- You don't appreciate it when people try to offer emotional support (because you think they're trying to take away your independence).

- You even become violent in your relationships.

- You keep changing sexual partners (you can't stick to one due to your fear of long-term commitment and intimacy).

- You aren't very excited about sharing personal thoughts with your partner.

- You are afraid of being smothered by love, raising your fear of vulnerability.

If these symptoms hold true for you, then you may have a paradoxical relationship with your partner. We can better understand it with the help of an interesting example.

Bojack Horseman, Avoidant Attachment Manifest

It's every psychologist's favorite exercise to review fictional TV/movie characters and see what sort of behaviors they exhibit. Since we're discussing attachment styles, it would be very revealing (and also lots of fun!) to discuss another fictional character dealing with avoidant tendencies.

I have watched the show Bojack Horseman four to five times on Netflix. It's refreshing how realistically the creators portrayed mental health decline in an anthropomorphic horse. We can also see that Bojack was going through avoidant attachment.

Here are three avoidant behaviors I noticed in him:

- Just like Chandler from Friends, Bojack Horseman scampers

away from intimacy like it's the bubonic plague. He will push people away and sabotage his romantic relationships because he both needs and is afraid of intimacy. Whenever a person comes too close to meet the real Bojack, Bojack will get out of that relationship, even though he needs to be loved.

- His prize possession is his independence, his self-reliance. He will do anything to preserve his "freedom" – which is, in reality, nothing more than loneliness – to the point of hurting other people. He also struggles to emotionally support his friends, romantic partners, and other people in his life.

- He's also dismissive of what his partners want or need from him. So, he downplays the importance of intimacy. Even a discussion about emotions will set him off. The moment he feels the conservation is gravitating toward their relationship dynamics, he'll deflect.

It took Bojack a lot of whacky adventures to get the help he needed. But you've got all the help you need right here. Remember cognitive reframing? We just talked about it a while ago. It can also help you overcome your fear of intimacy and start approaching every relationship without a shiver in your bones.

A Callback to Cognitive Restructuring

Feeling disoriented about intimacy? Don't want to be an open book but also hungry for love? Cognitive restructuring can help you overcome your fear of closeness. It's all about shifting your perception of intimacy.

Does your brain make it look like a source of threat and discomfort? Shift your perspective to start seeing intimacy as a source of love and compassion. Here's how to do it:

- What negative perceptions do you have about intimacy? Identify these negative thoughts. For instance, you may think, "Intimacy will make me lose my freedom" or "Showing vulnerability will make me an easy target."

- Now, challenge these bad thoughts. Don't accept them as scripture. "Am I afraid of intimacy because of bad experiences in the past? How would I start viewing it differently?" Tell yourself that your fear of intimacy is holding you back.

- Next, replace negative thoughts with positive ones. Tell yourself that you can be intimate and still keep your identity. "Intimacy will deepen my connections and make me closer to my partner," keep repeating this mantra in your head.

- There's no need to rush it; practice intimacy in baby steps. Start by sharing a few tidbits from your "mind palace," but don't reveal your innermost thoughts at this point. Slowly, you'll learn to share more as you'll notice the life-changing benefits of being intimate, e.g., having a healthy emotional connection with your partner.

That's how you can literally change your mind about intimacy and start seeing it as a very amazing growth opportunity. Don't forget to seek professional support and try couples counseling. A therapist's office will serve as a safe space where you'll learn that it's okay to be a little vulnerable in your lover's presence and see intimacy as a blessing.

Remember the different exercises we discussed before? I deliberately left out a very important one: mindfulness. It's one of the most

important and effective tools in the arsenal of avoidant attachment recovery. Let's see how mindfulness can help you alter your attachment style.

Mindful and the Rainbow-Colored Road to Recovery

If you want to escape the maze of avoidant attachment toward the open castle of secure attachment, make mindfulness or related meditative exercises part of your daily routine. Here's how it helps you:

- It makes you grounded in the present.

- It helps to stay in touch with reality.

- It keeps you from acting impulsively.

- It decreases your emotional reactivity.

Whether you want to attain emotional awareness or enhance emotional regulation, your go-to method should always be mindfulness. Since avoidant tendencies make it hard for people to recognize their or someone else's emotions, mindfulness will help them form a deeper connection with their inner selves. After a few tailored mindfulness exercises, you won't be out of touch with your feelings and emotions.

Here's how mindfulness helps people with avoidant attachment. If you practice it, you will see the following benefits:

- You learn to live in the moment and not the past.

- You stop overthinking stuff or getting paranoid about your partner.

- As a result, you don't distance yourself emotionally from your lover anymore.

In this section, we'll discuss how to practice mindfulness to target your avoidant and intimacy-hesitant behaviors. With enough practice, you'll be able to push away avoidant tendencies like earwax.

Mindfulness Practices to Remove Avoidant Tendencies

If you ask me to name the best tool for overcoming avoidant attachment, I'd day mindfulness without hesitation. Even research shows that mindful practices increase your resilience and make regulating your emotions easier (Yang et al., 2022).

Are you feeling overwhelmed and unable to make an important decision? Can't you feel the Earth beneath your feet? Try mindfulness and overcome emotional distress.

Here are three basic mindful practices you should follow in everyday life. Once you get mastery over these simple exercises, it'd be like having access to a magic potion that can heal your avoidant tendencies in a single mouthful:

- **Focused Breathing:** Place one hand on your belly and start breathing from the diaphragm. Focus on how your hand moves as the tummy goes up and down, like a baby sleeping. Place the other hand on your chest and ensure it doesn't move as much. The idea is that people breathe from their chests when they're anxious. So, focused breathing helps you breathe slowly and overcome your anxiety.

- **Sensory Mindfulness:** We all have five senses, right? But how often do we pay them any special attention? In sensory mindfulness, you notice what your senses are feeling. The things you see, hear, smell, taste, and touch – focus on it all. Just be like Spiderman and harness your "spidey senses." It'll help you live in the moment and always be there in the present.

- **Mindful Observation:** I'd like to call it the Rosetta stone of mindfulness. In the art of mindful observation, you simply observe what you see around you simply as a neutral observer. Be like the Watcher from the *What If...?* series. Your job is to concentrate on what's happening without judgment. It harnesses your ability to notice things without immediately rejecting or accepting them.

These beneficial practices will help change your avoidant tendencies. You will learn very slowly and gently to engage with your emotional side.

Incorporating Mindfulness in Daily Routines

Do you think these exercises are too much? Don't worry; you can simply incorporate the idea behind these different exercises into your everyday life. Check these simple tips and learn how to find time off your busy schedule to do the above three exercises:

- Take a few short breaths before getting out of the shower and starting a new day.

- Actively listen to folks when they're talking and pay attention to the conversation.

- Even when you're walking, pay attention to every step; paying attention to your bodily movements will ground you in reality.

- Eat your lunch in a distraction-free room where you can mindfully eat the food, chewing every morsel.

- Take short breaks at work and spend a few minutes alone in a room to prevent your thoughts from wandering.

- Set daily reminders to pause and check in with yourself; ask questions like, "Am I doing okay? Do I need a break from my daily routine?"

- Search for mindfulness apps online and use them to stay on track.

You may wonder how all of this helps you mend things with your partner and put your love life back on track. Let me explain the fantastic connection between mindfulness and a person's interpersonal relationships in more detail.

What Role Does Mindfulness Play in Interpersonal Interactions

If you want to improve the quality of your romantic relationships, mindfulness is the key to unlocking all the niceties necessary for a successful love life. That's not an empty promise either; several studies have shown that mindful practices can do wonders for intimate interactions (Khoury et al., 2023). Since you learn how to regulate your emotions thanks to mindfulness, you can:

- Easily accept when you're in the wrong.

- Increase your aptitude to engage in self-change.

- Pay more attention to your partner's needs and feelings.

- Never lose focus of what's important, i.e., your mutual love.

- Be mentally present in every conservation with your partner.

- Form more meaningful and connected relationships with people.

- Become a more kind and caring person, in tune with her feelings.

Combined with emotional awareness and regulation tips, these mindful practices will be your go-to tools for escaping the prison of avoidant attachment. Keep on reading as we uncover more secrets of attaining the perfect balance between your longing for freedom and your desire for intimacy.

Never let go of the strong rope of mindfulness in your life. Use it to open up a gateway to emotional excellence. It will make you more in tune with not just your but also your partner's emotions. That's how you embark on the next phase of your journey.

Key Takeaways

- Emotional attunement helps you recognize, understand, and validate your lover's feelings.

- Emotional check-ins, labeling, and body scanning are great ways to enhance your emotional awareness powers.

- Use breathing, cognitive reframing, and muscle relaxation techniques to regulate your emotions and prevent impulsive behaviors.

- Cognitive reframing is good for overcoming your fear of intimacy and embracing your desire for romantic affiliations.

- Incorporate exercises like sensory mindfulness and mindful observation into your everyday life to enjoy a healthier love life.

Sneak Peak - What's in Chapter 3?

You've learned the art of emotional awareness and beaten another monster in this quest. Another one bites the dust, I guess! So, what's next in our journey? Here's what you will learn in the next chapter:

- How to open up and communicate with your lover?

- Embracing your vulnerability as a newfound strength.

- Balancing autonomy with romantic relationships.

- Connecting with friends, family, and coworkers.

So, keep on reading and learn how to come to terms with your fear of vulnerability.

Chapter 3 - Step 3

Effective Communication and Embracing Vulnerability

"When people talk, listen completely... You should be able to go into a room and when you come out know everything that you saw there and not only that. If that room gave you any feeling, you should know exactly what it was that gave you that feeling."

Ernest Hemingway

Welcome to the third phase of our journey together. Your transformation into a more securely attached person is halfway done. You have learned to let people in and open up to them emotionally. In Chapter 3, you will find out how to turn vulnerability into your strong suit. So, let's get started with the third stage of this journey, shall we?

Priti's Story

Meet Priti; she's a shy 26 woman in an on-and-off relationship with her boyfriend, James. But she's always been avoidantly attached – the roots of her behavior go back to her childhood. Growing up in a house with nine siblings wasn't easy; Priti was always the least of her father's worries, overshadowed by more accomplished sisters.

She learned to keep to herself and mind her own business. While her avoidant behavior made her self-reliant and helped her cope with abandonment issues, it also crippled her communication skills. She sucks at expressing her emotions. That's the main reason why her relationship with James never seems to work out.

When he wants to talk, she tends to go back to her shell of minding her own business. When conversations touch on her deeper emotions or the future of the relationship, she tends to shut down. But one day, she realizes that she needs to make some changes.

Not-So-Fantastic Communication Barriers and Where to Find Them?

What does Priti do? Well, for starters, she picks up a book about avoidant tendencies and starts reading. This section is a brief account of what she learned about her avoidant tendencies and how to manage her lack of communication skills.

Priti realizes that certain communication barriers make her unable to talk about her emotions. So, check out these common communication barriers and see if they apply to you as well:

- Are you uncomfortable with expressing your emotions?

- Do you find it hard to show your emotions?

- Is it too embarrassing for you to show your emotional side?

How do these barriers play out in real life? Priti notices that she tends to:

- Avoid difficult conversations.

- Deflect hard-to-handle topics.

- Avoid dealing with other people's emotions.

- Get visibly disturbed when her partner brings up delicate topics.

Like Priti, you need to acknowledge that these barriers exist and that they make you very bad at communication. Your avoidant tendencies will only get stronger if you don't do anything to remove these communication barriers.

Effective Communication 101

Next, Priti learned the foundational principles of good communication. Spoiler alert: Merely talking doesn't make you good at communicating; you also need to listen. In the words of Hemingway, listen completely when someone is speaking.

So, here are the key pillars of effective communication for avoidant individuals:

- Clarity (the goal of communication is to be understood, so don't mince your words and be clear about what you're saying).

- Active listening is sometimes called the "highest level of listening" (Jahromi et al., 2016).

- Assertiveness, i.e., be bold and even brazen about what you're feeling; don't let anyone dismiss you easily.

- Be honest about what you want, even if it makes you uncomfortable; transparency is the root of effective communication.

Want to be better at communicating your thoughts and feelings? Priti learned these tips for better communication. They'll hopefully help you, too.

- Watch your tone; a bad tone can alter the whole message.

- Be concise; long talks tend to lose the listener's attention.

- Prepare a statement so you can talk more confidently.

- Body language and gestures are also part of communication.

- Use emotional awareness to see how well the listener is taking your message.

I hope these tips will make you an excellent communicator.

Overcome Avoidance with Effective Communication

Is there any way to overcome your avoidant tendencies with good communication? Yes, Priti learned a few very simple ways to use effective communication as a means to alter her attachment style. After all, good communication skills are a flag bearer of secure attachment, aren't they?

She tried the Gottman exercise described in Chapter 2, where you use "I" statements to have a heart-to-heart with your partner. You express your emotions without judging the other person or accusing them of anything.

Does verbal communication still make you uncomfortable? Then, write down your inner thoughts and feelings. Use journaling as a medium of self-expression.

Communication-Boosting Exercises for Avoidant Attachment

In the end, she found some awesome controlled exercises to boost her confidence, get good at communication, and express her thoughts more clearly, such as:

- Identify your emotions and what triggers them. Then, you can use "I" statements in a conversation to take ownership of your feelings. So, don't say to your partner, "You make me feel small and unimportant;" instead, say this: "When our mutual conversations are interrupted, it makes me feel unimportant."

- Again, active listening will come in handy when communicating with your partner. It helps you understand their perspective. Listen to your partner and paraphrase it in your words. Suppose your partner says they feel like you don't care about their feelings. You could respond with, "It seems like you're feeling invalidated, right? You don't feel heard."

- If you need some time off for self-reflection, communicate your boundaries to your partner calmly yet assertively. Suppose you need some "me time" to relax and recharge. You could tell your partner, "I value the time we spend in each other's company, but right now, I need to be alone. Can we please schedule some time apart?"

- It's never too late to seek feedback from your partner, family, and friends about how well you're communicating. Is your communication style good enough? So, you could say, "Please tell me how to improve my communication style?" Your loved one can give you examples of times when you could've communicated in a better way. Use this feedback to go nuts on effective communication.

Using all these strategies, Priti mended her relationship with James. Thanks to the power of effective communication, she and James are in a good place right now. Realize similar benefits for yourself! Implement the tips we've discussed and watch your life transform for the better.

In the previous chapter, you learned to overcome and embrace your fear of intimacy. In this chapter, I'll teach you to do the same with vulnerability. You'll stop thinking of it as a weakness and instead accept it as one of your many strengths.

Are you tired of cowering at the mere idea of vulnerability? The time has come to introduce a major paradigm shift; find out how to get over your fear of vulnerability and embrace it as a powerful tool to spice up your love life.

You and Your Vulnerability: A Brief Self-Assessment Exercises

The first step to making sense of your vulnerability is to identify the barriers. Ask yourself these questions:

- When you think about opening up and being vulnerable, which emotions do you experience?

- Are you afraid of vulnerability due to your bad experience with it in the past?

- Why do you think you struggle to trust others with your emotions?

- What kind of people or situations make you feel uneasy with vulnerability?

- How do you react when feeling vulnerable? Maybe you tend to withdraw, become defensive, or try another coping mechanism.

The second step is to understand the depths of your emotional patterns. Ask yourself these questions:

- Think about the times when you were feeling vulnerable. Did any specific thoughts and feelings come to your mind at that time?

- What is your current coping mechanism against vulnerability? Is it effective? Does it have harmful effects on your romantic life?

- What are the recurring themes in the way you react to vulnerability emotionally? These themes may give us a peek into your emotional state.

The third step is to develop different strategies based on your experiences. Ask yourself these questions:

- What steps can you take to be more comfortable with vulnerability?

- How do you create a supportive environment that makes you willing to open up more?

- Can you think of any specific communication skills or techniques to be better at self-expression?

- Is there someone you trust enough with whom you can practice being vulnerable? Maybe this person is none other than your partner.

- Are there any fears, worries, or negative beliefs that hinder your ability to open up and be vulnerable? How do you plan to challenge this negativity?

This simple self-assessment exercise will help you understand the deeper meaning behind opening up and being vulnerable.

Vulnerability - Turning Wounds into Resilience and Strength

The key to overcoming avoidant attachment is to get in touch with your feelings. But one thing keeps you from doing that: the fear of vulnerability. You hate being criticized and judged, don't you? It is natural. Your fear of rejection, making a spectacle of yourself in public, never lets you be open about your feelings.

In simple words, you never want to face your true emotions and feelings. This is called a fear of vulnerability that prevents you from needing others. As a result:

- You always try to be perfect.

- You close yourself off to friends.

- You keep everyone at arm's length.

- You may even get depressed (Murray et al., 2021).

Does the very idea of being open about emotions embarrass you? Do your ears get red hot when you're trying to express your sentiments (probably because you don't want the world to see the inner you)? But that's just a defense mechanism.

You're protecting yourself from the world by creating a shell of emotional distance, and vulnerability feels like UV rays trying to penetrate the Earth's ozone defenses. Some common signs include:

- Sharing information embarrasses you.

- You are always wondering, "What are they thinking about me?"

- You are afraid of being neglected, rejected, or laughed at.

- You tend to be ruminative over past events or bygone conversations.

In this section, we'll explore a few myths about vulnerability, the reasons why being an open book is important, and how to be vulnerable without overexerting yourself.

Busting Common Myths about Vulnerability

What do people often get wrong about vulnerability? By people, I mean not merely the individuals with avoidant attachment but also the general public.

- *'I can avoid vulnerability.'* Nobody can avoid it.

- *'Vulnerability means letting it all out.'* No, it means sharing your private concerns with people you trust.

- *'Vulnerability isn't needed.'* You simply can't ride the train to secure attachment without it, my dear reader.

- *'Trust comes before vulnerability.'* On the contrary, vulnerability is important in building trust.

It's time to dispel these misconceptions. Vulnerability isn't a weakness; it's a normal and quintessential human experience that needs to be embraced with open heart. It helps us:

- Build meaningful connections.

- Let people understand our flaws.

- Lend authenticity to our friendships.

- Show our romantic partners that we trust them.

We'll now explore some exercises that can help you develop your vulnerability.

How to Boost Your Vulnerability in a Healthy Way

Opening up can be scary! Let's learn how to navigate vulnerability in a way that empowers you, not exposes you. A lot of people will be ready to pounce upon exposed vulnerabilities and exploit them. Building trust is key to healthy vulnerability. Consider opening up to reliable friends, confidants, or even a therapist who can offer a safe space to share. You can share your uncertainties and concerns with them so they can help you find a way out of it.

When you don't share your vulnerabilities wisely, you may (Thomas, 2016):

- Be prone to personal attacks.

- Seem unstable.

- Be portrayed as a victim.

Let's explore how to share your vulnerabilities authentically without feeling emotionally drained. You must choose the right person(s) to be vulnerable before; ask yourself, "Does this man or woman even deserve to see the real me?" This person mustn't dismiss your feelings, try to judge you, or force a solution without suggestion.

Once you find such a kindred soul, you can start taking these steps:

- Practice vulnerability in safe spaces, i.e., in the presence of your family, friends, and lover.

- Always start small and disclose snippets from your innermost thoughts with other people.

- Establish trust through vulnerability and grow the courage to share more with the person you love.

- Slowly, you'll learn to recognize where it's safe for the hidden you to come out of the shell and share a glimpse of your authentic self.

It's equally important to understand your emotions and validate your experiences. Developing self-compassion will naturally increase your desire for closeness with others. This, in turn, will help you dismantle your defenses and become more open to vulnerability. Ultimately, self-compassion paves the way for secure attachment.

Priti is a living-and-breathing success story here. It significantly improved her sense of self-awareness and enabled her to form deeper connections with her lover. Priti also earned a greater capacity for empathy and compassion. In short, she learned to:

- Come out of the protective shell.

- Open up to her boyfriend.

- Communicate honestly.

- Rekindle her romantic life.

Remember, a successful love life requires you to be vulnerable. True love isn't afraid of sharing feelings and emotions. So, learn to be an open book in the presence of your partner, and use vulnerability as your strong suit in any relationship.

In the next section, we'll explore how to balance your need for independence with your desire for connection. You can be self-reliant and be intimate with your loved ones. Keep on reading to know the secret of autonomous connectivity.

Striking a Balance between Autonomy and Connectedness

We've come full circle to the same old discussion, i.e., the everlasting battle between your longing for connectedness and the fear of losing your identity. In avoidant attachment, it can be very challenging to move toward the seemingly distant room of connectedness by letting go of the comfy couch of autonomy.

However, just as you need to strike a balance between your work life and private affairs, it's equally important to create an equilibrium between autonomy and intimacy. Sadly, like the concept of vulnerability, autonomy also gets a bad reputation, and people have certain unfounded notions about what it entails.

So, we'll discuss the concepts of autonomy and interdependence in this section. Let's see what these ideas actually are in terms of romantic relationships.

Autonomy: Don't mistake it for emotional detachment; autonomy means your partner has to respect your boundaries. You don't lose the individual in romantic relationships, and your partner shouldn't try to suppress your identity for the sake of "love." You still have control over your life choices and can pursue hobbies and friendships outside this relationship.

Interdependence: You and your partner should be able to address their needs as individuals. You're attached to your partner, but still, you two can make your own decisions without stepping on each other's toes. In simple words, the idea of interdependence teaches you to value your emotional connection with your partner without losing the sense of self (Clarke et al., 2023).

Don't think for a second that these two concepts are mutually exclusive. Both of them are essential ingredients of healthy romantic ties. You can't function without both of these tools in your backpack.

Next, we'll explore a few reasons why both autonomy and interdependence are important. Hopefully, it'll help you understand how embracing the idea of connectivity lets you maintain your individuality and makes you successful in a relationship.

Autonomy: Never Give Up Your Identity

Do you now realize what autonomy is and what makes it different from isolation? It's not the act of shutting yourself out and acting like a closed book. Autonomy means you have to retain your identity. It means three things, in general:

- Choice

- Freedom

- Control

Keeping your identity alive after engaging in a romantic relationship is important. You don't want to forget your individuality for the sake of love, don't you? Maintaining your individuality strengthens your relationship. It shows your partner they love the complete you, not just you as part of a couple.

Studies have shown that individuals whose autonomy needs are met do better romantically. Success in one's love life depends on both partners retaining their freedom to some extent (Oz-Soysal et al., 2024). You are autonomous in a relationship if you:

- Pursue hobbies of your own.

- Take control of your own actions.

- Have freedom in decision-making to some extent.

You can see that even securely attached people have a "me time." They too often need a few moments alone. When you complete your transformation from avoidant to secure attachment, you won't lose your identity or your sense of self-reliance.

Interdependence: Shared Success is Real Success

Interdependence is the other major ingredient of a healthy, happy, romantic relationship. In this scenario, you and your partner will contribute to each other's well-being, never letting one person down so the other can rise to the occasion.

If you and your partner are interdependent, you two will:

- Listen to each other actively.

- Respect each other's boundaries.

- Make important decisions together.

- Support each other emotionally in dire times.

- Take responsibility for your own shortcomings.

- Communicate properly with each other.

- Never be afraid to be vulnerable in other's presence.

- Enjoy a heightened sense of self-esteem.

Also, interdependence isn't codependence, where you can't even function without your partner; it's an unhealthy relationship characterized by poor self-esteem and a lack of goals or desires outside the relationship. It kind of reminds me of Jerry and Beth from the sci-fi show Rick and Morty, who:

- Try to control each other.

- Can't communicate properly.

- Wallow in self-pity and blame each other.

- Engage in people-pleasing behaviors.

- Can't connect with each other emotionally.

This relationship is the complete opposite of autonomy. Secure attachment thrives on a healthy balance between connection and independence. While complete enmeshment can be stifling, so can a lack of closeness. Aim to create a partnership where you both feel supported and can still pursue your own interests.

Secure attachment in a relationship flourishes when there's a beautiful balance between independence and togetherness. You can be both a strong individual and a supportive partner. There's no need to sacrifice your identity for love or your connection for personal growth. Keep both aspects of your personality equally balanced.

Intimacy and Connectedness - Beyond Romantic Affiliations

I bet you thought these tips and tricks only apply to romantic flings, didn't you? Let me tell you, dear reader, that the principles of open communication are universal. The importance of open communication goes beyond romantic partners. It's a cornerstone for building strong relationships with friends, family, and colleagues, too. That's because these principles can enhance any relationship, romantic or simply amicable. Why is that?

That's because when you show vulnerability, you're essentially communicating with all the people around you. Here's how it happens:

- You talk about how you feel the way you do.

- You discuss the reasons why you feel the way you do.

- You let others understand where you're coming from.

- You openly express your thoughts and perspectives.

- They develop empathy for you.

You can see how vulnerability makes communication powerful, driving trust and empathy in every relationship. I can practically sense your suspicion. How does it help to be vulnerable – open about your emotional scars and psychological wounds – in front of the people you work with? Well, I have the perfect case study for you.

Rosa Diaz: The Importance of Vulnerability at Work

I'm not ashamed to say that Brooklyn Nine-Nine (B99) has always been a guilty pleasure of mine. I connected with these cops and enjoyed how their adventures protected the streets of Brooklyn from dirty criminals.

While my friends were obsessed with the characters of Jake Peralta and Capt Ray Hold – who is everyone's favorite, not gonna lie – I was in awe of Rosa Diaz, one of the best depictions of avoidant attachment on modern television.

- While she's hesitant to open up about her love life, she learns to talk about it little by little, starting with telling her pals merely the name of her partner.

- She grows from a person who doesn't even share her home address with people to giving her coworkers a glimpse of her private life.

- She opens up about her bisexuality and the problems she's faced with her family because of it.

- She slowly starts to share the details of her romantic life with her coworkers.

- When her boyfriend gets kidnapped, she opens up about how she's afraid of losing him.

Hopefully, Rosa's example has helped to see how applying the principles of vulnerability in communication can enhance any relationship.

Vulnerability in Communication with Friends and Work Buddies

When was the last time your friends had a heart-to-heart? Don't be afraid to discuss any deep-seated fears and insomnia-inducing concerns with your friends. It's completely fine to admit fears or insecurities and talk about how afraid you are of something. Here's a straightforward exercise to check if you're communicating well with your pals:

- Do you usually express concerns with your friends?

- Do you often share personal achievements with them?

- Do you talk to them about your personal life?

- Do you take them in confidence when making important decisions?

Showing vulnerability will deepen your friendships. It will also allow your friends to be vulnerable and open up to you about their feelings, leading to mutual emotional support and growth. Maybe one of your friends is growing through tough times. When they will see you opening up about your concerns, it'll give them the courage to seek help.

Even in professional settings, showing vulnerability is important for your productivity. So, you should be open about how much of a workload suits you. Don't be afraid to say, "I don't know how to do this," and seek someone's help. It'll lead to these fantastic benefits:

- Increasing your self-awareness.

- Better decision-making capabilities.

- Demonstrating the strength of your character.

- Showing how honest and frank you are.

- Letting you share the stress of your job with the manager.

They say, "Sharing is caring," and this saying rings true in the context of workplace relationships as well.

Again, I should remind you to avoid oversharing. There's a difference between healthy vulnerability and oversharing. Sharing deeply intimate things and overtly personal information can be problematic. It might make others uncomfortable. So, we need to talk about setting boundaries. Also, it's equally important to clarify to your friends that you will decide when to open up to them. Don't let someone force you to be vulnerable; be vulnerable when you feel the time is right.

Setting Boundaries When Communicating

While Rosa Diaz is an excellent example of how to open up about your feelings, Jake Peralta's best friend Boyle is a fine example of how not to show vulnerability. This is what he does wrong:

- Overstepping boundaries by sharing overly personal information.

- Excessively talking about his passions and interests.

- Forcing his coworkers to be equally as vulnerable as he is.

- Unabashedly asking people about their private lives.

Setting visible and clear boundaries is essential when you're trying to communicate your feelings. That's especially true in workplace communication. For instance, strangers shouldn't meddle in your private affairs, and casual friends shouldn't ideally ask deep and personal questions. Here is how you can communicate your boundaries at work:

- "I don't have the energy to help you out with [--------] at this moment."

- "I don't have the emotional capacity to listen to [--------] right now."

- "It makes me uncomfortable when you do [--------], so I have to leave."

- "[---------] is not a topic I want to discuss with you right now."

- "I am not okay with you sharing my story on social media."

In short, you must not be afraid to let people see your soft side. It makes you easier to talk to and prevents you from burning out under the burden of unspoken emotions. But it's equally important to choose what to reveal and who to share your feelings with. Also, respect other people's emotional margins if you expect them to respect yours.

Now, you know that the concept of vulnerability applies to friendships, too. It isn't restricted to romantic relationships. Next, we'll discuss how people with avoidant attachments can reach out to people, make new friends, and be the ones to initiate friendships. Stay tuned and expand your social circle.

Expand Your Social Circle - The Bridge to Secure Attachment

We've arrived at the last section of Chapter 3: The fine art of communicating effectively with people. You may wonder how to expand your social circle and make new friends. How do you initiate conversations? How do you extend the first hand of friendship? How do you make new and long-lasting connections without overwhelming yourself?

You may get overwhelmed by the idea of making new friends. As a person with avoidant tendencies, you may have shown these features (Thompson et al., 2023):

- Withdrawing from friendships to avoid intimacy.

- Not taking any initiative in forming friendships.

- Breaking friendships out of the fear of vulnerability.

- Avoiding friendships due to abandonment issues.

Don't worry; I'll explain how to form new friendships and always be the first to initiate a new amicable relationship. You can now expand your social circle and start the move toward secure attachment at a faster pace.

Good Communication Demands Baby Steps

There's no need to go fast and all in! Take baby steps. That's how you can get in the zone and prevent burnout. I'm not asking you to do something you're uncomfortable with right away. Maybe you're more comfortable creating a Facebook account and making new friends online.

It would help if you always started small. Let's explore some easy first steps towards building friendships, all at your own pace! There's no need to rush out of your comfort zone:

- Feeling shy? Start with group activities where there's no pressure on you to be the one to start the conversation. They offer a relaxed environment where you can connect with others through shared interests, and you're not pressured to have one-on-one conversations right away. This allows you to ease into meeting new people at your own pace.

- Don't invest too much energy in forming new friendships right away. Always set clear-cut personal boundaries. Take your time to find people who share your values and make you feel good.

- Then, focus on nurturing these new friendships. It's always better to have a few nice friends than lots of random acquaintances. Strengthen these bonds first and then move on to expanding your circle of friends further.

Remember, it's not about increasing your number of friends in the real world. We aren't talking about LinkedIn or X (formerly Twitter) here, where your number of followers matters. In real-world settings, true friendships involve a deep understanding, trust, and mutual support. Even if you manage to find one true friend out there among 8 billion souls, you've done well.

Making new friends is key to altering your attachment style. However, you can't make new pals without communicating the right way. So, let's review some fantastic tips to be excellent at communicating with strangers.

How to Communicate Well? A Few Useful Techniques

Are you still overwhelmed by closeness? Is the idea of intimacy something you're working through? Don't fret; There are two strategies to help you communicate well despite your fear of connectedness:

1. **Active Listening:** It simply means paying attention to what the other person is saying. Active listening is an integral part of effective communication. It helps build empathy and creates a bond of understanding between two people without the need to be overtly

vulnerable. If you don't want to disclose too much information, try active listening to make new connections without overwhelming yourself.

2. **Nonverbal Communication:** What happens when your body language shows you aren't interested in a conversation? Focus on nonverbal cues like gestures and facial expressions. Open body language is a welcoming sign and shows how friendly you are. Maintain eye contact when listening to someone and nod to show you're engaged.

Try these tips to excel as a communicator. But don't forget to set boundaries; after all, a new friend must show they can value your privacy and independence.

Healthy Boundaries for Independence and Connectedness

Remember, secure attachment isn't about losing your independence and being 100% vulnerable. It's about striking a balance between the two extremes of ultimate freedom and warts-and-all-nothing-off-the-books frankness. You must set healthy boundaries to ensure people respect your need for privacy.

Here's what you should remember about boundaries:

- Setting boundaries is your right, and there's no need to apologize for it! You choose who you open up to and how much.

- Communicate your boundaries to others assertively. Be very clear that you don't want to talk about a certain topic or discuss private affairs with a casual friend.

- Use polite, clear, and assertive words when conveying the need for the "me time." Say, "I value your company, but right now I need some space," "It's always good to talk to you, but I want to be alone right now," or "Please give me time to myself to recharge, and we'll talk later."

It goes without saying – it's equally important to respect someone else's boundaries. Even your partner may need space and ask for some "me time." Maybe they miss their friends and hang out with them. Or, there are some topics they can only discuss freely with their parents and siblings. In a secure, avoidant-free relationship, you will respect your loved one's privacy by:

- Honoring their needs for freedom and "me time."

- Not feeling rejected by their yearning to be alone for a while.

- Not feeling distant when they try to connect to you later.

Hopefully, you now understand that good communication is a matter of give and take. You have to give up some of your freedom by showing a few glimpses of vulnerability; as a reward, you receive people's trust and get to see them opening up to you.

Empowered with these simple tips and strategies, you are now ready to go on this exciting quest and use communication tools to build healthy connections and move beyond avoidant attachment. Just remember to spread your wings thin and start small.

Key Takeaways

- Recognize common communication barriers, e.g., deflecting specific topics.

- Learn the pillars of good communication: clarity, honesty, assertiveness, and active listening.

- Realize that you can't live without showing vulnerability; it's key to alter your attachment style.

- Practice vulnerability in baby steps; reach out to trusted friends, divulge bits of info, and establish trust.

- Embrace autonomy and interdependence, the two pillars of secure attachment.

- Learn that the need for intimacy and connectedness goes far beyond romantic ties; you should also work on expanding your social circle.

- Openness is key, but it's important to find a balance.

What's Next in Chapter 4?

We're more than halfway done, right? That's a relief. Well, you're now closer to altering your attachment style – much closer than ever before. We can move on to the 4th stage in our journey. Here's what awaits you in the next chapter:

- Intimacy challenges you might face due to avoidant issues.

- How do you express your feelings to your partner?

- A step-by-step guide to building intimate connections.

- Showing physical affection made easy.

Want to sweep your lover off their feet? We've got some winning communication strategies to help you build a deeper connection!

Chapter 4 - Step 4

Intimacy and Affection

"Real intimacy is only possible to the degree that we can be honest about what we are doing and feeling."

Joyce Brothers

Finally, we're drawing closer to your transformation into a securely attached person. This is the fourth stage of our journey together. In this chapter, you will learn the subtle art of intimacy and find the proper way to express your love for your partner.

Individuals with avoidant attachment often struggle with showing intimacy. They have a hard time expressing affection or telling their loved ones how much they care. Don't you get annoyed when your avoidant tendencies stop you from expressing intimacy like all other couples?

Miriam feels torn between her desire for intimacy and freedom. Growing up as the only child of a bedridden mother and deadbeat father, she was raised by an awesome stepdad who was always there for her – except when he was engulfed in his job, working as a traveling salesman. She learned to live alone, constantly fighting off heart-crunching concerns about her ailing mother.

She was so afraid to lose her mom that she distanced herself from her emotions. But assuming a stoic attitude toward life's barrage of miseries didn't do her much good either. She lost the ability to articulate her emotions openly; intimacy became a concept lost to poor little Miriam.

Now, she's a grown woman, working for a telemarketing agency. She is a good worker and has many friends. But while she's doing great on many frontiers of life, her love life is filled with hiccups and setbacks. She always imagined an ideal wedding as a kid – she would be dressed in white, walking down the aisle with her stepdad, and her partner's face would drop at the sight of her angelic face.

Miriam is in her late 30s and has no idea what went wrong. "What did I do? Where did I go wrong?" She practically had no idea about her avoidant tendencies until she met a counselor and learned what it means to be avoidantly attached.

We'll see what she learned and how she started her journey toward secure attachment. First, let's take a brief look at intimacy as a concept.

Intimacy: The Concept and its Multifaceted Dimensions

You may understand "intimacy" as a fleeting passion that leads to reproduction. But in reality, it's far more complex than the major driving force behind a healthy sex life. You express intimacy when you feel close to someone, as if there's a special bond between you and that other person.

Psychologists believe intimacy in terms of romantic relationships means five ideas (van Lankveld et al., 2018):

1. Love

2. Warmth

3. Sexual intimacy

4. Tenderness

5. Connectedness

But don't think that intimacy is something physical; it's about connecting with your lover and being vulnerable in their presence. It's also about sharing not just thoughts or feelings but entire experiences.

- **Physical:** You hug and kiss your partner, cuddle with them, and find comfort in their presence. When your partner touches you, you feel safe and find pleasure in this physical connection.

- **Emotional:** You and your partner can share their innermost thoughts when they are alone. You enjoy a bond of trust and empathy with them. You feel safe to be vulnerable in front of your lover.

- **Intellectual:** You can talk with your partner about literally anything. It's all about stimulating each other's minds and sharing ideas without mocking each other.

- **Experimental:** You share experiences with your partner. You guys travel and explore new hobbies together. You like spending quality time with each other and creating shared new memories.

Sadly, Miriam and many other women like her struggle to be intimate on an emotional level. She feels uncomfortable with emotional closeness and always prioritizes freedom over connection. That's because her instincts tell her to create distance from those who love her. Subconsciously, she's afraid she might lose her autonomy in pursuit of love.

Consider these two scenarios:

- Your significant other wants you two to spend more time together. But your fear of engulfment is in the way; you don't want to lose yourself in the relationship, so you grow anxious and withdraw.

- If you have experienced betrayal in a previous relationship, it might be difficult for you to trust others. Emotional scars run deep and force you to push your lover away. While you think your mistrust of people is protecting you, actually, it's just ruining your chances at a healthy love life.

But there's no need to lose hope. Do what Miriam did and get your romantic liaisons back on track. Try out these simple exercises to overcome all barriers to intimacy:

- Take some time to reflect on your fears and apprehensions. Ask yourself, "Which past experiences influence my current behavior?" Probably something from your childhood? Abandonment issues? Abusive exes? Once you find the root causes of these barriers to intimacy, addressing them won't be an issue.

- Once again, you'll learn how to communicate your boundaries to your partner calmly and respectfully. Ask them to give you some space and let you open up to them on your own terms.

- Do you have a nurturing and supportive environment where you can be vulnerable and share your innermost thoughts? Maybe a friend, family member, or therapist who can provide empathy and understanding?

It all starts with building trust in small steps. Healing needs to come naturally to you. There's no need to rip the Band-Aid off or try to rush the process. Here's what you have to do:

- Start by sharing minor, harmless details about your life. A funny story from work or personal anecdotes. A non-threatening piece of information will do. It makes you comfortable to share more intimate stuff with your partner later on.

- Play games like Two Truths and A Lie, in which you and your partner will tell two truths and one lie about each other. The other person has to guess which one's the lie. It's a lighthearted way to build trust by sharing information.

- Give it time, and you'll slowly regain your ability to trust others.

Next, I'll share a step-by-step process for mending and building romantic ties. You will learn how to get back on your feet and take control of your love life.

A Step-by-Step Process to Build Intimate Relationships

Let's start a new journey of healing. How do you build intimacy and grow closer to your loved ones? For that, we need to hear your thoughts and understand what you mean by intimacy. Ask yourself these questions first:

- What are your relationship goals? What do you wish to achieve from this bond? Where do you see this relationship going?

- How do you define intimacy? What is your interpretation of "being intimate?"

This four-step exercise will empower you to overcome barriers to intimacy. Keep these two simple questions in mind, and you'll be well on your way to stronger connections.

Step 1: Sharing is Caring

The best way to deepen the connection with your romantic partner is to share personal stuff. It's like entrusting them with a part of your personality, deep secrets you don't feel comfortable sharing with anyone else. It shows how much you trust them and value them.

- Start with easy conversations! Share your passion for a hobby or a funny work anecdote. This creates a relaxed atmosphere for deeper conversations later.

- Once you feel comfortable sharing small stuff, practice sharing your innermost thoughts and feelings with your partner.

- After that, you can try telling them about the things that disturb you. Your fears, vulnerabilities, insecurities, bad memories, etc.

- Encourage your partner to share similar stuff about them. It'll deepen the bond that you share with each other.

Whether you want to get closer to your lover, friends, or family members, sharing these intimate details about yourself will do the trick.

Step 2: Active Listening

This topic was covered before. You need to pay attention when the other person is talking to show them how much they matter to you. In simple words, it's about validating your loved one's feelings and experiences. Here's how Miriam did it and made her partner feel heard:

- Her partner talks about how a customer accused her of giving her the wrong pair of shoes at the shoe store.

- She makes eye contact to show that she's listening.

- To show that she's engaged in the conversation, Miriam nods occasionally; her partner then knows they aren't just talking to a wall.

- She asks appropriate questions and makes harmless comments like, "It seems like you were in a difficult situation." or "You really handled it poorly, I think."

- She asks for clarification and summarizes some parts of the story to show that you're invested in the story. She says, "In the end, the manager realized you were right, and the customer was just being an idiot."

- She shows empathy and offers emotional support by saying, "It must have been a tough day for you."

Step 3: Shared Activities

Even shared experiences can help you and your partner rediscover that spark and grow closer to each other. In Miriam's case, she realizes that her passion for anime cosplaying is something she shares with her partner, who is an otaku like her.

This discovery brought them closer to each other and became a great excuse for them to spend time together and get to know each other. Studies show that couples who spend a lot of time talking to each other and engage in shared activities (Hogan et al., 2021):

- Grow closer to each other.

- Are more satisfied with the relationship.

- Perceive their relationship in a more positive light.

So, find excuses to talk to your partner and be with them whenever possible.

Step 4: Rising from Challenges

Have you fought with your partner and don't know how to deal with it? Relax, every couple fights. A healthy relationship isn't about how often you fight but how you resolve these conflicts.

Take Miriam as an example again. Her partner once made plans with friends without asking for Miriam's input. Even though Miriam was hurt, she decided to constructively discuss the problem with her partner. Here's how the conversation went.

Miriam: "I felt excluded and neglected by your actions."

Partner: "I didn't mean to ignore you, I just wanted to hang out with friends."

Miriam: "I understand. Let's hang out sometimes, only us."

Partner: "Nothing will make me happier."

See? This is how you can resolve any conflict with your partner. Hey, disagreements happen! But instead of letting anger take the wheel, try talking things out calmly. Finding common ground is way better than yelling at each other.

If you want to create deeper relationships with your loved ones, especially your spouse or partner, keep applying these simple strategies to your life. It will make your love life more meaningful, taking you deeper into the warm oceans of intimacy. The key to a happy sex life is to understand the fundamentals of intimacy by using the strategies enshrined in this section.

Don't forget that building intimacy is an ongoing process and takes time. It doesn't just require your efforts; your partner should also be involved in it. That's why, in the next section, we'll discuss how to make your lover part of the healing process.

Involving Your Partner - The Foundation of Intimacy

In the everlasting words of Joyce Brothers, intimacy is about honesty; we need to be honest about our feelings and actions. But it isn't enough if only one person is trying to be honest and vulnerable. A relationship is like a bicycle; both wheels need to work harmoniously for the bicycle to progress on the road.

Similarly, your partner needs to take part in this intimacy-building exercise too. Only then can you alter your attachment style and move from avoidant to secure.

Here's what your partner does for you:

- They support you emotionally during the journey.

- They are the receiver of your innermost thoughts.

- They help you hone your communication skills.

- They respect your boundaries, making you feel safe.

- They give you regular feedback on your progress.

But you may ask, "Isn't this journey supposed to be deeply personal?" That's true. However, it is crucial to have a supportive partner by your side to make this transition easier. No journey, no matter how personal, is incomplete without your significant other's intimate contributions and feedback. They can support your personal growth and speed up the healing process.

Joint Reflection Sessions

So, how do you make your partner part of this journey? One exercise is called the "joint reflection session," in which you and your partner reflect on each other's feelings. You can do it like this:

- Share your feelings with your partner.

- Tell them about your negative/positive experiences.

- Listen to them when they share their feelings/experiences.

- Discuss these shared pieces of information.

This and many other simple exercises have been explored in detail in the books written on avoidant attachment. Why don't you share some academic resources with your loved one? Help them learn more about your attachment style.

Tips for Your Partner

Dealing with an avoidant partner can be exhausting, but your loved one needs a strong, supportive environment, a place where they can be vulnerable and express their needs.

Here's how you can do that:

- Listen to your avoidant partner when they have something to say.

- Validate their feelings and experience.

- Check-in with them about their well-being.

- Don't force them to be vulnerable without their consent.

For instance – and this example might seem a little too personal – surveys have shown that people with avoidant attachment avoid sexual intercourse with their partner if they feel sex makes them vulnerable and is emotionally overwhelming (van Lankveld et al., 2021).

Tackle Relationship Challenges Head-on

Here's what you need to hear about relationship building. Focus on these simple strategies to tackle any challenge that thwarts the integrity of your budding romantic ties:

- Find a safe space where you and your lover can be vulnerable without judgment.

- Share any concerns you two have with each other openly and honestly.

- Whenever a challenge arises, brainstorm possible solutions with your partner.

- Always be willing to compromise and adjust your behavior per your partner's request.

- Don't hesitate to refer to a therapist or relationship counselor when things get out of control.

You're now ready to move toward the final phase of this journey.

With your lover's hand in yours, you can walk the road of attachment, making way from avoidant to secure in record time. Just learn to embrace vulnerability, share your fears and desires with your partner, and open up to the warmth of touch.

The Warmth of Touch: How to Show Physical Affection?

We've broken down emotional barriers. Now, it's time to get physical and learn to show affection through the warmth of touch. It's a powerful way to build secure attachments. A person suffering from avoidant attachment is hesitant to physical touch; they prefer if others don't touch them or get too close. "Personal space" is a concept that is very dear to them.

So, do you tend to recoil when your partner touches you? Do unexpected touches make you uncomfortable? It's common for introverted individuals as well to view the idea of physical affection suspiciously.

However, it would help if you opened up to the warmth of touch. It is possible only if you understand how physical affection comes in various shapes, sizes, and forms. It can be:

- A pat on the back.

- A simple handshake.

- A warm hug.

- Cuddling gently.

- Kissing someone on the cheek.

EMOTIONALLY CONNECTED   241

- A passionate kiss.

- Fondling and pre-sex activities.

From a gentle touch to a warm embrace – there are different forms of physical affection. So, you can choose which "physical level you're okay with" right now. Maybe you will find it okay if someone shakes your hand. Or, you're OK with a simple hug. Probably, getting a quick kiss on the cheek from family members will feel "not that bad." Slowly and with time, you can teach yourself to grow more accustomed to higher levels of affection.

Physical affection is good for your well-being, too. It releases the hormone oxytocin. It is associated with a feeling of glee, happiness, and a stress-free attitude. Data shows that physical affection lowers the stress-causing chemical cortisol and boosts the production of oxytocin in your body (Schneider et al., 2023). Here is how this chemical will benefit your journey toward secure attachment:

- Your brain gets used to physical affection when it associates it with feelings of glee and happiness.

- You begin to trust your partner, and the bond between you two grows strong.

- It strengthens your sense of connection with your loved ones.

That's why you'll see that folks with secure attachments are okay with not just receiving but also expressing physical affection. Here's a fascinating study I was reading the other day. It surveyed 13 men and 27 women from different backgrounds and observed their attachment behaviors. It turns out that the warmth of touch makes a person feel a lot less lonely.

In other words, married couples suffering from loneliness and feeling like their relationship is going nowhere are – pardon me for using Internet slang – basically touch-starved. So, embracing the warmth of touch is the fastest way to reduce loneliness and speed your journey toward secure attachment (Tejada et al., 2020).

It kind of reminds me of a certain Internet phenomenon in which youngsters claim to be "kiss-less, hug-less" individuals, complaining about loneliness and mourning their highly avoidant behaviors. It seems that there really is a connection between the warmth of touch and loneliness.

That is because a "touch" isn't merely an act of making contact with another person's body with yours; it's a deeply personal act that conveys a deeper meaning. Physical affection hides the following secrets within it:

- It tells the other person, "I'm right here".

- It shows an unspoken bond of love.

- It conveys emotional support.

I would even say that receiving physical affection from your partner is a sign that there is still hope; you two can still make it work. Similarly, expressing physical affection will show you that a person with avoidant tendencies has the potential for growth. You have the room and the capacity to make everything better and work on yourself. That's how the act of touch, the warmness of physical contact, gives an unspoken yet deeply felt message to your partner.

It is a silent way of saying how much you love your partner.

But what should you do if you are touch-avoidant? How do you grow more accepting of physical contact with your loved one?

It's challenging to change your habits overnight and become desensitized to touching in a snap. You must gradually overcome your abhorrence for physical contact with your loved ones. For instance, try these exercises:

- **Hand-Holding Exercises:** Imagine you're walking side by side with your lover or friend. It's a safe environment, such as a park where you like to go to clear your mind. While you two are walking, reach out and hold the other person's hand. It may feel weird for a moment, but after a few minutes, you will enjoy touching the person you love/care about.

- **Shoulder-Rubbing Exercises:** Stand next to your lover. Ask them if you want to give them a brief massage. If they consent to the idea, you can rub their back (or have them rub yours). Relax your muscles, do deep-breathing exercises, and enjoy the experience. Slowly make this shoulder-rubbing session last longer, and you'll soon grow accustomed to it.

- **Progressive Touching:** In this exercise, you can let your partner touch you on the less sensitive body parts, such as your back and forearm. Once you stop being weird about it, you can ask them to touch you on sensitive body parts, such as the forehead, hands, neck, and belly. It'll help you overcome any anxiety or hesitancy associated with the warmth of touch.

- **Self-Touching:** Try massaging your own hands and shoulders. You can comfortably do this exercise using only your body. Slowly, you'll grow desensitized to the idea of touching and familiar with the physical sensation of being touched.

There are just a few points to remember here:

- Always ask for your partner's consent.

- Communicate your fears of physical affection to them.

- Ensure your partner is also comfortable with these exercises.

- Always start slowly.

What you can now do is create touch rituals to ensure physical affection doesn't become something you and your partner do out of the ordinary. Make it part of daily life. Try to make these simple routines the new normal in your daily habits:

- Hug your partner when greeting them.

- Kiss them before going to bed every night.

- Sit close to each other when watching a movie.

These simple strategies will make you more open to the idea of touching as a means to show your love and affection. But don't just do "touching" like a mindless activity. It needs to be meaningful; it needs to be full of emotion. So, incorporate mindfulness into the art of touching. Grab your partner's hand in your hand. What do you feel? What are your emotions?

What goes on in your head when you're being physically intimate with the love of your life? Focus on this sensation, this warmth oozing from something deep within your heart. Set your mind on this emotion to enjoy this experience. If you still do not feel at ease with physical affection, here's what you can do:

- Set boundaries with your partner by saying, "I am okay with holding hands, but hugging seems just too much right now."

- Ensure your partner knows that you're not refusing physical touch out of loathing but due to sheer aversion to the act of touching.

- Respect your boundaries, and don't pressure yourself into making physical contact.

These simple tips will make you a more touch-friendly person, opening you to a whole new world of affection and emotional connection. The warmth of touch will also speed up your transformation from avoidant to secure attachment style. And this concludes the fourth phase of our journey together.

In this section, you learned how to slowly increase your disposition toward physical closeness. The key is to ensure you're comfortable with it and only let trusted people into your "personal space." It will melt the icy remnants of your emotional state, making you more open to emotional connections.

Key Takeaways

- Intimacy has multiple dimensions, such as physical, emotional, sexual, and others.

- Share words and activities with your lover, listen to them actively, and stay strong in the face of challenges.

- Ensure your partner becomes a part of this journey as you're strong together.

- Learn to tackle relationship challenges to grow more intimate and never block the communication process.

- Embrace the warmth of touch via exercises like hand-holding, shoulder-rubbing, and self-massaging.

What's Next in Chapter 5?

We've successfully finished four out of five steps of this journey. Your transformation is nearly complete. In the final phase of this adventure, here's what you will learn:

- Celebrate the change, appreciate your efforts, and recognize the new you.

- Remember the tips you learned and make them part of this ongoing journey.

- Create a robust support system to avoid relapse (i.e., you going back to your avoidant style).

- Develop a foolproof follow-up plan and take extra good care of yourself.

So, let's see each other in Chapter 5 and finally say Sayonara to your avoidant attitude.

Chapter 5 - Step 5

Sustainable Growth and Personal Development

"It's a funny thing about life; once you begin to take note of the things you are grateful for, you begin to lose sight of the things that you lack."

Germany Kent

Welcome to the fifth stage of this quest, the stage where we complete your transformation into a secure person. Let's start by celebrating your success and hard work. Recognize the progress you've made in the past few days, going from Step 1 of the journey to Step 5. It wasn't easy reaching the finish line; I get it.

It takes a strong person with an iron will to alter their attachment style like you did! Celebrating small victories will encourage you to achieve even bigger goals (Reid, 2023).

This is the point: Don't belittle your achievements, no matter how small they seem. Even minor personality changes require a lot of hard work. Imagine sending your kid to their first day at school. You can boost their self-esteem and encourage them to excel in their academics by celebrating their first week at school, first month, sixth month, and first year.

You may think these victories are small. But, in retrospect, you'll realize these small victories lay the foundations of bigger changes. That's because:

- Your brain is wired to work with a reward-based mechanism; celebrating your small achievements is a great way to boost your sense of self-reliance.

- Tracking minor achievements will motivate you to achieve more and motivated to stay on track for the remainder of your journey.

- Celebrating smaller goals will encourage you to achieve bigger goals because your brain will find pleasure in goal achievement.

- Recognizing and consolidating change is a fantastic way to rediscover your sense of self-confidence and start believing in yourself.

After all, I always ask my clients to embrace SMART goal-setting as the go-to method to bring out major changes in their personalities. I hope you've heard of this term before. It is an acronym that stands for:

- **S**pecific

- **M**easurable

- **A**chievable

- **R**ealistic

- **T**ime-bound

Surveys show that setting SMART goals will lead to long-lasting behavioral changes and help a person alter their bad habits easily (Bailey, 2017). That's because SMART goal-setting leverages your brain's reward-dependence nature to boost your self-motivation. In other words, you will focus on bringing small changes in your personality.

Once you overcome minor manifestations of avoidant attachment, you can move on to overcoming major symptoms of avoidance. For this reason, you should celebrate your victories, no matter how small. Also, celebrate your success after achieving major milestones, such as:

- When you acknowledge that your part trauma is responsible for your avoidant attitude (Step 1).

- When you learn to regulate your emotions and balance your fear of intimacy with the desire for emotional connection (Step 2).

- When you learn to be vulnerable in a safe space and rely on others for emotional support while maintaining some degree of freedom (Step 3).

- When you overcome the barriers to physical affection and learn to embrace the warmth of touch (Step 4).

If you are still wondering why small victories matter, here's a breakdown of their major benefits:

- They make a seemingly difficult task easily manageable.

- They improve your momentum and speed up the journey.

- They make it less likely for you to resort to your bad ways.

- They create a positive feedback loop that promotes continued progress.

- They help you jump to the next stage of the journey with minimal distractions.

Now, I'm sure you are asking yourself one other question: How do you celebrate your wins? Well, I don't want to be the one to tell you how to celebrate your success. Do it the way you please. Do you want to spend some "me time" celebrating your victory? Want to have dinner alone? Looking forward to that hot shower? Thinking about taking a stroll in the park?

It's all up to you; celebrate your small victories the way you seem appropriate. But here are some general ways people in recovery, i.e., people close to the transformation from avoidant to secure attachment, tend to celebrate their achievements:

- **Say it out loud:** Talk about your winnings, tell someone, or simply tell yourself how much you've achieved.

- **Write it down:** Pick up your journal and write about it; tell dear diary how far you've come in your journey.

- **Share it online:** If it feels comfortable enough, share your success story online. Maybe it'll inspire other people with avoidant tendencies to focus on change.

- **Think about it:** Even quiet contemplation will do wonders as you reflect on how much better your life is when you don't avoid physical intimacy and are available to your partner emotionally.

These simple tips will help you turn secure tendencies into long-lasting habits. In simple words, it's all about replacing avoidant tendencies with secure ones. You should find the strategies that help you the most and facilitate the process of replacing your bad habits with good ones. This is what you should do at the final stage of this journey:

- Go through all the exercises in this book.

- Rate every exercise for helpfulness on a scale of 1 to 10 (1 indicates the exercise was not helpful at all.

- See which exercises are rated 5+ on this scale; stick to these exercises in the future.

- Make these exercises part of your daily routine, and soon, you'll notice that you do not experience avoidant tendencies at all.

Create a list of strategies that have worked for you during this journey and stick to them. One exercise may work for you but not for others. So, focus on what is helpful; prioritize that exercise and stick to it faithfully. Consistency, hard work, and gratitude – these are the three ingredients to complete your transformation into a securely attached person.

It's important to be grateful for what you've achieved. Only with a grateful mind can you hop on to the next stage of this quest, maintaining your secure attachment style. Let's see how to maintain your security and never go back to your avoidant tendencies.

Quest Forever - How to Maintain the Newfound Security?

Security isn't something you can simply achieve and keep somewhere. It's a state of mind, a continuous process that needs to be nurtured from time to time. It's a journey that never stops. You must keep building upon these secure behaviors and developing the thought patterns wired in the previous steps.

Stop thinking of secure attachment as a final destination of some sort. It's an ongoing, dynamic journey. All the steps discussed before were meant to put you on this road. You were supposed to be able to walk the path of security. With your hard work and utmost dedication, we're finally there!

You've overcome the barriers that kept you from making emotional connections and expressing yourself appropriately. In the world of attachment styles, however, progress isn't something you achieve; it's something you experience.

Your goal throughout the first four chapters was to escape the hurricanes of avoidance and enter the calm oceans of security. In the final chapter, you'll learn how to maintain your newfound security. Watch out for relapse, and don't let your avoidant tendencies make an appearance. Ask yourself these crucial questions from time to time:

- Am I detaching myself emotionally from my partner again?

- Am I uncomfortable with physical intimacy again?

- Am I failing at communicating my needs to my partner?

- Am I deliberately avoiding new friendships at work?

- Am I surrendering before my old wounds once more?

A relapse will simply undo all the progress we made in the past few chapters. So, you always need to be on guard for changes in your behavior patterns. Whenever you notice yourself going back to your old ways, you may try the following to avoid a relapse:

- Monitor your thoughts and feelings.

- Check-in with your attachment patterns.

- Watch out for major or minor changes in your behavior.

- Ask your support system to inform you if they see your behavior changing.

Whenever you find yourself relapsing, go back to the relevant chapter tackling the issue you are dealing with. For instance, let's say you start experiencing emotional regulation issues again. In this case, you'll review the relevant sections from Chapter 2.

Similarly, if you notice a change in your sensitivity to touch, such as a growing discomfort with warmth, refer back to the discussion in Chapter 4 for strategies to manage this.

However, there are some general tips to help you stay on track and avoid relapse:

- Pick up a notebook and start journaling. It will help you reflect on your thoughts, actions, and behaviors – giving you a fantastic self-reflection opportunity. It does seem a little repetitive to talk about the benefits of journaling again, but I will say this: Journaling is a great way to learn new things about how your mind works and get the hang of your complex thought patterns.

- Meditation is yet another great way to peek into the hidden corridors, labyrinths, and basements of your mind. Besides reducing anxiety, meditation can help you regulate your behavior and unlock the keys to maintaining your security forever (Krishnakumar et al., 2015). You can practice yoga to calm your mind, using this momentary calmness to understand the inner workings of your brain.

Use these simple strategies – most of which have been explored before in this guide – to assess key areas of success. Find out what you've been doing right. What kind of hobbies promote your security? What kinds of friendships keep your avoidant tendencies at bay and kindle an intense desire for bonding emotionally with other people? Your lifestyle, the food you eat, the activities you engage in, the people you hang out with, the places you visit, and even the thoughts you choose to entertain – all of this affects how steadily you'll keep on acting in a secure-attached manner.

All you have to do now is be mindful of your current behavior and how it differs from your past behaviors. A little dose of mindfulness will:

- Help you understand the correlation between your actions and emotions so you will avoid activities that promoted avoidant tendencies in the past.

- Let you observe your thoughts like an open book so you can avoid harmful and stress-inducing thought patterns and embrace security throughout your current relationship.

- Allow you to boost pro-social behaviors that are linked with emotional maturity and a deep desire to help others (Luberto et al., 2018); these behaviors reinforce security in a person's every single act of public dealing.

So, monitor your behavior as you communicate with friends, engage with your partner, and carry on with your normal life. Participate in activities that support your health – both physical and emotional.

But how do you face challenges and deal with relapse? In the next section, you'll learn how to apply resilience in different situations. Use the key skills explored in the next section to maintain your new-found security and avoid the recurring of your avoidant tendencies.

How to Stay Strong When Dealing with Challenges?

I always tell my clients to be resilient when faced with challenges and a lot of them come up with the same question: "How to be resilient? What do you mean by resilience?" Resilience has many definitions, such as:

- The capacity to bounce back from a misfortune.

- The ability to recover quickly from adverse situations.

- The motivation to go through change and adapt to new circumstances.

But my favorite definition is this: Resilience is a person's capacity to "successfully adapt to change, resist the negative impact of stressors, and avoid the occurrence of significant dysfunctions. (Babić et al., 2020)" In simple words, it is your ability to recover from any major or minor difficulty; the way you adapt to change determines how resilient you are.

However, I refuse to treat resilience as some of an innate ability. In my line of work, we do not believe that some people are brave or cowardly, strong or weak, strong-willed, or folks of weak resolve. People are either very resilient or less resilient. A resilient person is:

- A person of great willpower.

- Emotionally strong and well-endowed.

- A courageous, gutsy person.

But resilience isn't something you are born with; you develop the trait over time. It can be learned and, once learned, become a key player in your ongoing journey to maintain a securely attached romantic lifestyle. But developing resilience isn't a quest you should undertake alone. If you wish to face every setback with courage and determination, then learn to build resilience via:

- Relying on your support system to always have your back, the least they can do is tell you when you start showing symptoms of avoidance again.

- Hone your problem-solving skills so you can take on every challenge with 100% confidence and be strong in the face of adversity.

- Never let your emotions get the best of you. A resilient person is very good at the art of emotional attunement.

Still confused about how to practice resilience in real life? Check this example:

- Take deep breaths when you're faced with a difficulty instead of panicking. For instance, imagine you're slowly losing trust in your partner or feeling like they're trying to control you. Don't allow your emotions to dictate your next action; take a few deep breaths and tell yourself, "It's all under control."

- Then, reach out to a mutual friend or someone you trust. Tell that person what they think. Maybe you're being overtly suspicious, and your pal can add a neutral perspective to the whole situation.

- Talk to your friends and prepare for the possibility that your suspicions are true. Be brave and ready to move on if necessary.

- Be prepared to forgive your partner when you realize that your fears are unfounded.

Cognitive Reframing

Cognitive reframing is one of my favorite exercises. It's a fantastic way to change the way you are thinking and alter the entire narrative around setbacks. Here is how it goes:

- Take an inventory of your thoughts.

- Determine which thoughts need to go.

- Recognize the emotions connected to these thoughts.

- Ask yourself, "What's the actual purpose behind these thoughts? What are these thoughts trying to achieve?"

- Find new ways to achieve that purpose via a different thought pattern (possibly via a positive or neutral thought pattern).

- Voila! You've successfully replaced your negative emotions with positive ones.

This simple practice will help you deal with setbacks. Also, you have to lower your stress levels. Reduced stress levels are associated with better emotional resilience; a regular workout routine is associated with lower stress levels (Childs et al., 2014). You can overcome your stress and become mentally relaxed by staying physically active.

Pick hobbies that keep you on your toes, such as gardening, jogging, mountain biking, even dancing, judo lessons, or other exercises.

Resilience Building

However, there are other ways to build resilience. In simple words, "resilience" as a concept means being tough – mentally and emotionally – tough enough to navigate life and its many unique challenges with ease.

Do you want to grow tougher mentally and become strong-willed? This is what you should do:

- **Reflect on Your Past:** Think about the challenges you dealt with in the past. Ask yourself how to overcome those challenges. What worked well? How could you have responded to recurring avoidant tendencies before?

- **Be Thankful:** Assume a grateful attitude and always remember what you are grateful for in your life. Your partner, your family, an excellent job, a nice house, or something else that can help shift your focus from negative to positive.

- **Keep a Positive Perspective:** Always maintain a positive outlook on life. You must focus on things you can control and remember that setbacks are always temporary. Keep telling yourself, "These bad times will pass, and soon, I'll become a securely attached person."

- **Keep a Resilience Diary:** Write it all down – your daily challenges, how you overcome them, and what you learn from these experiences. Looking back, it will motivate you to work harder on maintaining your secure attachment style. It is a great way to remind yourself of your achievements throughout our journey together.

Create a contingency plan in case your resolve grows weak, and the power of stress compels you to go back to your old ways. This future planning involves keeping a solid support system at hand, people you can call whenever you're feeling down.

In the end, your family and friends are the ones who come to your help. You will have to rely on your support system to prevent future

setbacks. I know I've talked about creating a support system before. In the next section, you will learn how to do it right.

The Role of a Strong Support System in Attachment Theory

Let's talk about your "support system" in detail. I'm sure you have a rough idea of what it means. A support system is made of "facilities and people who interact and remain in informal communication for mutual assistance." In short, these are the individuals, people, professionals, or institutions that offer you the emotional support needed to live a particular lifestyle. In the context of our discussion, a support system will help you live a securely attached lifestyle.

Remember what I said about not taking this route alone? You don't have to be a lone wolf going your separate way. Your quest from avoidance to security must be a joint effort – at least between you and your partner.

Studies show that having a strong social support system will lower your stress levels and allow you to maintain your newfound secure attachment style for a long time (Acoba, 2024). Studies show that folks with secure attachment were less prone to psychological distress when living in isolation (such as COVID-caused lockdowns) than people with avoidant tendencies (Adar et al., 2022).

I hope you realize why having a strong support system is essential to maintain your newfound attachment and ward off the inklings of stress.

Support systems come in many shapes and sizes, including but not limited to:

- Your partner (the foundation of your support system).

- Your family members (parents, siblings, kids, or extended relatives).

- Your friends (the ones you know will always be there for you).

- Community groups (online or in-person support groups).

- Professionals (such as counselors like me and other qualified therapists).

However, you need a robust support system, a mixture of at least three from the many examples mentioned above. Regarding the last one, you should keep in mind that mental health counselors and psychologists come in many shapes and sizes as well.

Just ensure your preferred counselor/therapist specializes in Attachment Theory and realizes the weight of your struggles. Finding the right person to be your professional guide can be difficult. So, let me share some trade secrets with you:

- Do some research and collect the names of certified professionals in your locality.

- See if they specialize in treating people with avoidant tendencies and understand the challenges of this attachment style.

- Don't just check their experience or credentials, but also check online reviews and testimonials to ensure you're working with credible therapists.

- Ask for recommendations from your family and friends. They may know someone who can help you maintain your newfound security for good.

- Tell your therapy goals to the counselor so they understand what you wish to get from your sessions together and tailor their counseling style as per your needs.

These simple will help you find a good fit and get in touch with the perfect support group. If you want to maintain your security over a long period, you need to meet people who share your struggles and understand what you've gone through.

Find a platform where you can meet like-minded individuals and talk to people suffering the same problem as you are. But these platforms don't always have to be in-person. You can find plenty of online support groups as well.

- **In-Person Support:** You'll meet folks with avoidant tendencies or struggling to maintain their newfound security. A guest speaker may show up from time to time. Group discussions help attendants explore the depths of their avoidant behaviors.

- **Online Support:** You may join a chat room or an online forum to talk to people who are going through avoidant attachments. Some virtual support groups communicate via virtual calls as well.

A robust support system, therefore, is the key to maintaining your security. These online or in-person support groups will give you a sense of community. This is what you get by contacting a support group:

- You feel like you belong somewhere.

- You'll find opportunities for growth.

- You can share your stories without the fear of judgment.

- You get validated and encouraged.

- You may gain new perspectives on your experiences.

Don't think for a second that you're alone; you always have someone by your side who will help maintain your security and avoid relapse.

Hopefully, now you understand the different types of support available to you such as therapy, support groups, and others. But you must focus on building a personal support network. This support system should be a vital part of your Relapse Prevention Plan.

Relapse Prevention Plan: The Key to Maintaining Your Security

What happens when you feel inclined to go back to your old patterns and start acting avoidantly again? For that, you have to recognize the telltale signs of potential relapse. Maybe you won't notice the recurrence of these behaviors that easily.

So, here is a straightforward breakdown of some common indicators that you may be losing your grip on your newfound security:

- **Social Withdrawal:** Are you trying to avoid social interactions again? Do you try not to attend social events? Noticing a pullback from social activities? It may be a sign that you're reverting to your old patterns.

- **Rejection Sensitivity:** Do you feel fearful of getting rejected or being criticized once again? Do you tend to react defensively or withdraw emotionally to avoid getting hurt? Being too sensitive to rejection may be a sign of relapse.

- **Avoiding Intimacy:** We worked a lot to make you relaxed with the warmth of touch. So, are you avoiding physical affection and trying to maintain a surface-level connection with your partner? It may indicate you're relapsing.

- **Emotional Numbness:** Do you feel emotionally numb or disconnected? What are your motivation levels? Do you not enjoy activities you previously found a lot of pleasure in? This emotional numbness indicates relapse.

- **Escapist Tendencies:** Do you use social media excessively, binge-watch shows, take an unhealthy amount of "me time," play video games excessively, or overeat? These escapist tendencies may indicate that you're having trouble maintaining your newfound security.

But how do you counteract these early signs of relapse? It can be a bit difficult to nullify the effect of these signs. You need to address the underlying issues – the root cause of why your mind is pulling back toward avoidant tendencies. Here are some proactive steps to developing healthier coping mechanisms and nip the offshoots of your avoidant style in the bud:

- Realize that your avoidant behaviors may still be lurking somewhere in the dark entrails of your subconscious. The remnants of this avoidant attachment style can take at least a few months to disappear completely.

- Don't let negative thoughts bring you down. Refer to the cognitive reframing tip explored. It'll help you replace negative, discouraging thoughts with bright, encouraging ones.

- Stay away from situations (or people) that awaken your avoidant tendencies. It'd help a lot if you start recognizing the situations, places, or activities that trigger your slumbering avoidance. Staying away from these situations is a surefire way to avoid relapse.

Practice self-care to maintain baseline emotional stability. Self-care involves the following simple rituals:

- Get enough sleep (seven to nine hours every night).

- Drink plenty of water.

- Avoid a sedentary lifestyle.

- Perform meditation and mindfulness to ground yourself.

- Socialize with your loved ones and leverage your support system.

Once again, you shouldn't neglect the importance of a strong support network in this journey. Your partner, loved ones, friends, therapists, and others play a very important role in keeping you on track. They keep you accountable and encourage you to maintain your newfound security.

Most importantly: create a Relapse Prevention Plan tailored to your unique needs and situations. Your loved ones can help you make such a plan, and then you can tweak it how you see fit.

Personalized Relapse Prevention Plan

Here is a simplified prevention plan for you to take action. It has ten steps, but, of course, you can always add more:

- **Step 1 – Identify your trigger:** Recognize the telltale signs of relapse when they show their nasty face for the very first time.

- **Step 2 – Understand avoidant behavioral patterns:** Mind your behavior and realize when you are acting the way you did before.

- **Step 3 – Create effective coping strategies:** Find the most effective exercises (e.g., mindfulness, deep breathing, or yoga) you can use to cope with the chances of relapse.

- **Step 4 – Create a support system:** Strengthen your support system by excluding people you can't trust or who are no longer available to you for emotional support.

- **Step 5 – Set realistic goals:** Set both short-term and long-term goals to keep yourself from going back to the old patterns. For example, your goal is to attend every social event you're invited to or say "I love you" to your partner every night for a whole week.

- **Step 6 – Take good care of yourself:** Practice self-care, which will significantly reduce the chances of a relapse.

- **Step 7 – Learn how to be more assertive:** Assert yourself by clearly communicating your needs, wants, and desires. Set boundaries with other people and draw the line as politely as possible.

- **Step 8 – Remember how it affects others:** Don't forget that your relapse affects your loved ones, especially your significant other. Whenever you're about to act avoidantly, picture how your partner will feel about it.

- **Step 9 – Keep track of your progress:** Track your goals and monitor your progress. Once again, I'd like to remind you to keep a journal in which you narrate your quest from avoidant to secure attachment.

- **Step 10 – Celebrate small winnings:** Celebrate your commitment to secure attachment.

Don't forget that relapse prevention is an ongoing process, a part of the whole journey. So, keep reviewing and updating your plan as time goes by. Check in with your support groups regularly to stay on track, and soon your avoidant tendencies will become a long-forgotten memory.

Next, we'll move closer to ending our journey together. I'll share some tips with you on how to create a follow-up plan.

What's Next? Crafting a Follow-Up Plan

Do you remember the Germany Kent quote I shared at the beginning of the chapter? When you start taking note of the things you're thankful for, you lose sight of your flaws and weaknesses.

Gratefulness is just a part of the framework we'll discuss here. A follow-up plan does the following for you:

- Consolidating the changes you've achieved.

- Integrating these new habits sustainably.

- Keep a healthy mindset moving forward.

- Avoid the recurrence of your avoidance.

- Make this transformation permanent.

So, how do you come up with this plan? How do you make your newfound security a lasting change? A follow-up plan consists of these simple strategies. I have created a list of strategies for you to utilize. Grab your journal or note-taking app and write your thoughts and opinions. Think of it like a small homework at the end of this exciting adventure.

1. **Self-Reflection:** Reflect on your journey. Ask yourself how

much you've changed since you started reading this book. Can you spot any lingering avoidant behaviors? Do you still need help from a professional, or can you continue on your own from now on?

2. **Goal-Setting:** Set SMART goals to maintain your newfound security. Write down your goals. You can aim to improve your communication skills or build deeper connections with people.

3. **Develop Action Steps:** How do you plan to achieve your goals? For instance, you may attend more social events. Hang out with friends more often. Cuddle more with your loved one. Write down these action plans.

4. **Review Your Progress:** Write down which strategies have worked well for you. Which strategies have been the most effective?

5. **Maintaining Security:** Write down different ways to maintain your secure attachment style. For example, you can write which healthy activities you engage in to be in a healthy romantic relationship.

6. **Celebrate Achievements:** Don't forget to pat yourself on the back a few times. You should write down your winnings (the milestones you have achieved).

We've now moved on to the final part of our journey together. I feel it's only appropriate to end this chapter with a small section on self-care. Stay strong, stay secure, and don't let anyone bring your hopes down. Change is possible!

How to Take Care of Yourself?

Self-care makes you more resilient in the face of challenges (Martinez et al., 2021). I like to describe self-care as the foundation upon which you build the home of emotional as well as relational well-being.

Unless you're in the best of your health – both mentally and physically – you can't maintain your newfound security successfully.

Don't think of self-care as an indulgence; it's a necessity. Do you want to reinforce the key changes you've made in your personal growth journey? Then, practice self-care. In fact, self-care is a multi-faceted journey that tackles your:

- Mental health, you will notice reduced anxiety and depression.

- Physical health keeps you healthy and disease-free.

- Behavioral health allows you to avoid bad habits and behaviors.

- Emotional health keeps your emotions and feelings in check.

- Spiritual health gives you a sense of calmness and makes you feel connected to the universe.

I briefly discussed some self-care exercises previously in this chapter. Whether it's pre-scheduled quiet time, finding new hobbies, meditating, or routine physical exercises, all these activities can be part of your self-care routine. However, don't forget that self-care needs to be part of your everyday life as well.

When you're at work, home, or any other place, make self-care a priority – regardless of time constraints or lifestyle choices. This is what you can do:

- Start small. Incorporate brief, easily manageable activities into your life, such as taking a walk during a lunch break or practicing five minutes of deep breathing exercises before starting work.

- Spend pre-scheduled self-care time. You can set aside a period in the morning during your lunch break or before bedtime. Use this time to meditate or be with your own thoughts (positive ones, I hope).

- Multitasking can be a great way to make self-care part of your daily routine. For instance, I like listening to music when doing household chores.

- Say no to activities that make you uncomfortable.

- Excessive limit screen ruins your health and lead to sleepless nights (Nakshine et al., 2022). So, don't use blue-light-emitting devices (your tablet or phone) right before bedtime. Less screen time is good for your mental health.

- A sedentary lifestyle will only bring back your avoidant tendencies. You should try to make physical activity part of your everyday lifestyle. Whether you're doing yoga, dancing to your favorite tunes, or taking a short walk – find excuses to move your body.

These simple tips will set you on the path of a lifelong transformation. You can maintain your newfound security only if you're taking great care of yourself. Your focus should be boosting the mind-body connection. It's the surefire way to keep acting securely attached and stay out of the dark valleys of avoidant attachment for good.

There you go, folks! You have successfully transitioned from your avoidant attachment style to a secure attachment pattern. Self-care tips will help you stay on track and avoid relapse. I hope you can

now navigate the pathways of security on your own. **Bidding you congratulations on this transformation par excellence!**

Key Takeaways

- The subtle art of setting SMART goals is specific, measurable, time-bound, etc.

- Celebrating your success (even minor achievements count!).

- Maintaining your newfound security and watching out for relapse.

- Staying strong in the face of challenges and practicing resilience.

- Engaging in exercises like cognitive reframing to replace negative thoughts with positive ones.

- Creating a Relapse Prevention Plan and building a strong support system.

- Creating a follow-up plan and taking good care of your well-being; self-care is the most crucial takeaway here.

What's Next in Conclusion?

We've come a long way. Our journey together is about to end. But I won't let you go without a final word of advice. So, here's what you'll see in the Conclusion:

- We'll reflect on the journey and discuss the key points of the five steps; you will see how these stages are all interconnected.

- We'll celebrate your transformation and discuss exactly how you are changed now.

- Looking back at our quest together, you'll see how far you've come and what sort of changes you've made in your behavior/personality.

- How do you stay committed to personal growth and explore new challenges to keep yourself motivated and securely attached?

- How do you share your experiences with others and help other folks dealing with the same issue?

You have now completed the fifth and final step of this journey.

Conclusion

The End of the Journey

"There is only one corner of the universe you can be certain of improving, and that's your own self."

Aldous Huxley

The quest is complete, and through your hard work, you've gained the tools and knowledge to build secure attachments. Be reminded that:

- You are the catalyst of this transformation.

- You control the journey, and success is in your hands.

- You can choose to either go back to your old ways or maintain your newfound security.

So, let's review what we have learned!

Let's Celebrate Your Transformation

See how much you've grown. Notice the changes in your personality – the changes you have made in your behavior. In the past five steps, you have learned to treat yourself and others better.

You don't avoid emotional connectedness anymore. You don't try to pull yourself away from romantic affiliations or friendships.

- Have your thoughts changed regarding attachment and relationships? How do you perceive romantic ties? What changes? Do you look at your love life and past relationships from a new angle?

- In what ways have you noticed yourself becoming more open to your emotions? Are you more sensitive to other people's emotions? Or do you still have trouble reading people's emotions?

- Can you identify any specific situations where you acted differently than you'd have in the past? Did your new insights into Attachment Theory make you act or think differently? Are you a more emotionally intelligent person?

- Have your senses of self-esteem and self-worth changed? Do you value yourself and your romantic liaisons in a more positive light? Do you no longer prioritize your freedom and autonomy over having a long-term partner?

- Can you think of any concrete examples of healthy boundaries you've set, shown, or respected in your relationships recently? Are you more open about setting new boundaries or refusing to engage in things that make you uncomfortable?

Looking Ahead: Eyes on the Future

Congratulations! You read the whole book and applied the tips explored in the five chapters. You have now finished all five stages and transformed into a secure, attached person. Do you feel different? Do you see visible changes in your personality? How should life look like for a person with a secure attachment? Let me paint you a pretty rainbow-colored picture here.

- You realize the roots of your avoidance and learn to overcome old wounds.

- You are the one in control of your emotions and not the other way around.

- You overcame your fear of closeness and learned to balance your desire for emotional connectedness with a yearning for freedom.

- You're better at communicating your fears and concerns; the blazing hounds of vulnerability have turned into tame little kittens.

- After strengthening your romantic ties, you started reinforcing your friendships, familial bonds, and work relationships.

- You have embraced the warmth of touch and grown fond of intimacy; you don't hesitate to show physical affection anymore.

- You have made secure attachment part of your daily routine and embarked upon this lifelong journey, never to fall into the trap of avoidance ever again.

Let me remind you again, as I did in Chapter 5, that secure attachment isn't a milestone to achieve or a goalpost you reach. It's a constant journey, a lifelong process. Many clients I've met in my career think of personal growth as some sort of an objective, a mission that needs to be completed.

I always tell them, "That's a very counterproductive way of viewing progress." Self-improvement is like an ocean without a beach, a train with no station, and a cake that keeps re-spawning after it's been eaten. In the next section, I'll discuss how to make personal growth easy to tackle.

Final Words

As you close this book, I want you to embrace every moment in your life as an opportunity to practice secure attachment.

Take care of your well-being, go easy on yourself, and have some self-compassion. Significant changes take time to become permanent and setbacks are also a natural part of the process.

So, don't let failure discourage you from living life to the fullest. Keep in mind that every step forward – no matter how small or insignificant it may seem – is a step toward greater and better emotional well-being.

In addition, you now have a chance to go back to Chapter 1 and re-do your self-assessment. Evaluate the areas you can see clear improvements and the possible areas you think you still need to work on. This is a great way to keep on the journey of self-improvement towards a Secure Attachment Style.

As you keep walking this road toward secure attachment, may you find the strength you need! Keep the light of hope bright and vibrant in your heart.

Make love your bread and butter, and don't avoid those who love you back with sincerity!

Glossary

Affection: A gentle feeling of fondness or liking towards someone or something.

Assertiveness: The quality of being self-assured and confident without being aggressive.

Attachment: A deep and enduring emotional bond between individuals.

Autonomy: The ability to make independent decisions and act on one's own.

Avoidant Attachment: A style of attachment characterized by avoidance and dismissiveness in relationships.

Controlled Exposure: Gradual and controlled exposure to feared situations or stimuli to reduce anxiety.

Cognitive Reframing: A technique to change negative thought patterns into positive ones.

Cognitive Restructuring: see Cognitive Reframing.

Connectedness: The feeling of being connected or in tune with others emotionally.

Cortisol: A hormone released in response to stress and helps regulate metabolism and immune response.

Emotional Attunement: The ability to understand and respond to the emotions of others.

Emotional Pairing: Associating positive emotions with specific stimuli or experiences.

Emotional Awareness: Being conscious and understanding of one's own emotions and those of others.

Emotional Pacing: Regulating the intensity and timing of emotional expression.

Endorphins: Neurotransmitters that act as natural painkillers and mood elevators.

Focused Breathing: A technique involving mindful and intentional breathing to reduce stress and increase focus.

Guided Visualization: A relaxation technique that involves imagining positive and calming scenarios.

Intimacy: Close familiarity or closeness between individuals, often involving emotional and physical connection.

Interdependence: Mutual reliance and support between individuals or groups.

Introvert: A person who tends to be more reserved, reflective, and energized by solitude.

Extrovert: A person who is outgoing, sociable, and energized by social interactions.

Journaling: The practice of writing down thoughts, feelings, and experiences for personal reflection.

Mindfulness: The practice of being present and aware of one's thoughts, feelings, and surroundings.

Oxytocin: A hormone associated with bonding, trust, and social connection.

Positive Affirmation: Encouraging and positive statements used to challenge negative thoughts or beliefs.

Paradox: A seemingly contradictory or absurd statement that may reveal a deeper truth.

Paranoia: Excessive or irrational distrust or suspicion of others.

Resilience: The ability to bounce back from adversity, challenges, or trauma.

Relapse: The recurrence of symptoms or behaviors after a period of improvement or recovery.

Secure Attachment: A healthy attachment style characterized by trust, security, and comfort in relationships.

Self-Discovery: The process of gaining insight into one's own identity, values, and beliefs.

SMART Goals: Specific, Measurable, Achievable, Relevant, Time-bound goals used for personal development.

Subconscious: The part of the mind that influences thoughts, feelings, and behaviors without conscious awareness.

Support System: A network of individuals who provide emotional, practical, and social support.

Therapy: Treatment or intervention aimed at improving mental health, emotional well-being, or relationships.

Trauma: Emotional or psychological distress caused by a distressing or disturbing event.

Triggers: Stimuli or situations that evoke strong emotional or psychological reactions.

Vulnerability: The state of being open to emotional or physical harm, often associated with authenticity and emotional connection.

References

Acoba EF. Social support and mental health: the mediating role of perceived stress. Front Psychol. 2024 Feb 21;15:1330720. https://doi.org/10.3389%2Ffpsyg.2024.1330720

Adar T, Davidof M, Elkana O. Social Support Mediates the Association between Attachment Style and Psychological Distress during COVID-19 in Israel. Viruses. 2022 Mar 27;14(4):693. https://doi.org/10.3390%2Fv14040693

Babić, R., Babić, M., Rastović, P., Ćurlin, M., Šimić, J., Mandić, K., & Pavlović, K. (2020). Resilience in Health and Illness. Psychiatr Danub, 32(Suppl 2), 226-232. https://pubmed.ncbi.nlm.nih.gov/32970640/

Bailey, R. R. (2017) Goal Setting and Action Planning for Health Behavior Change. Am J Lifestyle Med, 13(6), 615-618. https://doi.org/10.1177%2F1559827617729634

Childs E, de Wit H. Regular exercise is associated with emotional resilience to acute stress in healthy adults. Front Physiol. 2014 May 1;5:161. https://doi.org/10.3389%2Ffphys.2014.00161

Clarke, J. & Snyder, C. (2023). How to Build a Relationship Based on Interdependence? Very Well Mind. https://www.verywellmind.com/how-to-build-a-relationship-based-on-interdependence-4161249

Hogan, J. N., Crenshaw, A. O., Baucom, K. J. W., & Baucom, B. R. W. (2021). Time Spent Together in Intimate Relationships: Implications for Relationship Functioning. Contemp Fam Ther, 43(3), 226-233. https://doi.org/10.1007%2Fs10591-020-09562-6

Iyengar, U., Kim, S., Martinez, S., Fonagy, P., & Strathearn, L. (2014) Unresolved trauma in mothers: intergenerational effects and the role of reorganization. Front Psychol, 5, 966. https://doi.org/10.3389%2Ffpsyg.2014.00966

Jahromi, V. K., Tabatabaee, S. S., Abdar, Z. E., & Rajabi, M. (2016) Active listening: The key of successful communication in hospital managers. Electron Physician, 8(3), 2123-8. https://doi.org/10.19082%2F2123

Karantzas, G. C., Younan, R., & Pilkington, P. D. (2023). The associations between early maladaptive schemas and adult attachment styles: A meta-analysis. Clinical Psychology: Science and Practice, 30(1), 1-20. https://psycnet.apa.org/doi/10.1037/cps0000108

Khoury, B., Manova, V., Adel, L., Dumas, G., Lifshitz, M., Vergara, R. C., Sekhon, H., & Rej, S. (2023). Tri-process model of interpersonal mindfulness: theoretical framework and study protocol. Front Psychol, 14, 1130959. https://doi.org/10.3389%2Ffpsyg.2023.1130959

Kogan, L. R. &Bussolari, C. (2021) Exploring the Potential Impact of a Virtual Body Scan Meditation Exercise Conducted With Pet Dogs on Recipients and Facilitators. Front Psychol, 12, 698075. https://doi.org/10.3389%2Ffpsyg.2021.698075

Kozubal, M., Szuster, A., &Wielgopolan, A. (2023). Emotional regulation strategies in daily life: the intensity of emotions and regulation choice. Front Psychol, 14, 1218694. https://doi.org/10.3389%2Ffpsyg.2023.1218694

Krishnakumar, D., Hamblin, M. R., & Lakshmanan, S. (2015). Meditation and Yoga can Modulate Brain Mechanisms that affect Behavior and Anxiety-A Modern Scientific Perspective. Anc Sci, 2(1), 13-19. https://doi.org/10.14259%2Fas.v2i1.171

Lampe, L., & Malhi, G. S. (2018) Avoidant personality disorder: current insights. Psychol Res Behav Manag, 11, 55-66. https://doi.org/10.2147%2FPRBM.S121073

Luberto, C. M., Shinday, N., Song, R., Philpotts, L. L., Park, E. R., Frichione, G. L., & Yeh, G. Y. (2018). A Systematic Review and Meta-analysis of the Effects of Meditation on Empathy, Compassion, and Prosocial Behaviors. Mindfulness (N Y), 9(3), 708-724. https://doi.org/10.1007%2Fs12671-017-0841-8

Martínez, N., Connelly, C. D., Pérez, A., & Calero, P. (2021). Self-care: A concept analysis. Int J Nurs Sci, 8(4), 418-425. https://doi.org/10.1016%2Fj.ijnss.2021.08.007

Mohammadi, K., Samavi, A., &Ghazavi, Z. (2016) The Relationship Between Attachment Styles and Lifestyle With Marital Satisfaction. Iran Red Crescent Med J, 18(4), e23839. https://doi.org/10.5812%2Fircmj.23839

Momeni, K., Amani, R., Janjani, P., Majzoobi, M. R., Forstmeier, S., & Nosrati, P. (2022.) Attachment styles and happiness in the elderly: the mediating role of reminiscence styles. BMC Geriatr, 22(1), 349. https://doi.org/10.1186/s12877-022-03053-z

Monti, J. D. & Rudolph, K. D. (2014) Emotional awareness as a pathway linking adult attachment to subsequent depression. J Couns Psychol, 61(3), 374-82. https://doi.org/10.1037%2Fcou0000016

Mueser, K. T., Gottlieb, J. D., Xie, H., Lu, W., Yanos, P. T., Rosenberg, S. D., Silverstein, S. M., Duva, S. M., Minsky, S., Wolfe, R. S., & McHugo,

G. J. (2015). Evaluation of cognitive restructuring for post-traumatic stress disorder in people with severe mental illness. Br J Psychiatry, 206(6), 501-8. https://www.ncbi.nlm.nih.gov/pmc/articles/PMC4450219/

Murray, C. V., Jacobs, J. I., Rock, A. J.,& Clark, G. I. (2021) Attachment style, thought suppression, self-compassion and depression: Testing a serial mediation model. PLoS One, 16(1), e0245056.https://doi.org/10.1371%2Fjournal.pone.0245056

Nakshine, V. S., Thute, P., Khatib, M. N., & Sarkar, B. (2022). Increased Screen Time as a Cause of Declining Physical, Psychological Health, and Sleep Patterns: A Literary Review. Cureus, 14(10), e30051. https://doi.org/10.7759%2Fcureus.30051

Ocklenburg, S. & Frye, D. (2023). How Many Children Are Securely Attached to Their Parents? Psychology Today. https://www.psychologytoday.com/intl/blog/the-asymmetric-brain/202306/how-many-children-are-securely-attached-to-their-parents

Oz-Soysal, F. S., Bakalım, O., Tasdelen-Karckay, A., & Ogan, S. (2024). The Association Between Autonomy Need Satisfaction and Perceived Romantic Relationship Quality: The Mediating Role of Openness. Emerging Adulthood, 12(2), 187-200. https://doi.org/10.1177/21676968231220074

Reid, C. (2023, August 5). The power of celebrating small wins | Know thyself, heal thyself. Medium. https://medium.com/know-thyself-heal-thyself/the-power-of-celebrating-small-wins-and-their-positive-impact-on-life-f2fd17c3dc51

Riggio, G., Gazzano, A., Zsilák, B., Carlone, B., &Mariti, C. (2020). Quantitative Behavioral Analysis and Qualitative Classification of Attachment Styles in Domestic Dogs: Are Dogs with a Secure and an Insecure-Avoidant Attachment Different? Animals (Basel), 11(1), 14. https ://doi.org/10.3390/ani11010014

Schneider, E., Hopf, D., Aguilar-Raab, C., Scheele, D., Neubauer, A. B., Sailer, U., Hurlemann, R., Eckstein, M.,&Ditzen, B. (2023). Affectionate touch and diurnal oxytocin levels: An ecological momentary assessment study. Elife, 12, e81241. https://doi.org/10.7554%2FeLife.81241

Schumann, K., & Orehek, E. (2019). Avoidant and defensive: Adult attachment and quality of apologies. Journal of Social and Personal Relationships, 36(3), 809-833. https://doi.org/10.1177/0265407517746517

Semeraro, A., Vilella, S., & Ruffo, G. (2021). PyPlutchik: Visualising and comparing emotion-annotated corpora. PLoS One, 16(9), e0256503.https://doi.org/10.1371%2Fjournal.pone.0256503

Taibbi, R. (2014). The 5 Whys to Self Understanding. Psychology Today. https://www.psychologytoday.com/intl/blog/fixing-families/201401/the-5-whys-self-understanding

Tan, T. Y., Wachsmuth, L,& Tugade, M. M. (2022). Emotional Nuance: Examining Positive Emotional Granularity and Well-Being. Front Psychol, 13, 715966. https://doi.org/10.3389%2Ffpsyg.2022.715966

Tejada, A. H., Dunbar, R. I. M.,& Montero, M. (2020) Physical Contact and Loneliness: Being Touched Reduces Perceptions of Loneliness. Adapt Human BehavPhysiol, 6(3), 292-306. https://doi.org/10.1007%2Fs40750-020-00138-0

Thomas, P. (2016). Health is wisely sharing vulnerability. London J Prim Care (Abingdon), 8(3), 33-34.https://doi.org/10.1080%2F17571472.2016.1193590

Thompson, S., Deaner, K., & Franco, M. G. (2023). How to Help Clients Make Friends. J Health Serv Psychol, 1-9. https://doi.org/10.1007%2Fs4 2843-023-00085-w

Tull, M. & Block, D. B. (2020). How Journaling can Help with PTSD? Very Well Mind. https://www.verywellmind.com/how-to-use-journalin g-to-cope-with-ptsd-2797594

van Lankveld, J., Dewitte, M., Verboon, P., & van Hooren, S. A. H. (2021). Associations of Intimacy, Partner Responsiveness, and Attachment-Related Emotional Needs With Sexual Desire. Front Psychol, 12, 665967. https://doi.org/10.3389%2Ffpsyg.2021.665967

van Lankveld, J., Jacobs, N., Thewissen, V., Dewitte, M.,&Verboon, P. (2018). The associations of intimacy and sexuality in daily life: Temporal dynamics and gender effects within romantic relationships. J Soc Pers Relat, 35(4), 557-576.https://doi.org/10.1177%2F0265407517743076

Wang, S. K., Feng, M., Fang, Y., Lv, L., Sun, G. L., Yang, S. L., Guo, P., Cheng, S. F., Qian, M. C., & Chen, H. X. (2023). Psychological trauma, posttraumatic stress disorder, and trauma-related depression: A mini-review. World J Psychiatry, 13(6), 331-339. https://doi.org/10.5498%2Fwjp.v13.i6.331

Wardecker, B. M., Chopik, W. J., Moors, A. C., & Edelstein, R. S. (2020). Avoidant Attachment Style. Encyclopedia of Personality and Individual Differences, 345 to 351. Cham: Springer International Publishing. https ://doi.org/10.1007/978-3-319-24612-3_2015

Webb, J. & Sills, D. (2023). Why Emotional Attunement is So Important, and So Healing? Psychology Today. https://www.psychologytoday.com/intl/blog/childhood-emotional -neglect/202211/the-opposite-emotional-neglect-emotional-attunement

Weber, R., Eggenberger, L., Stosch, C., & Walther, A. (2022). Gender Differences in Attachment Anxiety and Avoidance and Their Association with Psychotherapy Use-Examining Students from a German University. Behav Sci (Basel), 12(7), 204. https://doi.org/10.3390%2Fbs12070204

Yang, F. & Oka, T. (2022). The role of mindfulness and attachment security in facilitating resilience. BMC Psychol, 10(1), 69. https://doi.org/10.1186%2Fs40359-022-00772-1

Emotional Intelligence

A Practical Guide for Personal Growth and Building Stronger Connections

Amy Harper

Introduction

How Understanding Others Starts with Understanding Yourself

"The greatest discovery of my generation is that human beings can alter their lives by altering their attitudes of mind."
William James

If you have ever watched an episode of *Suits* and liked Donna's uncanny ability to intuit her peers' emotions, motivations, and needs- considerably better than they could on their own – you probably know emotional intelligence matters. It is mission-critical.

Have you ever had that feeling or perceived that your friend needs a hug before they even say a word? Maybe you know somebody in your office whose anger and frustration erupt like a volcano. It will probably leave you dumbfounded, with no clue about what happened.

We are all acquainted with people who are pretty good listeners in our personal lives or at work. Regardless of your situation, they somehow seem to know precisely what to say – and how to express it – so that you aren't upset or offended.

These types of people are masters at managing their feelings and emotions. You will seldom find them getting angry or losing their composure in stressful situations. Instead, they're considerate and caring and have the innate ability to look at a complex problem and calmly come up with a solution.

No doubt, we all deal with challenging emotions and tricky situations. Yet some navigate them like Donna from *Suits* and trust their intuition. What about others? They may feel lost in the chaos. Individuals like Donna are excellent at making decisions and have high emotional intelligence.

What if you could be like Donna, sniffing out a nasty power play faster than anyone else? Her emotional intelligence and social perceptiveness aren't merely TV magic and should not be reduced to a TV trope. It's a set of skills broadly known as emotional intelligence, and you can learn it, too.

Hone it properly, and it may develop enough momentum to help advance your career. After all, it catapulted Donna from overlooked legal secretary to powerful COO.

Why this Book is Worth Your Time

If close relationships fizzle out, leaving you with a longing for deeper connection, or you are unable to sense other people's emotional needs, *Emotional Intelligence - A Practical Guide for Personal Growth and Building Stronger Connections* will help you.

This book deals with the often messy yet glorious reality of being human. As you peruse this guide, you will find that our unfettered emotions can be like rogue waves. They can crash over our relationships and drag us under.

Remember we started with a quote from William James? Those words underscore the importance of changing your mental attitude. But altering our attitudes requires understanding them first. This is where emotional intelligence is so valuable. Learn to manage your emotions and to connect with others in a way that fosters empathy, communication, and trust.

Although working on and improving your emotional intelligence basically starts as an inward journey, you will see that people around you often feel the results. This introspective journey begins with more self-management and self-awareness and flows outwards to others through higher social awareness and perceptiveness.

Imagine a world where:

- Contentious arguments dissolve into calm and meaningful conversations fueled by understanding rather than blame.

- Misunderstandings are consigned to oblivion and replaced by mutual respect.

- Relationships blossom into gardens of trust, nurtured by honest, transparent communication and empathy.

This isn't an abstract fantasy; it's a tangible, achievable reality facilitated by emotional intelligence. Mastering emotional intelligence empowers you to manage impulsive behaviors and emotions, seize initiative, and uphold commitments. However, there's a crucial catch—it demands extensive practice, unwavering dedication, and acute self-awareness.

What You Will Learn

Do you want to know how this book will guide and inform your growth journey? We'll equip you with practical tools, tips, and strategies to:

- Identify, understand, and manage your complex emotions healthy and positively. No more emotional mystery tours! With my help, you'll become a master detective of your inner world. Stop feeling like a puppet on a string of your feelings.

- Build healthy and lasting relationships. Boundaries, communication, and empathy – we'll unpack all the essentials for creating thriving connections.

- Improve your health and well-being. Improving your emotional intelligence starts with self-care. We'll show you how to nourish your mind, body, and spirit.

Find out What's Next

So, are you ready to ditch the emotional blindfold and step into the light? The next chapter will equip you with quick exercises to recognize and label your emotions. Think of it as a personalized learning experience minus the awkward grade reports and packed with empowering insights. Is that intriguing? So, let's start.

Chapter 1

Beyond the Facade: Recognizing and Understanding Your Emotions

"It's impossible to live a meaningful life without under-standing your own heart and mind."

Dalai Lama

Experiencing emotions such as anger or fear often resembles navigating the complexities of high school – each sensation seems amplified, commanding our entire focus. Yet, once it subsides, it leaves us pondering its significance. Identifying an emotion isn't always straightforward. While we might hastily label it as anger at the surface, delving deeper might reveal a different truth. It could be rooted in resentment, frustration, or even a tinge of annoyance.

Have you ever felt like your complicated emotions are running a puppet show of their own, and you're merely the flummoxed audience member? Have you ever snapped at your partner for no good reason, leaving them bewildered, and you're left contemplating, "Where did that even come from?" This is a more common occurrence than you may realize.

Some people have difficulty controlling or regulating intense emotions, such as jealousy, and might feel at the mercy of their strong emotional reactions. Others try to ignore or downplay their emotional reactions and let feelings build up.

What is the result of this denial of your emotional experience? A lack of self-knowledge and impaired ability to use your emotions productively! Both are equally powerless places to be, as both types of individuals have trouble recognizing, regulating, and managing emotions.

Emotions are seldom one-dimensional, and it is completely normal to know you are feeling something but can't put it into words.

However, as Dalai Lama eloquently puts it, you can't live a meaningful and rewarding life without understanding your emotions, and being aware of your feelings will help you identify them in others. More importantly, it can enhance how you interact with people you meet.

Dealing effectively with emotions, especially conflicting feelings, is an important leadership skill. Maybe you can relate. Have you ever had mixed feelings about somebody you love? If yes, you are probably familiar with the intense discomfort that ensues.

Let's say your feelings were purely positive and brought joy and happiness; obviously, the relationship would be blissful. Having purely negative feelings is also less complicated since the course of action would be straightforward: Say goodbye. The tricky thing about mixed feelings is that they baffle you about the right thing to do.

It's crucial to navigate emotions deliberately for their effective use. Understanding your feelings requires creating a mental 'space,' allowing room for mindful examination from a neutral standpoint. By distancing yourself enough to observe your emotions—be it fear or excitement—you gain insight into their message. This perspective positions you to make informed, healthy decisions.

Naming emotions, known as labeling in psychology and psychiatry, stands as a pivotal initial phase in effectively handling them. However, this seemingly straightforward task poses complexities. Numerous individuals encounter difficulty in pinpointing their precise emotions. At times, the apparent emotional label may not accurately encapsulate the experience.

The Case File - Lack of Self-Awareness

If you asked Luke, an experienced lighting designer at a high-end construction and architecture firm, whether his feelings and emotions affect his work performance, he'd laugh. He'd likely tell you that what matters is his uncanny ability to turn a client's vision for their home or office building into an aesthetically pleasing and practical design. Feelings, what do they have anything to do with it?

However, inquire among Luke's colleagues, and you'll encounter an entirely different narrative – a version more dependable and credible. According to his peers, Luke's performance with clients fluctuates. Smooth sailing occurs when Luke is in high spirits (radiating smiles and positivity). Yet, when annoyance or anger sets in, his interactions tend to falter.

For instance, he doesn't listen well, showing contempt or hostility toward the client's suggestions or recommendations. Inevitably, clients disapprove of Luke's initial designs because he failed to incorporate their feedback and wishes accurately. Clearly, Luke's failure to identify his feelings – resentment or apathy - and how they impact his behavior don't do much good to his work performance. What Luke lacks is emotional self-awareness.

Picture this: The Chief Technology Officer (CTO) at a prominent innovation incubator possesses all the traits of a bully. The snag? He remains blissfully unaware of it. Despite excelling in his role, the CTO displays favoritism and dictates tasks to his team rather than managing them collaboratively. His selective listening sidelines those he doesn't favor. Attempts to address specific incidents with him are met with denial.

Like Luke, this IT wizard lacks self-awareness, no matter how good he is at his job. For one thing, a supervisor or boss who is a self-obsessed bully or is stubborn or arrogant is usually viewed by employees as incompetent. Those traits also correlate with lousy financial results.

Lacking self-awareness is like navigating a city blindfolded. Every stumble, every wrong turn, every awkward encounter is the direct consequence of not seeing the map. If you are not self-aware, you will likely stumble through life, reacting from impulse rather than responding from understanding and empathy.

This inability to recognize and understand your thoughts and feelings often manifests itself in misunderstood conversations, stress, and strained relationships. For instance, anxiety may coil around you like a serpent, squeezing the pleasures out of everyday moments.

The Missing Key - Emotional Intelligence

Fortunately, mastering the recognition of your emotions and understanding their influence on your decisions is a skill that can be cultivated, much like refining your tennis or swimming technique. Emotional self-awareness, often the most understated among a range of emotional intelligence abilities, serves as a remarkably crucial cornerstone for other competencies.

Individuals possessing robust emotional self-awareness typically exhibit ten or more of the twelve competencies. Consequently, they are better equipped to consistently employ positive leadership styles, fostering optimal working environments for their teams.

Do you want to learn to recognize the subtle emotions that guide your thoughts and actions? Emotional intelligence will get you there, and unlocking it starts with self-awareness. Learn how to befriend your feelings rather than bury them and harness and nurture them for a fulfilling life.

Your emotions and feelings are simply feedback mechanisms that let you know whether things are going well (as planned) or not. Yes, that's it. But what you later do with that info is a completely different matter (and considerably more crucial, as we'll see).

Emotions, such as joy or fear, often serve as tools to achieve an end. Confused? Well, consider this: they propel us toward our goals and sometimes uncover a sense of purpose. Yet, they aren't the ultimate goal; there's a crucial distinction there, isn't it? Sadly, many stumble at this juncture, mistaking emotions for the destination rather than recognizing them as pathways. It's akin to reliving high school days—a misinterpretation where feelings reign supreme as if they were the sole importance.

Why is Labeling Emotions Important?

I think saying, "I feel frustrated or irked when you interrupt me," is more constructive than just snapping in irritation. Do you agree? Learning to convey or express your emotions appropriately is an important part of healthy emotional and social development.

Fortunately, emotions are much easier to express when you're aware of your feelings and can label them. Also, for most people, the intensity of their emotions decreases after they explicitly express how they feel. If you describe how you feel using an "I feel" statement, you will notice that you can manage your emotions better.

Do you need an example? Sure! If you're feeling fearful (maybe after watching a horror or slasher flick like the Texas Chainsaw Massacre or witnessing a dreadful accident), verbalizing 'I'm scared' might assist in unraveling the reasons behind your emotions. This conscious acknowledgment can either help dispel these negative feelings or prompt you to delve deeper into understanding the root cause of your unease.

Cracking the Code - Tools for Recognition

Before diving into the benefits of integrating emotional awareness exercises and assessments into your daily routine, let me address something: I understand the complexity and intimidation that comes with trying to label emotions and boost emotional intelligence. It's a maze—where do you even start, right? I completely relate! Especially with the flood of must-try emotional wellness trends flooding the internet, it's natural to question: 'What makes this exercise worthwhile? Is it truly worth the time and effort?' Valid concerns! My resounding 'yes' stems from the fact that there's no downside to enhancing self-awareness and emotional intelligence; the potential personal and professional gains are manifold.

If you still need convincing, here are some other reasons to work on your emotional intelligence:

- Wanting to be successful in a leadership position.

- Trying to acclimatize to or fit in with a new organization or team.

- Looking to branch out of your network, socialize, and make new contacts or friends.

Moreover, understanding and labeling your emotions to boost your emotional intelligence isn't solely about professional pursuits. It's about unlocking a profound understanding of yourself and the people you encounter daily. There's a wealth of activities, self-assessments, and exercises designed precisely for this purpose and more.

It's time to channel your inner emotional Sherlock Holmes. Uncover the clues, gain self-awareness, and nurture a sharper perception of those around you!

The BodyScan Blitz

You have probably heard a lot about the benefits of mindfulness and meditation, such as improved sleep and stress relief, but did you know that it can also help with self-awareness? The main goal of a body scan meditation also called the body scan method, is to improve present-moment awareness. Cultivating this awareness helps deepen the connection between your body and mind.

Close your eyes and take a deep breath. Scan your body, paying special attention to any aches, itches, or tension. You may start with noticing your bodily sensations while listening to a song or watching a movie that you know triggers sadness, joy, or fear.

So, where are your emotions hiding? Maybe your shoulders are uptight with concern or worry. Tight shoulders can physically manifest various emotional states. Remember Ben Stiller's portrayal of Walter, a timid photo editor stuck in a dull and mundane routine? Throughout *The Secret Life of Walter Mitty*, Walter's hunched posture and tense shoulders visually represent his stress, anxiety, and lack of fulfillment.

Does your stomach or fists clench with anger, like Bruce Banner's, when he transforms into the rage-fueled Hulk? Similarly, you may remember Walter White's transformation from a calm, mild-mannered chemistry teacher to a ruthless drug kingpin. These scenes are punctuated by moments of clenched fists.

Observe these physical signals and cues without judgment – they represent your body's subtle narrative. Engaging in the body scan technique allows you to attune to your individual bodily sensations more mindfully. When confronted with intense emotions such as fear, connecting them to bodily sensations can foster a deeper comprehension. This awareness becomes a compass, simplifying the process of addressing both emotional and physical discomfort, thereby fostering enhanced mental and physical well-being.

Using a Wheel of Emotions

Understanding emotions, particularly complex ones like distrust, can be challenging without a comprehensive range to reference. Emotions often present a tangled web, sometimes allowing contradictory feelings to coexist—a concept vividly depicted in the insightful visual portrayal of human psychology in the film "Inside Out." Yet, despite this complexity, it's common to struggle with fully comprehending our emotions and how to navigate them.

What's a wheel of emotions, you ask? To simplify the complex landscape of human feelings, renowned psychologist and professor Robert Plutchik devised an emotion wheel, aiming to distill the spectrum of emotions we experience.

Beyond being a vibrant array of colors, the emotion wheel portrays eight fundamental emotions: ecstasy, admiration, terror, amazement, grief, loathing, rage, and vigilance. These emotions form the core of our reactions, experiences, and sensations. While this tool may seem simple at first glance, delving deeper reveals a guide that enhances emotional literacy and comprehension.

Numerous versions of this tool exist. Among the most notable are the Plutchik wheel, the Geneva wheel, and the Junto wheel. These wheels categorize various emotions, such as love or joy, along with their corresponding sensations.

The emotional wheel usually consists of a central circle housing eight core emotions, surrounded by outer rings that encompass more nuanced and specific feelings related to these primary emotions.

The emotional wheel simplifies the process of connecting the feelings you experience (middle and outer circles) to their corresponding core emotions (central circle).

To break it down further, let's consider an example: when you recognize feelings of anxiety or terror and identify fear as the core emotion associated with these sensations, you can delve deeper. How? By pinpointing the underlying thought driving these emotions. Then, explore the typical features or expressions of fear—an automatic physical response to a perceived threat commonly known as fight, flight, or freeze. This instinctive reaction serves to protect you from danger, prepare you for immediate action, ensure your safety, or signal that additional resources may be required for upcoming challenges.

Imagine Karen, a technically competent yet socially awkward finance professional, standing poised to deliver the presentation of her career. Her heart raced against her ribs, matching the frantic beat of an anxious hummingbird trapped in a cage. Her palms, once clammy against the cool, sterile surface of the podium, now served as evidence of her mounting unease. This was the moment Karen had been eagerly anticipating for three months—the presentation on Valuation and Financial Modeling for Startups. Yet, as she gazed at all the faces filling the auditorium, a surge of terror rooted itself in her chest. Doubt crept in; could she effectively articulate the complexities of IRR (Internal Rate of Return), ARR (Annual Recurring Revenue), and other crucial metrics?"

"This is just anxiety," she pondered, acknowledging the tricky yet familiar adversary. However, beneath the surface, a more profound fear slumbered – the gnawing worry that she didn't measure up to her male counterparts and that her meticulously crafted financial slides might not endure the scrutiny of the audience.

But something else lurked beneath her anxiety: Uncertainty. Was it imposter syndrome whispering self-doubt in her ear?

She knew she had choices before her. The instinct to fight or take flight beckoned, tempting her to charge forward or seek an immediate escape. Perhaps she could feign sudden illness to slip away from the glaring spotlight. Yet, within this spectrum, Karen recalled an alternative route - to pause, not as an act of surrender, but as an opportunity to collect herself and gather resources.

Drawing on her mindfulness practice and guided by her understanding of emotions via the wheel of feelings, Karen gently shut her eyes. The serene image of a tranquil beach flooded her mind—the gentle ebb and flow of the calming waves imparted a profound sense of reassurance. Each deliberate breath anchored the financial analyst firmly in the present moment, gradually loosening the grip of fear with every exhale."

Opening her eyes, Karen met the audience's gaze. The once-daunting financial formulas no longer overwhelmed her, nor did she cower under their perceived judgment. Though uncertainty lingered, a newfound sense of assurance and conviction also took root within her. She was determined to share her story—not as a flawless performer, but as someone who recognized her worth and trusted in her preparation.

The Wheel of Emotions - Building Blocks of Emotional Literacy

Allowing your negative emotions to be named and identified can significantly reduce their intensity and perceived threat. Utilizing a wheel of emotions for this purpose proves invaluable in delineating the array of feelings you encounter and uncovering their core emotions. I believe you'd concur with this approach's merit.

Refining your awareness of specific feelings and emotions you're going through, distinct from others, stands as a pivotal step. Pinpointing and labeling these sensations typically marks the initial and crucial stride in maneuvering or enhancing any circumstance. Here's my input: anything fostering this awareness, such as a wheel of feelings, undeniably facilitates progress.

Understanding emotional complexity becomes more manageable through the wheel of emotions, which elucidates the intricate relationship between primary and secondary emotions. It unveils the myriad feelings that arise from their interplay.

The emotional wheel offers more than just a list of emotions; it provides precise and dependable terminology for expressing feelings. Utilize it as a tool to refine your emotional vocabulary, enabling clearer and more descriptive communication with others. Discerning nuances between emotions – such as distinguishing 'irritation' from 'rage' – enhances your self-awareness and understanding.

Assisting in the modulation and regulation of emotional responses to external stimuli is crucial for ensuring their efficiency and effectiveness. This ability aids in foreseeing potential emotional reactions, resulting in more informed decision-making, improved actions, and, ultimately, a heightened sense of happiness.

After employing the emotional wheel to pinpoint precise feelings and emotions, you'll likely find yourself more objective, enabling better management of your reactions to those emotions.

Mindful Breathing

"Name it, and you tame it." Labeling or naming difficult emotions, such as guilt or envy, helps you disentangle, or "unstick," from them. Don't take my word for it - research indicates that when we name difficult emotions and feelings, the amygdala—your brain structure that perceives and registers danger—becomes less active (Šimić et al., 2021). As a result, it's less likely to trigger a physical stress reaction.

Imagine gently saying, "Fear is arising," or "This is anger." You will usually feel a sense of some emotional freedom—like there's some space around that feeling. Rather than being lost or overwhelmed by the emotion, you can recognize that you're having the emotion and hence have more leeway or choice of responding.

Mindful breathing is popular for its many benefits, including pain and anxiety relief. However, this simple and effective practice that focuses on the breathing sensation can also help you observe thoughts and label emotions.

You can improve emotional intelligence by paying close attention to the present moment – particularly your sensations, thoughts, and emotions. Remember Po from *Kung Fu Panda* mastering his inner peace and channeling the "Wuxi Finger Hold"? No doubt, those slow, deliberate breaths were all about mindfulness!

Studies published in the eminent Journal of Psychiatric Research revealed that subjects who practiced mindful breathing drastically improved emotion regulation and control and decreased symptoms of depression and anxiety (Fincham et al., 2023).

Breathing Mindfully to Label Emotions

You can do it in various creative ways, but a standard technique involves sitting comfortably in a quiet place. The following steps and tips will guide you through it.

Keep your shoulders down, spine straight, and chin lifted. Are you feeling tense? Maintain a soft focus on the ground before you, and let your eyes take in light without seeking sensory input.

Remember Yoda's calm wisdom flowing through the Force? It is time to let your breath mirror that. Inhale slowly and steadily and exhale even longer, releasing worry and stress. After exhaling three times, let your breath find its natural rhythm and relinquish breath control.

If you find your mind wandering, don't fret. Thoughts will pop up. Learn to label them and bring patience, kindness, and humor to your wandering mind. Consider savoring the experience of the breath as you may savor a flavorful gourmet meal from your favorite eatery. Each breath and bite is delicious and unique.

As you continue mindful breathing, notice what emotions and feelings begin to surface. Try to shift your attention gradually from your breath and then ask yourself: What am I feeling now? You will likely feel contentment if you sit down comfortably for this exercise without any conflicting or strong emotions. Or maybe you're curious, or perhaps there's another strong emotion inside, like yearning or longing. You may have a lot of different feelings.

Label your most prominent emotion(s). Try to identify your strongest feeling and give it a name. Finding an accurate label for your emotions is important. For instance, there are several flavors or degrees of anger, such as annoyance, resentment, rage, and aggravation. Trust me, finding the most suitable label will give you the same feeling as striking a ball on the sweet spot of your baseball bat; it clicks.

If you are overwhelmed by the emotion, or it's pretty unnerving or disturbing, simply stay with your breath and wait until you feel better.

For the remainder of this meditation, relax and let your attention move freely to whatever sensation or experience is sufficiently strong to call it away from your breath. Note that it could be a sound, thought, or an image.

In the final moments, reflect on what truly matters to you. No overthinking. Just let a simple value or quality rise to the surface. Is it kindness, laughter, or resilience? Set an intention to bring more of that quality into your day.

Remember, mindfulness isn't about achieving perfection; no one expects you to do that. Focus on cultivating awareness and kindness towards yourself and your experience.

Watching Other People

Watching others express emotions and feelings, whether in real life or through media, will help you develop and improve your emotional intelligence. Two weeks ago, I sat on a bus and saw a woman's face change significantly at hearing a crying and sniffling baby in a nearby row.

Instead of judging or assuming, I silently tracked her thoughts, 'she's upset, her eyes are welling up, her face is red, she has a strong emotional response, and this little baby is certainly bringing up something inside of her.'

Select movies or television series known for strong emotional performances. Pay attention to close-ups of actors' faces and how they express complex feelings. For instance, Casey Affleck delivers a powerful and moving performance as a grief-stricken man haunted by past trauma in *Manchester by the Sea*. He conveyed various emotions through micro-expressions and unspoken pain on his face.

Documentaries like *My Octopus Teacher* and *Icarus* are also excellent resources, featuring real-life people expressing genuine emotions. And who can forget *Man on Wire* – a gripping and insightful documentary that tells the story of Philippe Petit's high-wire walk between the Twin Towers.

Follow the Emotional Map

When observing others, imagine yourself building a map of their emotion. Label what you see – "furrowed brow," "tightly clenched jaw," "tearful eyes." Connect these clues together to identify the likely emotion – "frustration," "grief," "overwhelm."

Empathy vs. Projection – Know the Difference

Understanding the difference between empathy and projection is crucial for building genuine connections with others. Empathy involves actively seeking to comprehend the emotions, experiences, and perspectives of others without imposing your own feelings or biases onto them. It requires active listening, validation, and a non-judgmental approach to create a safe space where individuals feel heard, respected, and understood. On the other hand, projection happens when you unconsciously attribute your thoughts, emotions, or experiences to another person, thereby distorting their feelings and inhibiting communication.

Recognizing and respecting the uniqueness of each individual's journey is essential in practicing empathy. By approaching interactions with an open and non-judgmental mindset, you acknowledge that everyone has their own set of experiences, beliefs, and emotions that shape their worldview. This perspective fosters trust, mutual respect, and deeper connections, allowing for meaningful interactions that transcend differences and promote understanding and compassion. By prioritizing empathy over projection, you create a foundation for building stronger relationships, enhancing communication, and cultivating a more inclusive and empathetic environment.

Keep Practicing

The more you notice and analyze, the better you will identify and understand emotions in yourself and others. Consider the context. Analyzing the situation will help you understand the potential causes of a person's emotions. Over time, you'll build a library of emotional cues and responses, enhancing your empathy and communication skills.

Journaling

I know it's not always simple to corner free-floating thoughts buzzing in your mind. To work through understanding complex emotions, consider using a journal to articulate your feelings and thoughts. Journaling has other benefits, too. It can help lower symptoms of depression and anxiety while increasing positive mood and overall well-being.

Journaling will help get out raw emotions and feelings in several ways:

- It feels safer and more private than telling someone else.

- It helps prevent thought rumination.

- It allows you to be more neutral and judgment-free.

Writing about your emotions and thoughts, especially the difficult ones, will help you identify and understand patterns in your thinking and emotional responses. This way, you'll be able to process difficult emotions. If you're feeling overwhelmed, stressed, or anxious, it is time to stop and process your emotions. And you will never go wrong with the power of writing. Journaling boosts emotional awareness, increases self-reflection, and improves emotional regulation.

Making Journaling a Habit

Journaling is a valuable personal practice. The best part is that you don't need to show your writing or notes to anyone. Plus, you can write about whatever feels or seems most relevant or meaningful to you. Maybe it was a harrowing experience when an unruly dog chased you down the street or when your request to work from home was turned down. There are so many choices! What better way to connect with your inner self or gain insights into your feelings or emotions?

Here's a simple guide on how to practice journaling to get a handle on your emotions:

- Begin by setting a goal or intention for your journaling practice. Be specific about what you hope to gain from this writing exercise. What thoughts or emotions do you want to explore?

- Start writing freely (no holding back) about your feelings, thoughts, and experiences. Don't censor yourself or worry about spelling or grammar. They are trivial in this context. Try to write as if you were speaking to a close friend.

- Reflecting on your writing is crucial. What themes or patterns do you notice? Is there anything you would like to explore further? How do you feel after writing?

- Practice self-compassion, and don't be too harsh on yourself. Be gentle and kind with yourself throughout this process. Steer clear of criticism or self-judgment.

The EQ Toolbox -Find Your Strengths and Weaknesses

Emotional intelligence, or "EQ," encapsulates your ability to recognize, manage, and evaluate your emotions. Have you ever wondered what your emotional fingerprint looks like? EQ assessments are like personality tests for your feelings and highlight your strengths and areas for growth.

Emotional intelligence tests and assessments are becoming increasingly popular as employers in all industries recognize the value and importance of emotionally intelligent employees.

Emotional intelligence tests, such as the 360 EQ (Talent Smart) or the Genos EI, range from brief online quizzes taking a couple of minutes to longer appraisals. These EQ tests and assessments provide brief scenarios to quickly and objectively quantify emotional intelligence along single or multiple dimensions like self-awareness, personal motivation, social skills, and empathy.

Knowing your score on an emotional intelligence test will help you better understand yourself and develop or improve your relationships with others. Emotional intelligence contributes so profoundly to career growth and success that many companies actively look for high-EQ candidates.

The Mayer-Salovey-Caruso Emotional Intelligence Test (MSCEIT)

Don't let the name deter you! The MSCEIT is a popular ability-based test that measures your capacity to understand and manage emotions. This reliable test focuses on four branches of emotional intelligence: perceiving, understanding, using, and managing feelings and emotions.

GlobaLeadership Foundation

With its mission to develop self-aware and emotionally healthy leaders and top executives, the GlobaLeadership Foundation aspires to help companies and businesses solve environmental and social issues globally. You can take this free emotional intelligence quiz with only 40 multiple-choice questions. It won't take more than 15 minutes to complete. What are the benefits? Get insights on your self-awareness, relationship management, and social awareness, to name a few!

The Six Seconds Emotional Intelligence Assessment (SEI)

This self-assessment tool measures a person's emotional intelligence using a unique combination of self-reporting and feedback from others. The SEI measures eight competencies associated with emotional intelligence, including empathy, emotional literacy, and collaboration. You can access this test through certified providers. Pricing varies based on the provider.

Mind Help

You may have heard of Mind Help. The organization advocates for better psychological and mental health across the comprehensive spectra of life, including personal happiness, professional growth and development, and better family relations.

With just fifteen simple questions, this straightforward emotional intelligence assessment challenges you to understand better your emotions and responses to other people's feelings. This short EQ test is free to take and provides an immediate score and a useful brief on your test results.

You can use these emotional intelligence tests, workshops, and training programs to get valuable insights, feedback, and guidance.

Life After Self-Awareness - The Butterfly Effect

Consider the ripple effect of just a single pebble dropped in a pond. That's the transformative power of increased self-awareness and higher emotional intelligence. While emotional intelligence appears to come naturally to some, like Donna from *Suits*, our brain's plasticity means we can boost our emotional intelligence. All you have to do is be willing to put in the work.

When you understand your emotions, you communicate more effectively and increase your chances of building stronger relationships and making conscious choices. For instance, as a manager with exceptional relationship management skills, you can inspire, guide, motivate, and develop your team members, significantly affecting team productivity and performance. You can also navigate conflict with empathy and embrace challenges with resilience rather than shying away.

Remember, becoming self-aware and emotionally intelligent is a journey. You can expect some stumbles, detours, and moments when you get lost in the fog. What is quite clear, though, is that being emotionally self-aware and working on your emotional intelligence is vital for leading a happy, productive, and fulfilled life.

Key Takeaways

- Emotions are not fleeting feelings but forces that shape our thoughts, actions, and choices.

- Identifying, understanding, and managing your own emotions and those of others helps promote strong relationships, facilitates wise decisions, and a fulfilling life.

- Recognizing the potential causes of your emotional reactions and experiences is vital. Recognize those gut butterflies and facial twitches – they have a story to tell.

- Use body scan meditation, the emotional wheel, and journaling to identify, name, and differentiate among various emotional experiences or reactions.

- Watch how others express feelings, from the bus stop to movie screens. Notice the cues and create an empathy map to further this exploration.

- Experiment with different emotional intelligence tests and assessments to know where you stand.

What's to Come

In the next chapter, we'll dive into the art of managing emotions effectively. Get ready to become the master of your inner world using short and long-term strategies for building emotional resilience and tools for managing stress. Let's keep exploring!

Chapter 2

Taming the Emotional Tigers: Strategies for Regulation

"Breathing is the bridge between thought and emotion. Master your breath, and you master your emotional tides."
Thich Nhat Hanh

E motions manifest in numerous ways and are a normal part of everyday life. Don't we feel annoyed when stuck in traffic? Similarly, we feel sad when we miss our families and loved ones or someone who passed away recently. We can get mad and lose our cool when somebody lets us down or does something awful to hurt us. What about deadlines looming like thunderclouds and emails pinging like angry hornets? Yeah, that's part of the daily grind, but it can get you on edge!

When the Inner Storm Rages

While it's normal to experience emotions regularly, some individuals find themselves grappling with more intense or volatile feelings, such as anger or jealousy. If you resonate with this, you might notice that your emotional spectrum encompasses higher highs and lower lows. Left unattended, these fluctuations can significantly influence your life. For instance, you might transition swiftly from a state of calm and composure to feelings of anger or sadness in the blink of an eye.

Emotional dysregulation, also known as affect dysregulation, refers to experiencing difficulty when trying to manage or diffuse strong emotions and feelings, particularly those considered negative, including anger, jealousy, and frustration. While your emotions may occasionally spin out of control and cause you to act recklessly, for some individuals, it happens regularly.

Their fickle and rapidly changing emotions may cause them to say or do things they later regret. Emotional outbursts may damage close relationships or even hurt their credibility with others.

When emotions like anger or envy impact your relationships, overall quality of life, or performance at school or work, explore healthy and proven ways to cope. Remember that feeling of finally calming a hyperactive pup? You may have to coax it with treats and engage its playful side until his frenzied barks morph into contented tail wags. Your emotions and feelings can sometimes feel like that puppy, bouncing off the walls and leaving you gasping for breath. In this chapter, you will learn how to calm the emotional chaos and remain composed when your emotions try to get the better of you.

The Toolbox for Inner Calm and Peace

There's nothing wrong with getting worried or upset from time to time. After all, it is a normal part of life and shows we are fallible humans. But what happens when your anger or anxiety takes over, and you just cannot calm down for some reason? Being able to calm yourself and stay cool is usually easier said than done.

So, how do the toughest and most resilient people summon the determination to keep going? Fortunately, being prepared for emotionally charged moments and periods of stress and anxiety can make it simple to get through them. Knowing how to manage your well-being will help you recover after a tense encounter or stressful event. Some people refer to our ability to handle stress as our resilience.

Having some strategies and coping techniques, you are familiar with will help you when your emotions or feelings are trying to get the better of you. Consider adding these calming tactics and strategies to your toolbox. They will empower you to navigate the choppiest waters with clarity and grace.

Immediate Calming Techniques

The Breath is Your Anchor

Breathing techniques, such as alternate nostril breathing, help relax your body. When anxieties surge, or emotions overwhelm you, specific patterns that entail holding your breath for a specific period enable your body to replenish oxygen.

Based on an ancient yogic technique known as pranayama, the 4-7-8 breathing technique was developed by Dr. Andrew Weil (Esmaile et al., 2020). When anxieties surge, inhale deeply for four counts, hold for seven, and exhale slowly for eight. This technique infuses your tissues and organs with vital oxygen, starting from the depths of your lungs. Repeated practice results in a noticeable slowing of your heartbeat and a gradual relaxation of your muscles.

Breathing practices are integral to regulating emotions, and now you will understand why we started this chapter with Thich Nhat Hanh's quote.

If you practice it frequently, it's possible that the 4-7-8 breathing technique could help you fall asleep quickly. So, if you have sleep issues, give this technique a try.

Visualize Yourself Calm

This is another immediate calming tip that requires you to practice some of the breathing techniques you've learned. How does it work? After taking deep breaths, close both eyes and imagine yourself calm and composed. See your body relaxed, and then imagine yourself working through an emotional, highly stressful, or anxiety-inducing situation by staying focused and calm.

Create a mental picture or image of what it looks like to stay relaxed and calm. This will help you refer back to that image whenever you're anxious.

Half Smile and Willing Hands

Emily's head felt like it would explode any minute. She was homebound on a super crowded subway train in New York City with her small child in tow. The kid was having a loud temper tantrum, his cries echoing through the crowded train. Emily had carried her son down the subway steps, screaming and kicking, while also lugging the heavy stroller (imagine being in her shoes). To top it off, she had a nasty migraine, and the overwhelming frustration and charged emotions threatened to push her over the edge. Emily's head was pounding; her temper was rising.

However, instead of getting carried away, she applied a valuable skill she had learned. She smiled. That's strange, right? It wasn't a genuine or natural smile but rather a forced one. Her lips were pursed, but she willed her mouth to stretch and slowly turn up at the clenched corners.

Emily also placed her hands in front of her. And her palms were up in a subtle gesture of acceptance. Don't know what's happening here? Emily was doing what's called "half-smile, willing hands," a proven practice that helps encourage acceptance of the current situation, acting as an effective distress tolerance skill (Christina, 2023). And believe me, it works like a charm. So, if you are in a similar situation and practice this technique, you will start to calm down.

These skills and movements can help increase the willingness to do what's needed in a stressful or anxious situation, help regulate your nervous system, and induce relaxation.

Challenge Your Thoughts

You may know that part of being emotional or anxious is having irrational thoughts and feelings that do not necessarily make sense. Often, these thoughts keeping you on edge are the "worst-case scenario." Like many people, you may be caught in the vicious "what if" cycle. It is not pretty and can cause you to sabotage so many things in your life.

Suppose you have a presentation coming up. It may look like a monstrous shadow swallowing your confidence. What if I stumble over my words? What if the audience laughed? The "what if" can spin like a chaotic carousel, fueling your dread.

When you have one of these thoughts, take a moment, stop, and ask yourself these questions:

- Is this probable or likely to happen?

- Why am I having this thought?

- Is this thought even rational?

- Has this ever occurred or happened to me in the past?

- What is the worst or scariest that can happen? Can I handle that?

The Power of Five Senses

Are you overwhelmed by loud noise? Consider taking a sensory break to calm yourself. Focus on five things you can see, hear, smell, taste, or touch. When you take some time to focus on your sensory experience, it will take you "out of your head" and out of your anxious and overwhelming loop of thinking. Ground yourself in the present moment, letting go of mental chatter. Sensory breaks calm your nervous system, improve concentration, and increase self-control.

Chew Gum

Fun and simple! Chewing on a piece of gum is a great way to help lower anxiety (and even improve mood and productivity). Actually, research studies show that individuals who chew gum regularly are usually less stressed than those who don't (Sözbir et al., 2019).

You know that feeling when the world throws a lemon at you, and you just want to chew it back? Instead of letting stress and anxiety get the best of you, try chewing a stick of gum. And the benefits of chewing gum go beyond mere distraction. Chewing actually stimulates your vagus nerve, your body's main highway for calming signals. Plus, your jaw muscles get a workout, releasing endorphins, which are your body's natural feel-good chemicals.

Listen to Soothing Music

Did you know that listening to favorite tracks and soothing music can have a calming effect? You will find many relaxing music videos for anxiety and stress relief online. So, the next time you feel your emotional or anxiety level cranking up, grab a pair of headphones a relaxing beverage, and tune in to your favorite music.

Long-Term Strategies for Building Emotional Resilience

When facing as much chaos and uncertainty as we have, especially over the past few years, emotional resilience springs to mind as an increasingly vital skill. Emotional resilience enables you to remain optimistic and calm in the face of uncertainty and disruption. Here are some ways to develop it.

The Gratitude Garden

Gratitude can be defined as a profound appreciation for the multitude of blessings, whether they manifest as a fulfilling job, cherished relationships like that with a partner, or the various experiences that enrich our lives. Yet, amidst the richness of these gifts, envy, cynicism, and the allure of materialism can stealthily lead us into the trap of taking things for granted. Truth be told, we're all susceptible to this oversight at times. However, recognizing and embracing gratitude for the positives in our lives can liberate us from the perpetual cycle of comparison with others' lives and possessions.

So, plant seeds of gratitude daily. Write down three or four things you're thankful for, like reliable friends, including even the little things. Rather than avoiding uncomfortable feelings, practicing gratitude allows you to sit with the emotion, no matter how intense, until it slowly melts into something new. Eventually, this improves your ability to choose a response rather than impulsively reacting. This is emotional resilience.

Maintain a simple and brief list of things you are grateful for in a paper notebook, or enter them regularly into a digital spreadsheet. You will even find digital gratitude journals, like Happy Gratitude or The Gratitude App, that you can download and use.

Although you'll likely feel a rush of joy and excitement after receiving a hard-earned promotion at work or winning the lottery, gratitude extends to the simpler and smaller blessings that are usually overlooked. Some are taken for granted, like savoring a delicious meal after a long day.

Even the smallest or seemingly trivial moments, like a chat with a close friend, a nice gesture from a total stranger, a peaceful morning stroll in nature, or a cool breeze on a sweltering day, are some things you can appreciate and be thankful for.

Block a regular time every day — for example, first thing in the morning or maybe at the end of the day — to add to and review these records.

Practicing Gratitude at Work

If you are a leader or manager of a team, consider dedicating time (even five minutes or so) in your team meetings to thank and appreciate a team member for their dedication and hard work with specific examples.

Encourage and motivate your team members to express gratitude to their colleagues and help them develop resilience by building meaningful connections.

You can also write a simple thank-you email or note. There's no need for a lengthy summary or being formal, but putting into writing your appreciation and gratitude towards somebody and then sharing it with them helps start a chain of positivity for you and that person.

Being Optimistic

Optimism is the label given to the unique personality trait exhibited by individuals who usually expect that good things will happen down the line. Looking on the bright side will help you maintain a positive outlook while facing challenges with resilience.

For instance, if you are an optimist, you will see bad events, such as a relationship failure or break-up, as temporary setbacks you can overcome with effort and ability. When you view problems as temporary, you can stop the never-ending cycle of negative tapes that may run through your head.

Optimists show more emotional resilience and composure when confronting challenges and obstacles, even if progress seems difficult or slow. There's also a reciprocal relationship between these two, which should not be overlooked. Optimism leads to or improves resilience, and emotional resilience creates more optimism.

Are you optimistic? See how many traits and characteristics you can check off. Optimists are more inclined to:

- Seek information and use it to their advantage.

- Ask for help and be more approach-oriented.

- Accept that they can't control all aspects of a situation.

- Devise strategies and plans to take action.

- View a difficult situation as a challenge rather than a threat.

- Use humor and positive emotion as a coping mechanism.

Truly resilient individuals who have to survive the most challenging and harshest circumstances and still achieve goals carefully balance a positive outlook with a realistic view of the world.

Similarly, resilient leaders have high levels of self-awareness, are adaptive and flexible in thinking, and display emotional strength, courage, and optimism. So, as a leader, assuming a resilient posture means embracing vulnerability and uncertainty in every learning experience.

The Sleep Sanctuary

If you are feeling stressed or anxious, prioritizing sleep will do you a lot of good in the long run! During sleep, our brain forms memories and processes each day's events. Your brain will also discard any unnecessary information and thoughts that might otherwise clutter your mind. Your emotions are balanced when well-rested, and your coping mechanisms work like well-oiled gears. Aim for seven to eight hours of quality sleep each night.

To improve sleep and develop emotional resilience, consider the following tips:

- Establish a Proper Sleep Routine: go to bed and get up at the same time daily, even on weekends, in order to create a consistent and stable sleep pattern.

- Create a Comfortable and Relaxing Sleep Environment: make your bedroom dark, comfortable, quiet, and cool to facilitate restful sleep.

- Manage stress: practice one or more stress-reduction techniques, such as deep breathing, meditation, or yoga, to reduce stress levels and enhance sleep quality.

Good sleep is important for your brain to function adequately and helps you better handle your impulses and emotions.

Spend Quality Time in Nature

It's hard to overstress the importance of spending time in nature as it is a balm for your soul. Spend some time outdoors, walk in the park, and listen to the wind. This can help lower stress and improve overall well-being. You could also try taking care of indoor plants, going for a hike, or spending time with animals.

From Frazzled to Focused — Tips to Tame Stress and Prevent Overwhelm

Nowadays, it is hard not to get stressed or overwhelmed every once in a while. There's so much on your plate. Between juggling family, work, and other commitments, it is easy to become too stressed or even have burnout. So, it is important to set some time aside to unwind; otherwise, your physical and mental health can take a toll.

Does it feel like you can't do anything about stress? Those bills will never stop coming, deadlines are looming, and there will never be more hours in the day. But let me tell you that you have much more control than you may think or are led to believe.

While managing stress and keeping your sanity intact isn't a one-size-fits-all system, it's valuable to have a comprehensive toolkit of stress management techniques and tips should you need them. Here are some techniques and steps you can take to destress and finally regain control.

The Time Ninja – Schedule like a Pro

Some people may feel stressed and anxious because they have so many things to manage. A pile of dirty dishes or laundry, PTA meetings, and someone has to take out the trash. You get the picture. In this case, changing how you organize time can help you feel more in control. Set realistic goals and delegate tasks where possible so you don't spread yourself too thin.

Try to identify when you're most productive or have the most energy, like in the morning. If possible, do your most crucial tasks around that time of day. This will help you concentrate better.

Create a list of things, personal and work-related, that you have to do. Arrange them carefully in order of importance. Make sure you focus on the most urgent task first.

Develop Your Interests & Hobbies

Engaging in activities that bring you joy and fulfillment can be a powerful antidote to the stresses and anxieties of daily life. Whether you find solace in watching a comedy movie that makes you laugh, immersing yourself in the tranquility of gardening, or losing yourself in the rhythm of a favorite rock song, these moments of enjoyment provide a welcome respite from nervous and stressful situations. By dedicating time to indulge in your passions and hobbies, you create opportunities to recharge, refocus, and regain a sense of balance amidst life's challenges.

Additionally, engaging in shared hobbies is a great way to build connections and form bonds with others, especially when you're feeling stressed, anxious, isolated, or lonely. Participating in group activities or clubs centered around mutual interests creates a supportive and inclusive environment where you can connect with like-minded people. Whether it's joining a gardening project, attending a comedy movie night, or becoming part of a local group of rock music enthusiasts, shared hobbies foster a sense of community and belonging. These interactions not only expand your social circle but also cultivate meaningful relationships that are based on shared experiences, values, and interests. By embracing shared hobbies as a way to meet new people, you can overcome feelings of isolation and enrich your life with new friendships, experiences, and perspectives, leading to a more fulfilling and connected life overall.

Speak Up for Yourself

If you perceive mistreatment, such as feeling overburdened by tasks due to your accommodating nature, it's crucial to address the issue directly and assertively. Silence can inadvertently perpetuate such behaviors, leading to increased stress and dissatisfaction. By voicing your concerns openly and constructively, you create an opportunity for mutual understanding, enabling both parties to identify underlying issues and explore solutions. Prioritizing open communication empowers you to advocate for your well-being and professional integrity, fostering a more equitable, respect-ful, and collaborative environment conducive to personal and professional growth.

Eat Well and On Time

Embracing a wholesome and well-balanced diet is not only beneficial for your physical health but also plays a pivotal role in enhancing your emo-tional well-being and overall happiness. Consuming a diet rich in fruits, vegetables, lean proteins, and whole grains provides your body with essen-tial nutrients, vitamins, and minerals necessary for optimal functioning. These nutrient-dense foods not only fuel your body but also help regulate moods and emotions by supporting neurotransmitter production and balancing blood sugar levels. Additionally, maintaining consistent meal patterns and avoiding skipping meals ensures a steady supply of energy throughout the day, preventing energy dips and mood fluctuations. By prioritizing a nutritious diet, you empower yourself to cultivate a harmonious balance between physical health and emotional vitality, laying the foundation for a happier, healthier, and more fulfilling life.

Get Organized

Maintaining an organized and clutter-free environment extends beyond aesthetics; it profoundly influences your mental well-being and overall sense of tranquility. A cluttered and chaotic outer world often translates to a disordered inner state, fostering feelings of agitation, overwhelm, and heightened stress levels. Conversely, cultivating a tidy and clean home or office space instills a sense of order, control, and harmony in your surroundings, which directly contributes to mental balance and emotional stability. By taking proactive steps to declutter and organize your environment, you create a conducive space that promotes focus, productivity, and peace of mind, ultimately enhancing your quality of life and overall well-being.

Don't Multitask

Engaging in multitasking may appear to be a way to increase productivity, but it often has the opposite effect. It compromises efficiency and effectiveness in your work. Rather than accomplishing tasks more efficiently, multitasking can lead to increased stress, tension, and a higher likelihood of making errors or overlooking important details. By dividing your attention among multiple tasks simultaneously, you dilute focus and concentration, hindering your ability to perform each task to the best of your ability. Instead of juggling multiple tasks at once, it's better to prioritize and focus on one task at a time. This approach enhances concentration, productivity, and overall performance, ultimately fostering a more balanced and effective work approach.

Mindfulness and Relaxation Routines

Now and then, you must plan on some actual downtime. This will give your mind some much-needed time off from stress. Practicing mindfulness and relaxation techniques is a great way to do that.

The Morning Meditation - Start your day with a few minutes (15 to 20) of mindfulness. Focus on your breath, observe your thoughts without judgment, and create a space of inner calm before the day's hustle begins.

The Evening Ritual - Unwinding before bed with a relaxing routine is a great way to keep your mind fresh. Take a warm bath, read a calming book, or practice gentle stretches. Ease into sleep with a mind free from tension.

The Mini-Breaks - Throughout the day, take tiny mindfulness breaks. Close your eyes for a minute, do some deep breathing, or simply step outside and notice the sky. These micro-moments of peace add up to a calmer day.

Handling Triggers - Facing Your Inner Dragons

We each possess emotional triggers—those moments that swiftly catapult us from calm to intense emotions. Identify your triggers, and then use relevant coping mechanisms to stay in control. For example, if you are impatient, take deep breaths.

Recognize situations, thoughts, or people that spark strong emotions like anger or envy. Awareness is the first step to managing them.

Stockpile healthy coping mechanisms. Exercising, journaling, healthy eating, spending time in nature, or creative pursuits. Having options empowers you to choose healthy responses.

Don't react in the heat of the moment; you will regret it later. Step away, count to ten, or write down your feelings. Maybe use a journal. This space prevents impulsive decisions and allows for a calmer response.

Challenge negative thoughts. Instead of "I'm overwhelmed or burdened," think, "This feels intense, but I can handle it."

Prioritize tasks, delegate when possible, and set realistic expectations.

Remember, regulating your emotions takes time and plenty of practice. There will be some stumbles, setbacks, and days when your emotional tigers roar. Don't let them overwhelm you. So, grab your toolbox, face your demons, and rewrite your emotional story.

Key Takeaways

- Master immediate techniques like mindful breathing, sensory grounding, and expressive movement to regulate emotions and navigate anxiety.

- Cultivate long-term resilience through daily practices like gratitude journaling, prioritizing sleep, listening to music, and repeating positive affirmations to strengthen your inner resources.

- Become a "Time Ninja" by managing your schedule, setting boundaries, and seeking solace in nature to minimize external stressors.

- Start your day with a mini-meditation, create calming evening rituals, and sprinkle micro-moments of mindfulness throughout the day to cultivate lasting inner peace.

- Identify your triggers and equip yourself with specific coping mechanisms for each.

Coming Up

This chapter helped us calm the inner storm, but true peace often comes from connecting with others in your personal and professional life. In Chapter 3, we will immerse ourselves in the art of communication. We aim to elevate our discourse, navigate conflicts maturely, and foster enduring friendships.

Chapter 3

Navigating Social and Interpersonal Relationships

"The single biggest problem in communication is the illusion that it has taken place."
George Bernard Shaw

Remember that awkward time you tried explaining your love for polka dancing to your goth friend? Was he scratching his head? Or maybe the awkward silence after disagreeing with your parents about religion or politics? I know that navigating personal or professional relationships can sometimes be like walking a tightrope blindfolded with juggling pins in your shoes.

Who doesn't crave fulfilling relationships, especially ones where you get to grow and mature? However, navigating the social dynamics can be fraught with challenges and complexities. Communication breakdown turns conversations into cacophonies of misunderstanding, and as George Bernard Shaw encapsulates, we often assume that simply speaking our words means communication has occurred. However, this "illusion," he calls it, often masks misunderstandings, misinterpretations, and unspoken assumptions.

If you long for healthy relationships and want to resolve conflicts harmo-niously, this chapter will crack the code to empathetic communication, where words become bridges instead of walls. You'll also learn to identify and nurture those friendships that make your soul sing, leaving the ones that drain your emotional battery behind.

The Power of Empathy

Empathy is an important yet relatively understudied topic. You probably know that empathy has something to do with emotion and, especially, emotional connection. Empathy in personal or professional communica-tion is the unique ability to share and understand another person's feelings. It could be your friend, spouse, or boss.

As an empathic listener or communicator, you must actively listen to your audience, acknowledge their emotions, and respond to show you genuinely care about them. Most business consultants and advisors — and definitely most employees — agree that empathy is one of the critical leadership skills. Sometimes, we even picture "CEO" as "Chief Empathy Officer."

Undoubtedly, the ability to step into another person's shoes, share their feelings, and understand their challenges and situation is a powerful trait that develops trust and faith.

Harper Lee's classic *To Kill a Mockingbird* explores the importance of empathy and understanding others, particularly in the face of injustice and prejudice. Empathy is the cornerstone of emotional intelligence in relationships.

Tips and Tricks for Communicating with Empathy

You are often told to "put yourself in the other person's shoes" or use words and phrases that make that individual feel safe and supported enough to express themselves. While nothing is wrong with that, it's not particularly specific advice.

So, what does it really mean to communicate with empathy and understanding? What are the skills that you need? And what does it mean to use understanding and empathy as a professional or business owner where your target audience is not yet engaged in a meaningful dialogue with your enterprise or brand? Let's find out.

Active Listening

This is about truly hearing what someone is saying, beyond the words, to their underlying emotions and needs. These could be fear, jealousy, or insecurity.

Use the following to improve your active listening skills:

- Make eye contact.

- Be inquisitive, show interest, and ask relevant questions if you do not understand something.

- Summarize or paraphrase the other person's words, ensuring you fully and correctly understand them.

- Try to validate the other individual's emotions. You can do this without agreeing with them.

- Avoid multitasking. That's a big no. Resist the urge to check your smartphone or write an email while somebody is speaking.

Mirroring

Mirroring, also known as imitation technique, is the practice of developing a connection with someone by subtly imitating their speech patterns, body language, and other nonverbal cues.

Why does mirroring work? The answer is simple: when somebody sees themselves reflected in another person's actions or eyes, it immediately builds trust, rapport, and connection. By using this technique, you can signal to your friend or romantic partner that you're in sync with them. The benefits are obvious, it breaks down barriers and creates a more productive and positive dialogue. If you want to promote effective communication with someone, reflect on their feelings in a validating way, showing you understand where they're coming from.

Consider these examples.

Scenario 1 - Frustration at work

Partner: "Ugh, this deadline is almost impossible! I've been working on this report for hours, and I feel like I'm hitting a wall."

You (mirroring): "Yeah, I can tell you're feeling really frustrated. This project sounds intense, and the pressure must be getting overwhelming."

Scenario 2 - Sadness after a breakup

Friend: "I can't believe it's over. I thought we were so good together. I feel like a complete mess."

You (mirroring): "It's okay to feel heartbroken. This is a big loss, and it's natural to be sad and confused right now."

Use Open-Ended Questions

Encourage deeper sharing and understanding by asking questions that go beyond "yes" or "no" answers. Examples of simple open-ended questions include "Tell me more about your relationship with your manager/supervisor" or "How do you see your future?" Combining open-ended questions with empathic responses and paraphrasing can provide a more meaningful explanation using their own knowledge and words.

Consider Sarah, who noticed her friend Alex seemed distant. He was slumped at a cafe table, staring into their lukewarm latte. Usually, Alex burst through the door with a joke and a contagious grin, but today, silence clung to him.

Instead of making assumptions or launching into her usual witty banter, Sarah observed how Alex avoided eye contact and played with the chipped rim of his mug. Alex sighed, and Sarah mirrored it with a sympathetic frown. "Rough day at work?" she asked, not as a casual greeting but with genuine concern.

Alex hesitated, then met Sarah's gaze briefly. "Yeah," he mumbled, a tremor running through their voice. "Just feeling overwhelmed, you know? Work is crazy, family stuff is, uh..." The sentence trailed off, and Sarah leaned forward, encouragingly nodding.

She also asked an open-ended question, "What's got you feeling overwhelmed?" It was a gentle nudge, an invitation to delve deeper without pressure. And Alex, sensing Sarah's genuine interest and support, took a deep breath and started to speak.

Alex spoke of the looming deadline at work and the strained relationship with a family member. As Sarah listened, she mirrored Alex's emotions, her brow furrowing. She asked follow-up questions, not to pry but to understand the emotional undercurrents swirling beneath the surface.

This opened up a conversation about Alex's challenges, strengthening their connection.

Emotional Intelligence – The Foundation for Effective Communication Skills

How refined and effective are your social skills? How adaptive and flexible are you when communicating with individuals of varied personalities and characteristics? Do you fare well in a new, awkward, or different communication setting? Effective communication involves being direct, clear, and concise in your message and actively listening to the other person. You must adapt communication styles and tones to fit the unique needs of different situations.

To be an excellent communicator, building your emotional intelligence is important. As we have seen, emotional intelligence is a crucial skill that builds and fosters effective relationships.

Clear communication is the bridge between minds and hearts. To refine your communication skills, use the following strategies.

Start with "I" Statements

In a difficult or sensitive conversation with a partner, accusatory language can halt the discussion. And you don't want that, right? As soon as you or the other person feels attacked, instinctively, those defensive walls come up, and effective communication becomes almost impossible.

Consider this statement: "You don't care about me or my feelings." It can come across as accusatory and lead to defensiveness in the other person. Take ownership of your thoughts and feelings and avoid accusatory "you" statements.

For instance, instead of saying, "You always leave your mess lying everywhere," say, "I feel annoyed when I see the mess everywhere."

Be Authentic

Authenticity means being true to your beliefs, personality, and values despite the pressure or urge to act otherwise. When you are more transparent, you will become a more effective communicator and express yourself better.

Here are some tips on how you can be authentic and transparent:

- Be unapologetically true to yourself.

- Be honest and open.

- Ask for assistance when needed.

- Set healthy boundaries.

- Learn to assert your feelings and clearly, respectfully, and professionally communicate what you need.

Improve Nonverbal Communication

Pay attention to facial expressions, body language, and tone of voice to better understand and convey emotions.

Facial Expressions

Emotions: Learn to recognize the subtle differences between genuine and forced smiles.

Eye Contact: Maintain appropriate eye contact to show engagement and attentiveness.

Body Language

Open vs. Closed: Uncrossed arms, relaxed posture, facing someone shows openness and interest. Crossed arms, hunched shoulders, and averted gaze signal disinterest or discomfort.

Micro-expressions: Fleeting facial expressions that reveal true emotions, like a flicker of anger before a smile masks it.

Tone of Voice

A higher pitch might suggest excitement, while a lower pitch can convey seriousness. Loudness can indicate anger or enthusiasm.

Resolving Conflicts with Grace and Respect

Are you tired of arguments and verbal clashes that go nowhere? Do passive-aggressive notes and slammed doors define your relationships? We've all been there. Caught in the crossfire of a heated exchange, wishing the ground would swallow us whole. With the right tools, you can transform disagreements into opportunities for growth and connection. We will help you learn to navigate conflict with civility and grace and emerge stronger together.

Conflicts are inevitable; there are no two ways about it. But they don't have to be discordant. For constructive conflict resolution:

Stay calm and collected: Don't let emotions hijack the conversation. Consider this example. Emily and Mike faced a disagreement about project priorities. Instead of blaming each other, they stayed calm, focused on the issue, and brainstormed solutions together, finding a compromise that benefited both.

Focus on the issue, not the person: Steer clear of personal attacks and blame games. A disagreement with your partner or spouse feels like a personal attack. Instead of firing back with harsh words, reframe the conversation. Say, "I understand you're upset about the dishes, but can we focus on finding a solution together?"

Brainstorm solutions together: Work towards a win-win outcome that meets everyone's needs. Are you stuck in a creative rut with a colleague? Instead of dictating your idea, turn it into a brainstorming session. Ask, "What other ways could we approach this project?" You might find a hidden gem even better than your own.

Building and Maintaining Positive Relationships

Are you tired of feeling lonely, misunderstood, or simply adrift in a sea of acquaintances? Have you ever gone on an awkward first date where you spilled your drink? You are not alone.

We all crave those connections that make us feel genuinely seen and valued. Here's the kicker: forging and sustaining strong relationships takes time and effort. In this section, I'll share practical tips to help you create a vibrant network of relationships that bring joy and purpose to your life.

Manage Mobile Technology

While tech tools and gadgets, including your mobile phone, are a lifesaver in an emergency, they can also be a complete distraction when people show a lack of mobile phone etiquette. Be mindful of the impact of technology on relationships and strive to minimize its harmful effects.

Before entering a setting where quality time with loved ones is the priority (dinner dates, family gatherings, meaningful conversations), make a conscious decision to put your phone away. Silence notifications or turn them off completely. You may even store your phone in another room to create a tech-free zone where genuine connection can flourish.

Celebrate Differences

Imagine staring at a blank canvas. Beautiful, yes, but devoid of life! Now, picture that canvas bursting with vibrant colors, each tile unique, each brushstroke reflecting a different perspective. That's the magic of relationships – a beautiful mosaic of minds forged from the richness of our differences.

Yes, it's tempting to crave clones of ourselves, people who echo our thoughts and validate our every move. But the truth is, sameness suffocates. Life thrives on diversity, on the kaleidoscope of viewpoints that makes every interaction a discovery.

So, ditch the cookie-cutter mold! Celebrate the quirks, the disagreements, the perspectives that challenge your own.

Fostering Empathy in Every Context

Empathy and understanding are the cornerstones of strong, meaningful relationships. They allow us to connect with others deeper, build trust, and gracefully navigate disagreements. But how do we cultivate these qualities in different social contexts? Here are some practical strategies to foster empathy and understanding in different contexts and situations.

At Work

Active Listening: Give colleagues or peers your full attention when they speak. Make eye contact, avoid interrupting, and ask clarifying questions to show you're genuinely engaged. Practice random acts of kindness. Small gestures can make a big difference in someone's day.

Perspective-Taking: Try to see things from your colleagues' point of view. Consider their workload, deadlines, and priorities before forming judgments or responding hastily.

Teamwork and Collaboration: Celebrate diverse perspectives and ideas. Encourage open communication and brainstorming sessions where everyone feels comfortable sharing their thoughts.

In Friendships

Offer Kindness and Compassion: Validate your friends' feelings, even if you don't always agree with them. Show willingness to help during difficult times and celebrate their successes. Show you're paying attention by saying things like, "I can see you're feeling frustrated" or "It sounds like you're worried."

Practice Open Communication: Share your thoughts and feelings openly and honestly and actively listen to your friends' perspectives. Respect differences of opinion and engage in constructive dialogue.

In Romantic Relationships

Show genuine interest in your partner's world. Ask questions about their day, their hobbies, and their feelings. Listen attentively and offer support without judgment. Instead of scrolling through your phone during dinner, put it away and ask, "Tell me about the most interesting thing that happened at work today." Actively listen to their response and ask follow-up questions to show you're engaged.

Practice active communication. Share your needs and desires openly and honestly, and give your partner the space to do the same. Choose a calm moment to share your concerns using "I" statements. For example, "I feel hurt when you cancel plans at the last minute without explanation." Offer solutions and listen to their perspective. Be willing to compromise and find solutions that work for both of you.

Celebrate differences: Don't try to change your partner or mold them into your ideal person. There is no such thing! Embrace their unique quirks and perspectives, and cherish what makes your relationship unique. Maybe they leave notes around the house for you to find or have a funny way of humming while they cook. These little things add charm and individuality to your relationship.

In this chapter, we saw how communication, honed with empathy and understanding, becomes the bridge connecting hearts and minds. We learned to embrace conflict as a chance for growth, not a chasm to fear. So, reach out to a friend, offer a listening ear, and embrace the vulnerability that fuels true understanding. Practice the art of constructive conflict, understanding that disagreements can pave the path to stronger bonds.

Key Takeaways

- Empathy is like the conductor's baton, weaving the instruments of relationships into a unified sound.

- Clear communication is the bridge that connects minds and hearts, fostering understanding.

- Conflict resolution requires staying calm, focusing on the issue, and finding collaborative solutions.

- Through investment, celebration, support, and forgiveness, strong relationships are built over time.

- Fostering empathy in every social interaction enriches the human tapestry and creates a harmonious connection.

Conclusion

Emotional Intelligence: Your Guide to a Fulfilling Life

As you've reached the end of this book, you've gained a valuable understanding of the power of emotional intelligence. You've learned to identify, understand, and manage your emotions, build resilience, create meaningful connections, and navigate relationship challenges. But this is not an ending but a vibrant beginning.

A Recap of Your Emotional Journey

Chapter 1: You tuned into the rhythm of your own emotions, deciphering their messages and recognizing their influence on your life. Emotions are not fleeting feelings; they are powerful signals influencing our thoughts, actions, and choices. Understanding them is essential for making wise decisions and living a fulfilling life.

Chapter 2: You discovered effective techniques to manage difficult emotions, regulate stress, and cultivate inner peace. These techniques, such as mindful breathing, grounding practices, and positive affirmations, can be used to navigate challenging situations and build long-term resilience.

Chapter 3: You explored the importance of empathy, clear communication, and conflict resolution in building strong relationships. You've learned how to actively listen, express yourself effectively, and find common ground even in disagreements.

Beyond the Pages - The Daily Rehearsal

Now, it's time to put this knowledge and insight into action in your daily life:

- Make emotional awareness a habit. Regularly reflect on your feelings and the emotions of others. Practice identifying and naming emotions to strengthen your emotional intelligence muscles.

- Incorporate positive practices. Continue to engage in gratitude journaling, mindfulness exercises, and healthy sleep habits to nurture your emotional well-being.

- Focus on communication. Practice active listening, clear communication, and empathetic understanding in your interactions.

- Invest in your relationships: Show appreciation, offer support, and practice forgiveness to strengthen your connections with loved ones.

The time to start is now. Take a deep breath, believe in your abilities, and embrace the incredible potential of your emotional intelligence.

References

Christina. (2023, June 2). Distress Tolerance Series #7 Half Smiling and Willing Hands - ACTivation Psychology. ACTivation Psychology. https://activationpsych.com/distress-tolerance-series-7-half-smiling-and-willing-hands/

Esmaile, S. C., Tort, A. B. L., & Lobão-Soares, B. (2020). Pranayamas and their neurophysiological effects. International Journal of Yoga, 13(3), 183. https://doi.org/10.4103/ijoy.ijoy_91_19

Fincham, G. W., Strauss, C., Montero-Marín, J., & Cavanagh, K. (2023). Effect of breathwork on stress and mental health: A meta-analysis of randomised-controlled trials. Scientific Reports, 13(1). https://doi.org/10.1038/s41598-022-27247-y

Šimić, G., Tkalčić, M., et al. (2021). Understanding emotions: Origins and roles of the amygdala. Biomolecules, 11(5), 1219-1238. doi:10.3390/biom11051219

Sözbir, Ş. Y., Ayaz-Alkaya, S., & Bayrak-Kahraman, B. (2019). Effect of chewing gum on stress, anxiety, depression, self-focused attention, and academic success: A randomized controlled study. Stress and Health, 35(4), 441–446. https://doi.org/10.1002/smi.2872